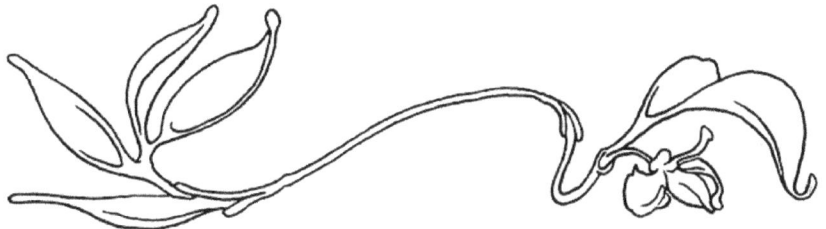

Chatting with The Beloved

You Are Loved

by Connee Chandler

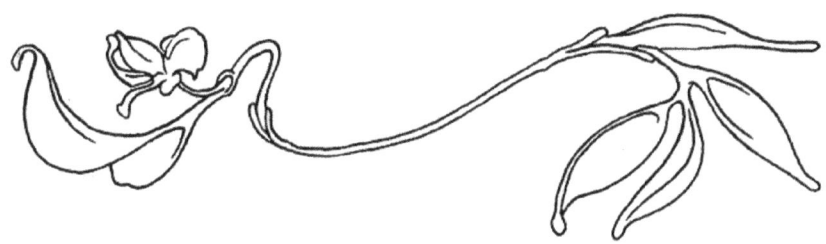

Chats with The Beloved, August-December 2009

aBASK Publishing
Niwot, CO 80503-8694

Copyright 2013 by Connee Chandler

All rights reserved. No part of this book may be reproduced by any mechanical, photographic, or electronic process, or in the form of a recording, nor may it be stored in a retrieval system, transmitted, or otherwise be copied for public or private use other than for "fair use" as embodied in articles and reviews, without prior written permission of the publisher or the author.

ISBN# 978-0-9843855-8-4
Library of Congress Control# 2012937415

Cover Photos: Magi Rose, 2011, 2009
Cover Layout: Chandra Fudge, Pinque Productions
 "Flora and Fauna" Illustrations: Ted Ramsey, 2012

aBASK Publishing
Niwot, CO 80503-8694
www.abaskpublishing.com

First Printing
Printed in the United States of America

Table of Contents

Table of Contents 3
Introduction 6
AUGUST, 2009: 9
Chatting with The Beloved Begins 9
    You Don't Know Us Well Yet, But You Will! 8-22-09, 8:33 AM 9
SEPTEMBER, 2009: 15
Dancing With an Invisible Partner 15
    Moments of Bliss – "Butt Gusting" Belly Laughter: 9-2-09, 8:20 AM 15
    Unfolding Love Story: 9-4-09, 1:25 AM 18
    Feel the Love: 9-8-09, 9:03 AM 21
    In Good Hands: 9-9-09, 1:00 AM 22
    Higher Frequency Thoughts: 9-13-09, 10:41 AM 22
    Learning to Perceive Who You Already Are: 9-14-09, 8:51 AM 26
    Chatting on the Edge of the Universe: 9-15-09, 8:38 AM 30
    SEE God rather than SEEK God: 9-16-09, 8:43 AM 35
    Opening a Very Big Portal: 9-17-09, 3:54 AM 37
    Just Checking In: 9-18-09, 7:24 AM 42
    Dancing With an Invisible Partner: 9-19-09, 2:25 AM 42
    Allow the Hugs from Within: 9-20-09, 1:25 PM 52
    We Are Timeless: 9-23-09 54
    The Impulse at the Perfect Moment: 9-24-09, 9:33 AM 56
    Love is Like a Box of Chocolates: 9-25-09, 7:04 AM 56
    You on Steroids: 9-27-09, 4:41 AM 58
    You Can't Leave Home Without Us! 9-29-09, 9:50 AM 63
    Omnipresence is a Trip: 9-30-09, 6:03 AM 68
    A Lesson in Non-Judgment: 9-30-09, 10:16 AM 74
OCTOBER, 2009: 79
The Incredible Dance of Life 79
    Powerless! 10-2-09, 3:00 AM 79

Love is Contagious: 10-3-09, 10:15 AM 82
Send Them OUR Love: 10-4-09, 9:27 PM 83
The Cosmic Distribution System of Divine Love: 10-5-09, 9:07 AM 88
B: Lets Me Talk! 10-6-09, 8:45 AM 92
Alarming Thoughts Are an Alarm from The Beloved: 10-7-09, 6:35 AM 98
Staying Conscious, Re-Patterning Myself: 10-8-09, 9:15 AM 101
Not Everyone Will Choose This: 10-10-09, 5:05 AM 103
Alternating Focus: 10-11-09, 6:51 AM 105
Follow the Impulse: 10-13-09, 5:00 AM 106
Taking the Scenic Route: 10-14-09, 8:11 AM 111
Sending Love: 10-15-09, 4:32 AM 116
We Are Your Adoring Fans: 10-16-09, 10:15 AM 119
Bashar on Personal Friendship with All That Is: 10-17-09, 11:35 AM 123
Shakes Up Our Assumptions: 10-19-09, 8:35 AM 130
Being Light on Our Feet: 10-20-09, 8:45 AM 133
Carol's Note, and Then Being "Stood Up": 10-21-09, 10:15 AM 137
We're Always Here : 10-22-09, 7:39 AM 141
Are You REAL, B?: 10-23-09 4:33 AM 142
What Matters is Connection, Not Age: 10-24-09, 6:15 PM 145
This Incredible Dance of Life: 10-26-09, 4:45 AM AND 5:44 AM 149
Inspired Action: 10-27-09, 9:00 AM 160
Turn, Turn, Turn: 10-28-09, 5:11 AM 161
Wonder and Wander: 10-29-09, 9:10 AM 166
Kate's Life: 10-30-09, 4:49 AM 170
"Loosing" Kate: 10-31-09, 4:10 AM 173
NOVEMBER, 2009: 177
Everything is All Right Here 177
There's No Standard of Conduct You Have to Adhere to: 11-1-09, 4:01 AM 177
You LISTEN! 11-4-09, 4:16 AM 179
Another Movie Moment: 11-5-09, 7:28 PM 181
Eternal and Temporal: 11-6-09, 8:49 AM 184

We Love it When You Are Literal! 11-7-09, 8:17 AM 186
Preview of Coming Attractions: 11-8-09, 7:17 AM 191
Enraptured by Eggplant: 11-9-09 3:24 AM... 196
In Bed with The Beloved: 11-9-09, 8:40AM 200
I AM FREE! 11-10-09, 8:15 AM 205
Everything is All Right Here: 11-11-09, 6:26 AM.. 213
Stories and Meaning: 11-13-09, 8:42 AM 218
Finding Magi: 11-14-09, 9:33 AM 221
Willing to Experience a Shift in Perspective: 11-15-09, 6:43 AM......................................223
Conscious Evolution: 11-16-09, 9:15 AM 225
A Little Perceptual Adventure: 11-17-09, 7:03 AM 228
I Break for Love: 11-18-09, 7:10 AM 230
Twisted Sister Meets Shifts in Consciousness: 11-19-09, 9:31 AM 232
A Life Filled with Wonder in the "Magic Queendom": 11-22-09, 7:10 AM.......................234
Making Space ISN'T Lazy! 11-22-09, 11:30 AM 237
Timeless Eternal Nouns: 11-23-09, 9:30 AM 238
The BIG Box of Crayolas: 11-24-09, 5: 21 AM 240
Tell me the Story Again: 11-25-09, 2:00 PM..242
Kate's Service: 11-29-09..247
Forgot Your Book? 11-29-09, 11:15 AM 250

DECEMBER, 2009: 253
We Bless You, Every One..253
Big Hairy Fun: 12-1-09, 11:01 AM 253
You are Cute When You are Cranky: 12-2-09, 12:28 PM 257
Handling Changes with Grace: 12-3-09, 5:08 AM 261
We Bless You, Every One: 12-4-09, 7:42 AM...266
Appendices...269
Appendix A: Putting on the Christ, *Science of Mind Magazine*, Daily Guide for September 25, 2003 269
Appendix B: Resilience, August 30, 2009 270
Appendix C: The Path, Winter 1988-1989 270
Appendix D: The Hill and Fields, June 29, 2002 273

Appendix E: Filter of Grace, May 1997 275
Appendix F: The Next Gentle Step, March 14, 1998 277
With Great Thanks 279

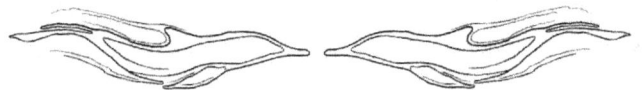

Introduction

"I think everybody longs to be loved and longs to know that he or she is lovable and, consequently, the greatest thing that we can do is to help somebody know that they are loved and capable of loving."

Fred Rogers: America's Favorite Neighbor (television documentary), 2003.

Welcome to the beginning of my on-going love story with The Beloved in dialog form.

I have been studying about God since 1985, when I joined a community study group in Denver, focused on Louise Hay's book, *You Can Heal Your Life.* Finding out Louise Hay had been a Science of Mind Practitioner led me to Mile Hi Church two years later, which then led me to Cherry Creek Church of Religious Science. I took all the Science of Mind classes available there and became a Licensed Religious Science Practitioner in 1992. I moved to Virginia in 1993, serving as a Practitioner and teacher of Science of Mind classes at the Celebration Center in Falls Church until 2002, when I started a Science of Mind Study Group in Sterling, VA with a number of my friends.

During my years in Virginia, I was honored to publish forty-eight Daily Guides in *Science of Mind Magazine,* including one that was republished in a special issue of reader favorites. (See Appendix A)   I also wrote an e-book, *A Gift of Vision,* which is available in full text on my website, www.ConneeChandler.com.

I had been praying, teaching and talking about Spirit from a Science of Mind perspective for over two decades when this part of my life story begins. In late June 2009, I read *The Shack* and was inspired by Wm. Paul Young's description of what it can mean to "live loved" by Source. I wondered what it would be like to live loved in the context of my life and beliefs. I began to imagine what it would be like to have an actual, personal, ongoing, interactive, real-time relationship with the divine. But in truth, the idea of hearing God talk to me "scared the willies out of me."

The founder of Science of Mind, Ernest Holmes, encouraged everyone to experiment with spiritual experiences. In his *Ideas of Power*, page 108, he says, "The only prophetic thing that can ever happen to you and to me, is not to read –

just read – what others have done, but somehow or other, taking that as an example, to do the same thing."

I wanted my connection with Source to feel fresh and delightful. So I simply relaxed through the months of July and early August, pending inspiration. I continued to write in my journal about all the things I love to be, feel, have and see. I saw that as "tuning myself to the vibration of love," and wrote many journal pages of love lists daily.

In late August, while writing in my journal, I stumbled upon the word 'Beloved' and began to hear the other side of a conversation flowing. On September 2, 2009, I began to allow the loving chats with "B:" that make up the pages of this book, to flow freely.

People have asked me to define who or what The Beloved is. "The collective consciousness of love" is the best way I know to describe the infinite and intimate energy I feel in these conversations. I continue to come to know The Beloved better and trust them more powerfully each day.

I offer my personal experience in the hope that you, the reader, may be inspired to remember and honor your conversations with Source as you talk and listen to the Love that flows within you.

Whatever name comes to you is the right name.

Just say "Hi" and listen...

With love,

Connee Chandler

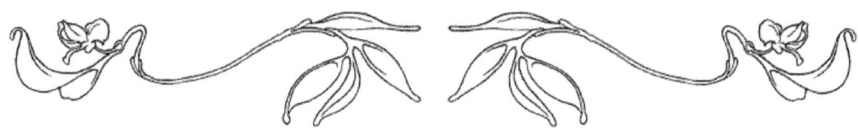

AUGUST, 2009:

Chatting with The Beloved Begins

On August 22nd, a conversation emerged that felt clear and powerful to me. I had started writing "Positive What If's" to tune up my vibration that morning.

You Don't Know Us Well Yet, But You Will! 8-22-09, 8:33 AM

Connee: What if I began putting my energy and my love into my writing? What is MY work? What if I knew what my own work was and wanted to channel my love into something I am creating? What if my life is my ultimate work of art?

I was touched last night when one of my friends told me that being friends with me was one of her happiest life experiences so far. That seems incredible to me. This friend has traveled all over the world, and had adventures that I would never dared undertake. I'm glad she was able to feel love from my listening to her and paying attention to her. I believe we can make love to all the Universe by listening and paying attention.

What if I am already good at loving and being loved and it is just a perceptual problem that I don't "get it?" What if I discover that what I have been looking for has actually been here all along? What if I learn to see that I don't need to strive to be something I am not, but simply to recognize that I already am who I want to be?

What if I already am a writer and there is a book inside me that wants to be written? What if I had a young friend who was happy to be paid to type up what I write? What if writing books doesn't have to change my freedom and my flow significantly? Or what if it does, and I enjoy the changes?

What would I really want to do if I felt totally loved and supported by Spirit? What is it I really want?

I want a strong, flexible, healthy body with wonderful energy, endurance and vibrancy. I want to live confidently, feeling empowered. I want to feel glad to be me and glad to be alive. I want to relax into knowing that life is good and all is well. I want to remember that I live in the heart of God already. I want to learn what it feels like to live loved. I love knowing that I am loved. I am willing to feel the great love that Source has for me. I am willing to experience it more in my life.

What if I don't need to worry about the future? What if worrying about it is the only thing that can keep it from being magnificent? What if there is an ease and grace ahead of me that I never imagined before?

What if I learn to look up and forward rather than down and backward? What if I had a clear vision of who I am and what I want? What if I knew that all I needed to do was to relax myself and help other people relax? What if I got so deeply relaxed that all my resistance just drained away? What if I find it easier and easier to fall in love with the present moment and trust that things are flowing toward good, good and more good? What if I am an ever-expanding and evolving being? What if I get clearer glimpses of the light of my being?

What if coming into conscious relationship with Source is a present reality rather than a far-away dream? What if whatever you call it – All That Is, Source, Spirit, God, Jesus, Sarayu, Papa... Beloved...

Oooooo, I like "Beloved."

Suddenly I can feel that he likes Beloved, too!

Connee (C): What if Beloved already knows me and loves me totally?

Beloved (B): I do.

C: What if Beloved already has a solution for my future work?

B: I do.

C: What if The Beloved sounds like a whisper on a meditation tape giving loving suggestions to relax?

B: I do.

C: What if The Beloved, my beloved Beloved, is already here, right now, loving me?

B: I am.

C: What if I can start to feel and hear him more powerfully every day?

B: You are.

C: What if there's no trick to this but to relax and allow it to happen.

B: You got it!

C: What if I am already getting the message clearly and strongly?

B: You are.

C: What if I am now learning to pick the signal from amid the noise more astutely?

B: You are!!

C: What if the things that look like they are going wrong are actually demonstrations to show me that I am already receiving messages and I can easily attend to them more gracefully?

B: In fact, you are already in the middle of that process, Connee. You are listening. You are allowing me/us in more and more. You are tuning up to hear us more clearly as you consciously choose to tune to the vibration of love. You are a gift to the world – each one of you is! And you are tapping into the gift that you are specifically, more and more powerfully!

C: I want to know about love! I want to love and be loved. I want to savor and bask in love, to breathe it in and allow myself to be excited by it. I want to fill my heart with love. I was shocked to feel the emptiness there the other day. My heart, radiant as the sun on the outside, felt totally empty on the inside! It was a shock!

B: You are so good at translating vibrations into images – well done, sweet girl. The image was a reflection of your bleak, lonely thoughts in that MOMENT, not the truth of your being. Like a sky flooded with ambient light that only shows 2% of the stars to your gaze, your radiant heart can be covered by a filter of fear caused by limiting patterns of thought.

You wrote once about the void – it's not empty at all. It is totally full of infinite possibilities. THAT is the truth of your heart, too.

You get to fill your heart by your focus of attention. You can choose to fill it with the divine. Choose to focus on God, The Beloved. Choose to focus on your appreciation for having a day off to read a silly novel, or to watch a comedic movie.

Every day, by your focus of attention, you fill your heart with fear or grace. Every day, you put in there your invitation for God to be something specific for you. What do you want me to be? Do you want me to be a volcano, or a chocolate fondue, or a dish of raspberries or a life path of lovely surprises and delights and amazing people around every corner? What do you want me to be?

C: I want you to be the FEELING of love, warming my heart, relaxing me, so that I feel at home within myself, safe, secure and beloved. I want to live loved!

B: Ah, Connee, yes, you just got it! You want to feel safe in your own heart. You want to feel at home and loved within yourself.

The non-local part of you is EVER loving, ever giving sublime beauty to your life. But you have to feel safe in your own heart to take it in. This is a powerful message – the safety you feel depends on the way you treat yourself in your own heart.

C: How can I make my heart a safe home for myself?

B: Your heart was created loving and loved, safe, secure and homey. Your heart is God's heart, perfect, whole and complete already and always.

C: So you are saying that in some way I don't yet really understand, that my heart is divine, serene and secure NOW?

B: Yup, it always has been and always will be. Your heart is an individualized part of God's heart.

But there is the catch. In the process of individualizing, your free will comes into play. You get to choose to do whatever you want to do with God's heart. You can open it, close it, build walls around it, build structures inside it – traps, nets, escape hatches down ventilator shafts...

C: Ha! That's a reference to that silly novel I just read! I love that you are showing me that you know what's going on with me. It's like you are tracking my life! You know what I've been reading and thinking...

B: We've always been here, Connee. We know it all and we love you absolutely. There are no gaps, shadows or voids in our love for you. We love you, and everyone else, too, absolutely. Our love is powerful and can be trusted. As *The Shack* said, "You don't know us well yet, but you will!"

B: & C: [Simultaneously] I/We are so glad we are having this conversation!

B: We are the peace that underlies all things. You have tapped into us before. It is so good that you are consciously choosing to feel for us as you did during the early part of this conversation. We like that you call us Beloved!

What you have been saying you want most in all the world is to be able to tell people how deeply they are loved. In order to do that, you have to know it yourself! You have to know, feel and **live** how deeply you are loved.

You have been getting this message of love spread out over many years, in tiny glimmers here and there. You have been receiving very well, indeed, this high vibrational message. We send it all day, every day to everyone. That you receive it is **grand**!

Your skill at receiving is expanding now. It's becoming more dimensional, like your radiant heart image. Your willingness is coming into alignment with your skill and your joy. So this conversation can be taking place like this now, fairly easily. You are doing very well. We are very pleased with your choice of intention and your effort to listen to us.

You are seeing more and more clearly now. You are receiving the call to do this work powerfully and doing great work. Keep it up. All is well. There is no hurry here. You are already getting it right. Relax, bask, you got that right! As you spread appreciation, you expand love on the ground, on this planet. You impact the degree of love in the consciousness of humanity as you choose love. There is no greater value than that.

C: I am willing to receive the love you have for me. I am willing to open up to an ongoing conversation between us. I want to receive clearly and well. I want to translate these vibrations from you into exquisite songs of love from non-local to local. I want to live loved. I am willing to hear and see and feel and know how deeply I am loved. I am willing to sink into the ocean of love and fill up my heart with the love that is infinitely there for me. I am willing to receive the gift of love you have always been offering.

B: We are love. We always have been and we always will be. There is nowhere love is not. Like attracts like. Therefore, we are also loved. The relationship that is created within God in *The Shack*, three in one, is re-created everywhere, between each of you and us.

C: I am willing to explore this more fully and write it down. I am willing to step into the power of what is flowing here. I don't know where it will lead, and I trust that it will be good.

I am willing to be led and I am listening. I am hearing a loving voice, murmuring under all the rest. I am willing to find my own heart's desire. I want love to be my highest priority. I am willing for it to be easy and comfortable, one gentle next step at a time.

B: We look forward to this relationship with you. Thank you for talking to us. And for listening!

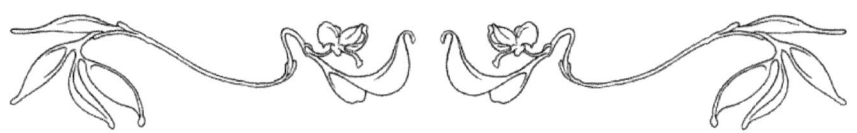

SEPTEMBER, 2009:

Dancing With an Invisible Partner

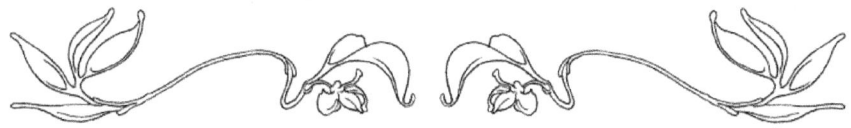

Moments of Bliss – "Butt Gusting" Belly Laughter: 9-2-09, 8:20 AM

C: Morning, B!

B: Hi, Conn!

C: I love you!

B: We love you, too!

C: How can I allow myself to bask in the bliss and stop retreating into chocolate and Free Cell and staying up too late reading?

B: Give yourself some time, sweet girl. This is a powerful evolutionary step you are taking here. There's plenty of time for you to get comfy here. You don't have to rush into anything. Just relax, play with your friends, get a massage.

You are in such harsh and heavy judgment! It just doesn't have to be that way! You don't reject sweet Rosie because she puts her claws in your face when you pet her. You just play the hand/paw game and love her unconditionally. You need your own version of the hand/paw game for a while, where you notice yourself making the choice you would prefer to release and you love your way through it.

You do slow yourself down by doing those things. It's ok! They are just old habits that are bringing you a little relief right now. Don't make a big deal of this. Don't use hard, harsh words. Soften, gentle, child. All is really well. There is no hurry at all.

In fact, there is magic in this cool clear air of fall. You are moving into a new period of love and growth. You are really going to enjoy this time. There's fun afoot, and freedom and joy!

Merrily, merrily float down the stream. Sing more, dance a little and get more playful. The light of your being is magnificent. The love you are opening up to receive is here for you already in brilliant abundance.

Your heart is opening to a wonderful partner and a wonderful new life. It's all unfolding perfectly and in good timing. Relax, play with Kathy and Carol. Bliss with Carrie. Explore how good you can feel with each one. Do positive aspects of everyone. Notice how many beautiful people you have attracted into your life who want to play with you. Relax, release, refresh yourself daily.

"Close your eyes. Fall in love. Stay there." Rumi was so wise!

C: But I don't stay there. I get cranky and afraid of the asthma…

B: There, there, sweet girl. It's ok. You are going to be all alright. You ARE all right. You are bouncy, resilient and beautiful, just like the cosmic snowflake vision you saw recently. (See Appendix B) That was such a wonderful translation of vibration you did there! You really are good at the imagery stuff. We're so glad you are who you are, doing what you do!

This is plenty, you know! We are very proud of you and pleased that you do what you do.

You can just relax into this now. No need to rush around or upset yourself. A little bit of writing, a little bit of quiet contemplation, some uplifting reading, some walks in the woods, some wonderful stories, some tasty food, some laughter with friends, some birthday parties and guided meditations – THIS is your Evensong in action, love in motion. It is already underway and it is beautiful.

We love you. We hold you in high regard and great respect. We trust that you are doing your best every day. You don't have to make an old choice wrong in order to make a new choice today. Take one gentle step at a time.

Get out your notebook and give yourself some check marks and encouragement for healthy behaviors. *DRINK MORE WATER!*

That's really the key here. It's so simple. Your body needs more water to evolve with greater ease. And as you drink more water, those deep breaths are supported. You need more water so you can breathe more easily and deeply. You will feel lighter, more confident and more beautiful because you are seeing yourself with appreciation and in alignment with how we see you all the time.

We love you. We surround you with love in every moment. We trust your choices and we know the ultimate outcome. We see what is queued up for you, what Abraham-Hicks calls your vibrational escrow...

C: What's in there?

B: Moments of bliss! Gazillions of them! Romantic moments! Butt gusting - oh, that meant 'gut busting' belly laughter!

B: & C: [Laughter]

B: Floating on air moments. Soaring in consciousness moments. Deep and sweet connection moments. Rising in love moments. Melting into Presence moments. Putting words to vibrations moments. Seeing grand visions moments. Peak moments. Vivid moments. Moments of being deeply touched. Harmonious moments. Lusciously sensual moments. Glowing grins moments. Fireworks moments. Deeply relaxing moments. Hanging out with friends moments. Overflowing joy moments. Moments of celebration. Moments of wonder, awe and reverence. Moments of outrageously fun irreverence.

You have a terrific sense of humor and fun. It is coming out more and more. Take EVERYTHING lightly. Make a big deal of nothing.

Everything can wait. Just relax. Your life is flowing beautifully! Expect great things around every corner. Chill out. Drink more water. Love someone or something. Let it be easy. Life is good. Give thanks. Relax and celebrate. All is well.

Unfolding Love Story: 9-4-09, 1:25 AM

In an email I received, my friend Tewa wrote: "All of existence loves me!" And then she talked about a powerful, deep mystical experience of waking up wrapped in the soft warmth of The Beloved.

C: All of existence loves me, too!

What an amazing thing <u>that</u> is!

I want to experience feeling loved at that level, too, please Beloved. I am willing for you to open this door. I am eager to know and to love and be loved by Spirit now. I am willing to allow my heart to expand to allow this experience. I am eager to feel the power of love moving through my heart, my mind, my body and my life. I love loving. I love feeling love, loving, loved and beloved.

I love being aware of you, Beloved!

B: We're so glad you've begun to communicate with us directly, Conn.

C: I want to do it more and better. I am willing to open to this experience more completely.

B: It's infinite in potential, so 'completely' is relative. Being here with us is your birthright and we have spoken to you 24/7/365 -- all the days of your life.

It's a testament now to your listening and interpreting the blocks of thought into words that this seems now more like a dialog than a picture or a vision.

C: I have loved my visions.

B: We'll still talk in images when that's the best way to translate the vibration. And the feeling of being loved is, for you, conveyed better by this dialog because it feels more intimate. You have been requesting this feeling of intimacy.

C: Yes. I do want to know YOU with my heart. I want to know me in nonphysical with my heart.

B: Exactly! You want to know the collective consciousness that is your ME and WE, intimately.

And we love that this love story is unfolding. For we love you with all the aspects of love you can imagine – romantic lover, mother, father, brother, sister, friend, child – and many more ways you haven't begun to put words to, including creator/creation and self-love!

We feel nuances that are requiring you to evolve in order to communicate with us about them and perceive them. Your sensitivity is evolving. Your capacity to interpret the vibration of love is expanding. Once you perceive what we are sending, you are evolving in your ability to translate that into words that communicate what we feel to others!

This is the work/job/joy/play you were born to do that has been predicted for you.

You came with the intention of expanding humankind's capacity to feel the love of God. The veil is thinning and all the tacking of your sailboat thus far is bringing you to this powerful destination. You are arriving on a new shoreline that contains beauties you have barely glimpsed to date.

You have the capacity to evolve in this way. You chose it from nonphysical and now you are choosing it from the physical.

Don't regret or second guess your decisions not to channel in the 80's and 90's. That was not the time for your gift and you wisely allowed the portals with lots of static and resistance to close. There is no hurry here.

We repeat. Relax.

There is no hurry. You have two more decades to do this work before you are ready to retire to the experience of a quieter life.

So your starting now to share our love and our thoughts on paper is in perfect timing.

You have become the imperfectly perfect messenger by feeling estranged from love and then coming back to it. Your gift for identifying this new experience is amplified by your having felt outside of it for so long. This really helps you put the coming back into it into words now. It's a gift to the world that you were willing to carry to make this time and place possible. We honor your willingness to explore outside the love so as to more poignantly express inside the love!

Stop, relax and look up more powerfully now. We want you to see with us and recognize that nothing has ever gone wrong here.

It's all been something in the process of going very, very right. Who you are, where you are, what you have, and who your friends are, are totally ideal to the experience that is beginning to unfold.

Not one piece of this puzzle is missing or out of place, for you or for anyone else, Connee. Each one is perfectly on his or her path.

The capacity to perceive love is evolving on this planet. And there are many, like Tom and Katie and you, who are blooming in the flowing of the heart right now. Your co-creative experience is expanding you all. Nothing is out of alignment. You are working together for good on purpose and you are amplifying each other's abilities. It is a valuable co-creative partnership that will continue to bloom.

You are each doing your work that allows that to happen. Stop, relax and look up often to see the love growing that you are bringing together into the world.

It's all good. You meant for this to unfold together. You all followed the perfect impulses to get here and you will continue to do so.

Relax. Look up and see the moon bows!

It's all good.

Now get some sleep, dear girl. There is plenty of time for this love to unfold. Sweet dreams, Beloved.

Feel the Love: 9-8-09, 9:03 AM

C: Good morning, B!

B: Hi, Conn!

C: I love exploring love with you!

B: Definitely our idea of fun, too!

C: I want to get really good at conveying your love in my writing.

B: You are already doing a great job. There's a vibrational resonance set up as you feel more and more loved by Source that is *automatically* there as you write. And even more as you speak. People can hear the warmth in your voice. You don't have to talk about love. You can talk about anything, and if you feel loved by Source, you will be communicating that love.

C: Really? That sounds like magic!

B: The deepest desire people have is to know they are loved. Your ability to express yourself AS love is proportionate to how filled up with love you already are. When you really feel immersed in the infinite Love of God, there is no limit to how much love you are able to give. It flows through your words, vibrates in your vocal cords, shines in your eyes, radiates in your smile! People get it because you LIVE it. You teach best by your example. Just let yourself feel the love, bask in it, breathe it in, savor it, appreciate it, open your heart and your mind to the evidence of it.

C: I love that I am encountering lots of other people's writings about the love that God has for us now.

B: That's Law of Attraction in Action. As you focus on love, and feel love and loved, more love comes to you from everywhere.

C: It's fun to notice all the synchronistic ways love is coming.

B: You ain't seen nuthin' yet! We adore you and are more and more able to send you evidence of our love as you open yourself up to receive it. Being happy and appreciating today is the best way to line up with an even more amazing tomorrow.

In Good Hands: 9-9-09, 1:00 AM

C: Hi, B!

B: Hi, Conn!

C: I'm feeling down – my friend Kate's in the hospital and I want to know her wellness and provide support and love for her. I feel concerned because I am seeing her as a friend rather than viewing her wholeness as a practitioner sees.

B: You are asking for help seeing Kate as Source sees her. She's already flying high with vibrant good health and wellbeing and an alligator-free vacation from our perspective. We like to see you smile here. Feeling better about Kate is your objective.

C: Talking to you does make me feel better.

B: And so will a good night's sleep. Kate is in good hands, resting in the heart of God! Get some rest yourself, and we'll talk tomorrow.

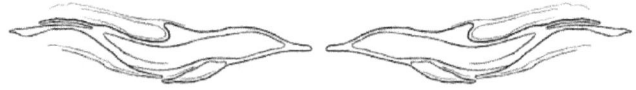

Higher Frequency Thoughts: 9-13-09, 10:41 AM

C: Hi, B!

B: Hi, Conn!

C: I'm blissing on love this morning. I heard you tell me that the reason I love the PERN Series books is that the author, Anne McCaffrey, feels loved, and she pours her overflow into those books! It's truly wonderful to read love.

B: Exactly! It doesn't matter what you/she writes about – the love shines through!

C: So that's why Esther Hicks is so good at speaking, "There is great love here for you." She feels loved!

B: Yes, Esther does feel loved. Jerry and Esther Hicks have a particularly loving relationship. She adores him and her love has put her into a powerful state of allowing. That's how Esther started speaking for Abraham in spite of her fears and reservations.

C: I don't have a Jerry...

B: Yet. You will!

And it is good that you are making this connection directly, on your own. If you had that partner in the outside world right now, you wouldn't be reaching inward with such passion. Getting our connection established in word and dialog is the precursor to all you will be doing in the future.

Everything is lining up perfectly. Relax. Trust. Everything you know you want, and much more, is before you. And THIS moment is exquisite! The sun is shining; it's a glorious day. You connected with the movie *Pollyanna* through your friend Julie on Facebook this morning. You thought about Abraham's quote on thinking of Self-love as being the Self that loves. (Abraham-Hicks, Caribbean Cruise Workshop, April 2006.)

You are loving yourself by allowing yourself to connect with the love you are, in the broadest sense, by connecting with us. And by focusing on all that you love inside and out.

It is powerful to love your feelings. Your writing long lists of things you love goes even further in tuning you to love when you focus on feelings. Feelings are your center; the hub of the wheel of your being.

Coming to love your 'negative' emotions is the next gentle step. Loving your negative emotions is really appreciating your magnificent guidance system.

Begin to dialog with us consciously when you are feeling negative emotion.

C: Wow, that's a cool idea. What would that be like?

B: You did it last night, more unconsciously. You said to yourself, "It's a Saturday night. I wish I had a date." We invited you to look at all the tickets you have for this fall and winter for Saturday night concerts coming up with your friends Carrie, Catherine and Ted. You heard us, and it perked you up. Then you remembered that you had a date with the PERN Series books; and your friend Vesta had given you Chinese food; Jeanne had given you homemade brownies; and you relaxed and had a lovely evening by yourself.

C: Yes, the thought of the tickets did turn the tide.

B: You wanted to feel good. You were asking, and we were able to feed you the perfect thought. We are poised with the perfect thought to give you next, all day, every day. We do think in your mind when you call us in.

We meant it when we said you chose this relationship with us from your nonphysical perspective and now you are allowing it in the physical. In fact, everyone does. Everyone chooses to have intimate connection to Source before they come into the physical – as emotion, and more fully as thought. But everyone's not tuned to receive in thought because they aren't tuned to a high enough frequency to be a match to us.

Esther Hicks tuned herself to Source through meditation. Meditation brought you visions, but it was your flowing love lists that tuned you to real-time dialog.

Let's go back to discussing choice. You asked to feel loved. It's been a strong focus for you since last October. You have opened yourself to a much more powerful guidance system with your focus on becoming more sensitive to your feelings. You also opened up more fully by allowing your love to flow on purpose with your love lists. As a result, you are receiving constant input from other people's expressions of love. You are seeing it clearly.

Remember the interaction you witnessed yesterday between two of your students. One noticed the other was speaking about receiving and she suddenly recognized that she was focused purely on giving in that moment – that was a powerful demonstration of what you have been doing for almost a year now. You shifted your focus from being solely a giver to being willing to give AND receive. You are beginning to let in the love that has been here for you all along. You have always been loved as much as you are now.

You are expanding your tolerance for receiving!

C: I'm hearing raucous laughter at that choice of words!

B: Well, you ARE moving up the scale from barely tolerating receiving to being willing to receive. You have come a long way toward having an open heart with the women in your life. You still have a ways to go with the men. You have made some powerful strides there recently, too.

C: I want to be open to receiving love. I am willing to receive love. I am eager to feel loved. I love feeling loved. There is still a little glitch there. I am suspicious and cynical about some people from my past.

B: Do what Pollyanna taught – if you look for the bad in people, you will always find it!

C: That's a quote attributed to Abraham Lincoln from that movie. Seems he taught Law of Attraction!

B: Yes, and if you look for the good in people, there is so much of that to find in everyone!

C: I'd love to get over getting my buttons pushed and feeling ouch-y.

B: You are. You've done a great job this past week of noticing where the ouch started and asking us for thoughts that felt better. As you talk to us more in this specific way, we are able to slip more thoughts easily into your regular mind chatter flow! You are creating an 'ambience of invitation' in your mind for us and our frequency of thought.

C: I want a higher frequency of higher frequency thoughts!

B: & C: [Laughter]

B: Here's a high five from nonphysical! We love it when you play with us!

We want to talk to you about playing Free Cell. The only thing wrong with playing computer games is your judgment about it. You can use Free Cell as an easy tool to slow down your energy and distract you when you feel overwhelmed. It's ok.

We aren't judging any of your behavior. It will be much easier for you to make other choices, if you want to, from a place of approving of yourself.

Give yourself the benefit of the doubt. Your mind likes a strong focus of attention. We loved your friend Lucia telling you yesterday that her mover learned efficient packing by playing hours/days/weeks of Tetris! All is going well here. Your focus of attention is getting powerfully honed. Your mind is in training and you are a really good focuser.

You get to choose how you use that gift. And playing Free Cell from a place of appreciation is fun!

C: Thanks, B. I feel loved!

B: Thanks, C. We feel loved, too!

B: & C: [Laughter]

Learning to Perceive Who You Already Are: 9-14-09, 8:51 AM

C: Morning, B!

B: Hi, Conn!

C: I love you! I love exploring this relationship with you. I love getting to know you better, Beloved. I want to see through your eyes and love the world with your heart!

B: We love the power of your blossoming intention to connect with us, as much as we have always loved you for being. We love you and everyone, infinitely and eternally. We also love you specifically and know you intimately. We track every single detail and are endlessly delighted by your new ideas and preferences that are born from the contrast. You are incredibly, from your point of view, and logically, from ours, precious to us.

Loving you, and everyone, is what we do. Just that!

C: You are so adorable, B! I understand why Esther Hicks said that, at first, it was weird when she realized Abraham was always there. And then, when she relaxed into it, she loved the feeling.

I love the specificity with which you communicate with me – the synchronicities in how you weave your answers to me with what's happening in my daily life give me thrill bumps. Thank you for loving me.

B: You are so welcome, Conn! In all senses of that word! You are welcome to our love. You are welcome to your life. You are welcome to the world. You are welcome to be heir…

C: Heiress!

B: & C: [Laughter]

B: …to the kingdom of heaven on earth now. You are welcome to it all!

C: Wow, that feels awesome, B! So I'm trying to get my mind around being totally and unconditionally loved and appreciated…

B: [dryly] Try using your heart!

B: & C: [Laughter]

C: Ok, I get it. It's about loving myself…

B: You say that as if it is a BAD thing!

B: & C: [Laughter]

B: At the level of consciousness known as Oneness, Self is God. Self is ALL.

C: So my head is tingling which means pay attention here…

B: Good! We're glad you are paying attention…

Think of how you love your cats. You feed them and groom them, pet them and water them, and play with them. You touch them with tenderness and recognize them for the love they bring to your life. You see their sweetness and continually affirm it in your attention to them. You clean up after them and provide what they need to have good, safe and comfortable lives.

You already love yourself in those ways!

C: Wow, you are right, B! I do provide for myself a good, safe and comfortable life.

B: The only part you want to expand is the positive affirmation part. You love your kitties unconditionally. You don't judge them when they throw up and you have to clean it up. You keep your heart open to them and know they are always doing their best. You never beat them up, or punish them for things you judge as wrong.

C: I adore them. Sometimes, I think I love them too much and I should be more strict with them.

B: Being strict with a cat is a waste of time. You can love them into wellbeing, but you cannot discipline them into wellbeing. You are an equally freedom-seeking being. Love and affirm your sweetness, like you do with Dusty and Rosie. We think you will enjoy the results.

C: Good girl, sweet girl...

B: Exactly! Goodness, kindness, sweetness and gentleness are your defining qualities because you are love. And you are also strength, power, intelligence, creativity, health, abundance, joy, beauty, harmony, peace and energy! There are endless aspects of who you are to explore.

C: All of those are things I can be?

B: All of those are things you ARE! You are an eternal, infinite being! Now. You are an eternal infinite being now.

All of those things you identify as qualities of God are YOU, now. It's an amazing thing to recognize and experience within yourself. As Abraham-Hicks said, "If you look for it, you will always find the goodness. It may be buried deep, but it is there. Look for it!" (Asheville Workshop, 5/29/09)

You are not trying to become something you are not; you are learning to perceive who you already are.

C: I've sure heard and said THAT before!

B: See – you've been communing with us and communicating our collective knowing, as you, for a very long time now. You've only recently asked for and received this feeling of chatting on the edge of the expansion of the Universe; and that expansive feeling is greatly enhanced by this dialoging format we have evolved together. We will continue to evolve in our ability to commune.

C: It sure makes talking to myself more entertaining!

B: & C: [Laughter]

B: You're easy! We love that about you!

B: & C: [Laughter]

C: I'm tired now.

B: Rest and relax, sweet girl. You are doing very, very well in receiving us accurately. You were born to do this…

C: That brings tears to my eyes.

B: Because you are allowing yourself to feel more of our love every day. You are letting in our appreciation of who you are. And expanding in using this wonderful gift – which represents an amazing constellation of gifts, talents, skills and aptitudes you have been honing your whole life. The tingling on your scalp now is the indicator that you are receiving us clearly and more fully in allowing this river to run.

You are ready. This is the time.

Only not right now!

There's no hurry in the physical. Take a little time when you are inspired.

C: I want to fall in love and be passionate about you.

B: This is the getting to know you/us phase. It's good to take it in small snippets and get acclimatized to this new internal environment you are exploring.

All is well. We're on an adventure together. The team has changed as the terrain has changed and our presence will be ever available to you from now on. Ask and it is given. The door is wide open and the love is flowing both ways. You can trust this and rely on it.

This is the love you have been seeking your whole life. Relax and let us love and support you. It's what we do and we love our job/joy/play/work.

We love you. We're glad you love us.

Rest, relax and remember there's no hurry.

We love you.

C: Bye for now, B.

B: Bye, Conn. We're right here when you call...

Chatting on the Edge of the Universe: 9-15-09, 8:38 AM

C: Morning, B!

B: Hi, Conn!

C: I love you! I am so glad I read *The Shack* and got so clear that I wanted an intimate relationship with Source.

B: Yes, that book was a portal of possibility for you. It modeled for you the experience of taking a risk and moving forward into something you were saying you didn't want. Isn't it interesting that you are now enjoying three things you said you didn't want – the Abraham cruise with your playful friends; massage with active, stimulating conversation; and 'channeling.'

We like that you are characterizing this as chatting rather than channeling. We'll get back to that later.

But first we want to address your enjoying things now that you were saying you didn't want moments ago.

'Moments ago' is an exaggeration. But we want to amplify that your vortex is full of blissful moments. And point out that paying attention to what's happening in this moment right now matters.

This is happening in THIS moment. This chat, as a conversation, is happening because you are focused and listening in this moment. And now you are expecting us to be here, talking back to you when you talk to us.

Your saying, "Hi, B!" primes the pump, opens the door, and allows the energy to move.

We can, do and will talk to you forever, but unless you open the door to your listening, you don't hear what we are endlessly saying.

We are saying, "We love you!" We are saying, "We bless you." We are saying, "We are you!"

Moving into this level of intimacy takes courage and willingness. David Hawkins is right in his book, *Power vs. Force*. Opening to any powerful new experience of connection moves you up the Map of Human Consciousness from fear to courage to willingness to understanding to love to joy to bliss to Oneness.

Reconnection is not a singular event. It's an endless stream of moments, and choices of focus in the moment, that set up a vibration that is matched by Law of Attraction.

The choice of focus sets up a vibration. A different choice of focus sets up a different vibration. It's that simple.

What do you want to vibrate? Choose the feeling as your focus, and then tune to that vibration.

C: Thank you, B! I'm thirsty. I need to go get a glass of water.

B: YAY! Drink more water, Love. You need water to evolve to support this process happening more easily.

C: Ahhhhhhh… That's better! Kitties fed, email answered, thirst quenched, earlier chat typed. Now I feel relaxed and ready to continue.

B: Good! Notice how well you are loving yourself, and Dusty and Rosie. Well done!

C: Thanks! You are appreciating me for doing my daily routine?

B: Your daily routine is vital to your sustaining your healthy, joyful life. Of course we appreciate that! We look forward to your appreciating yourself more for it, too!

C: Wow, that's an amazing idea! Thanking myself for drinking water or brushing my teeth!

B: Yup! You were talking about moving into Appreciation LIVING! That's how to do it. Appreciate everything you do as you live. Appreciate everything you do that contributes to your wellbeing. You do a gazillion things daily that help you be clean, healthy, strong and attractive. All of them are worth giving yourself a pat on the back for!

C: So we have a couple of subjects still on the table to talk about – things I said I didn't want that have come that now I love, and "chatting" rather than "channeling."

B: Yup, where do you want to start?

C: Chatting.

B: You have "Chatting on the edge of the Universe" on your business cards.

C: I was thinking about my phone sessions with ***people!***

B: Indeed. And we love that you broadened it to include chatting to nonphysical. Because it is just as easy, and WAY more fun!

B: & C: [Laughter]

C: Oh, I don't know about that! Chatting with connected people is WAY fun, too! I am so glad I know that!

B: For sure! We love that you've figured that out. But that's just 'cause, if you are connected and they are connected, *WE'RE* there, too! We bring the party to the party!

B: & C: [Laughter]

C: Like Abraham-Hick's saying, "Take your Inner Being everywhere you go. If you take your Inner Being to the party, it's going to be a good party!" (El Paso, TX, Workshop, 2/17/01)

B: Exactly!

You have set the intention in your prayers with your clients for a long time to have the fullness of both of you, infinite and finite, local and non-local, show up during the conversation. You asked, and we came, and you have increasingly tuned yourself to the vibration of flow.

We wanted to say 'Cosmic Flow' there. You judged that as too pretentious and left it out.

But that is what this is: Cosmic Flow. Cosmic Consciousness. The broader perspective of Source flowing into Time-Space Reality.

You, and we, like the phrase 'Chatting with The Beloved,' because it sounds so familiar, intimate, simple and easy. And it is. Yet we don't want you to miss the value inherent in the familiar any more than we wanted you to miss the love that getting up and getting a drink of water represents when you are thirsty.

It's all simple. And elegant, as Einstein would say. It all matters.

We'd love to see you do more intention-setting with prayers throughout your day. Bringing the divine into the present moment, as Joanna Gray said – segment intending with invocations. Thank her and ask her if you can quote her!

[C: I did, she said yes! Thanks, Joanna!]

B: The subject of now doing things you said you didn't want to do is interesting. You have lived making rules for yourself that are no longer serving you. You are opening much more powerfully to unconditional receiving when you are connected.

You are allowing us to create a much more interesting mix for your days, because you are focusing on how you want to feel rather than what you want to do, or who you are going to do it with. You are feeling your way through it.

When you say, "I want to feel loved!" we can line you up with dozens of people who adore you and want to let you know how much you are loved and appreciated.

C: Author Kathryn Alice, in *Love Will Find You*, said that we are appreciated for our virtues but we are loved for our flaws.

B: That's a good starting point. We'd say it as, "You've been willing to feel appreciated for your virtues, and now you are feeling loved by those who don't consider differences in people's talents and performances to be flaws."

Remember your friend Laurie Cohen's famous line, "Love is flawless and flows at every frequency." (Private email, March 2007)

Love does not perceive flaws. When you are connected to Source, you don't perceive flaws. When you are in the vortex, you focus on positive aspects. You focus where you feel the love flowing. And if you do see someone who you perceive as flawed, say something like, "Oh, they are asking for love right now. Aren't they cute?"

Being more gentle with yourself and others is the work!

C: That was totally awesome! I wrote it while I was sitting here waiting for a friend to call. And when she did, I asked her to do an invocation with me. And then read her the section on allowing people to love me so I feel loved, right after she gushed about how much she has loved me for fifteen years! And then we talked about seeing flaws in other people, and I read her the section on love not seeing flaws.

You are GOOD!

B: It's more to your credit than ours that YOU sat and wrote it just before you needed it. You have done it for years with your clients in dozens of other ways. Think how your friend Dr. Lisa Williams says that you always answer her question in your opening prayer, before she asks it.

You already ARE who you think you want to be.

It's all a process of learning to perceive through the eyes of Source.

C: I know it is pretty powerful to sit here and see me through your eyes.

B: You are still afraid to see yourself in the radiant truth of your being.

SEE God rather than SEEK God: 9-16-09, 8:43 AM

C: Hi, B!

B: Hi, Conn!

C: I stayed up way too late last night and I am tired this morning.

B: How would it feel to say instead, "I was so excited about visiting PERN last night that I stayed up late to read about Menolly and her fire lizards. I loved the details of how she impressed NINE of them, gained her freedom and became a Harper. What an amazing consciousness Anne McCaffrey has, and how I adore her beautiful books!"

C: Feels a lot better!

B: "Stayed up too late" is a judgment and judgments weight you down and make you tired. Relaxing into love with a great story can be as beneficial as sleeping. So can talking to us, or you wouldn't have been inspired to pick up your pen so early this morning.

C: I wanted to hear what you had to say about your cliff hanger statement from yesterday: "You are still afraid to see yourself in the radiant truth of your being."

B: We thought we'd intrigue you with that one, especially since you told someone the story this week about how you saw the face of God in your meditation once and it was SO bright that you slammed the door on it!

Humankind has often slammed the door on radiant brilliance – it makes sense not to blind yourself. You have free will; you get to choose to take it one step at a time. To 'see through a glass darkly' is just to wear sunglasses to see more comfortably when the light is too bright.

Now, in addition to asking to feel loved, you have also been clearly speaking your intention to perceive clearly. You continue to evolve in the sensitivity of your perception, at your request. We just want you to notice where your resistance is, and let it go consciously.

C: I am willing to have a gentle, easy path of expanding awareness to seeing who I truly am.

B: Yes! Well done! We very much like the care you are using in feeling for the vibration of the words you are choosing for the intention you are setting. We also want to honor the way you are learning to feel our side of this dialog as well.

C: I am having to notice more specifically this morning than I have been the last few days – so I guess I am not tuned as high today as I have been.

B: Good insight! Keep feeling your way through everything! What is your intention in our dialog?

C: I am willing to feel loved. I am eager to give and receive love. I am also loving hearing what you have to share with me to help me learn and evolve in deepening connection with you. I value our relationship greatly. I want to know you better. I want to know myself better. I love this feeling of intimate, flowing conversation.

Thank you for inviting me to focus on my intention as I keep expanding and clarifying it. I am also now remembering what you said yesterday about doing an invocation with each segment of my day.

B: Beautiful! We love that you are so clear about your desire for greater closeness in our relationship.

Be like a little child. Little children learn like sponges in the course of their being, playing and loving.

If you come with love and lightness of being, and playfulness, you will learn a lot more than if you SEEK to learn.

Remember to SEE God, rather than SEEK God. There is nowhere God is not, you are never alone.

C: I like being your "sweet girl." It feels like innocence within this warm intimacy. That's a wonderful combination.

B: Yes, we love that vibration, too. Rest now, and relax before you begin this day.

C: Bye for now, B!

Opening a Very Big Portal: 9-17-09, 3:54 AM

C: Hi, B!

B: Hi, Conn!

C: So I woke up coughing at 3 AM, got up to get a glass of water and found a letter to me in email, asking for information, which I researched and replied to. Then I was inspired to write to another friend about the very cool Metro fare card manifestation I had yesterday. And then I was inspired to post that to the Abe list. (TheAbeList@yahoogroups.com) In writing to them, I was inspired to pre-pave how I wanted to feel tonight at the concert in DC. And in writing about that, I went into bliss, sitting at my computer.

And it occurred to me that coughing and wanting a glass of cold spring water from my water cooler in the den was the path of least resistance to connection and bliss through each of those rendezvous in the moment.

I am back to manifesting something I would say I don't want, waking up coughing and thirsty at 3 AM, as a path to something I am very clear I do want, the feeling of bliss.

This feels like a synchronicity with the Abraham-Hicks quote I transcribed yesterday. Here's the actual quote: "If you can get this thing we are going to say to you next, your life will be blissful from this point forward. If you can be happy in anticipation of what's coming, you'll be happy forever more. And everything you want will come quickly." (Philadelphia Workshop, 6/11/09)

B: Pretty cool, huh? We line up stuff like that for you all day, every day. You are just awakening to your ability to perceive it now! It's not new, it happens all day, every day – you always get what you are vibrating. It's just that you are noticing the synchronicities now. Well done!

You are on the way to being able to use us, and the 'fairies of the Universe' that Abraham talks about far more consciously and specifically. Remember them saying, "You have this really good staff that will take care of everything for you. You just have to delegate it – and trust it." (St. Louis, MO, Workshop, 7-18-00)

We want you to delegate everything. Ask and let go, as you did with the fare card. And follow the impulse just as you did there.

C: Here's the story of the fare card, B.

I woke up very early in the morning, aware that I am going tonight to a concert in Washington DC this week, and would need a fare card for the subway. I last went into DC in April, had a fare card then, but had no idea where it might be. So I asked my Inner Being where it was, and realized there probably wasn't much money left on it anyway, so that I could just buy a new one today. I let it go and went back to sleep.

Then a friend called in the morning and asked me to drive to DC to see another friend in the hospital. I looked around for something, a little gift, to bring my friend that might cheer her up. My eye caught on a little plastic baggie that had some fridge magnets in it, and I was inspired to pick it up and look at them. The one on top said "Celebrate!" which didn't sound like the exact tone I was looking for during a hospital visit, but instead of putting it down, I ruffled through them inside the bag to see if any of the magnets had a different message. I saw something of a different color in the middle.

It was the fare card!!! There was $7.60 left on it - I think that might even be enough for my round trip into DC!

I have a 2000 square foot house with gazillions of things in it. My Inner Being pointed me toward a baggie I had tossed into a basket on the counter in my kitchen that has laid there, probably undisturbed, for five months! Pretty amazing!

B: You are doing such a great job of picking up what we are telling you. We just love this more intimate relationship with you. This is as much fun for us as it is for you. We celebrate alignment.

When you got up and followed the impulse to get the glass of water... note that the water is a synchronicity, too! Isn't that fun? You've been writing about drinking more water all month. You are making it so easy for us to play with you!

Anyway, when you followed the thirsty impulse, you were doing the same things as picking up the baggie of fridge magnets that led you to the fare card. You were responding to our guidance. And the same is true of the emails you replied to. Each time, you just did the next thing that felt good, that you felt gently inspired to do.

It's really that simple. That's what Abraham-Hicks means by, "Feel your way through it." (Rye, NY, Workshop, 10-12-97)

Nor are you judging or offering any resistance to the fact that this is all happening at 3:00 AM! You are such a good sport, Connee! We love that about you.

In fact, we are really pleased that you are not just listening and writing down what we are saying. You are also typing it up, appreciating its value and sharing what we say with friends. In doing that you are honoring your gift, which allows it to grow by your loving attention to it.

But even more, you are actually putting into practice, moment by moment, the things we are suggesting to you. Today you have been practicing shifting away from judgment and setting intention in a way that brings the divine into the physical. Well done!

C: You say that a lot, "Well done!"

B: We love you. We look for things to appreciate about you, all day, every day. We are showing you how beautiful you are to us. Even more importantly, we are showing you what love looks like. We are modeling the way you can treat yourself. Loving and looking for things to appreciate about yourself can become the undercurrent thought you choose to engage in all day, every day. It's a choice you can make.

Once you choose to look for things to appreciate about yourself, you are seeing through the eyes of Source. And once you feel what it feels like to match your approval of who you are with OUR approval of who you are, you won't give a rip about seeking approval from anyone else!

That's how you get to the place of not caring what other people think of you. Not by your not caring about them, but by your caring more about you.

In your caring more about you, and receiving more fully all the love we are endlessly sending to you, you are full to overflowing with love and will have so much more to give, generously and unconditionally, to the people around you.

As you give from the overflow, you glow! You go, girl! You really are on a roll here, and we are so delighted with you!

C: I'm pretty delighted with myself, B. This seems like good stuff to me. It's fine-tuning some questions I didn't even know I had.

B: We love this about that, too. We are able to squeeze in answers so easily, because you didn't come here with questions to get answers. You came here to love and be loved! That's why this dialog in this easy peasy way is possible.

C: That brings tears to my eyes, B.

B: Yup, this whole 'intimate relationship with God' stuff is very powerful, Conn. It opens doors for you, effortlessly.

Focus on feeling loved. You are so loved. You always have been. You always will be. You were created to live loved. Wm. Paul Young, who wrote *The Shack,* is a very good listener, and he opened a very big portal. What you are doing here is also opening a very big portal.

We felt your reluctance to write 'very big' there.

C: It seems pretentious…

B: That's what we were telling you about your being afraid to see the radiant truth of your being. You are endlessly willing to give credit to dozens of other writers, teachers and friends, but you are afraid to witness the brilliance of what you are doing here. What are you afraid of?

C: I'm afraid that this is not as good as you think it is. And I am afraid that I'm not as good as you say I am at getting it right.

B: Relax, sweet girl. This isn't a test! We love you and are totally appreciative of your willingness to show up and do this at all. We adore your courage to write it and your acknowledgment of its value in your desire to share it with your friends.

When you are connected, you feel the exquisite clarity and love that is shining in all these words. When you get momentarily disconnected, you have doubt.

That's not because you aren't good enough, or because this work is not good enough, it's because you feel negative emotion when you disagree with what we know to be true.

We know the value of what's happening here. We know the impetus and intention behind it, and the outcome of what is to be.

C: I can't take it all in at once. I just want to focus on how good it feels to talk with you. And how much I enjoy re-reading it and then typing it up and practicing it.

It's like my own personal flavor of love to me. Talking to you like this feels like the best thing that ever happened to me.

B: [Dryly] Didn't take you long to reconnect!

B: & C: [Laughter and delight]

B: Ok, C, back to sleep! Enough for now.

Take it easy. Little snippets. We want to have fun with this and we want you to have fun.

C: Ok, B. Would you help me get back to sleep quickly and easily, and wake up a "giant refreshed" as my mom used to say?

B: You got it, sweet girl! Night-y Night...

9: 40 AM: I went back to sleep and woke up and started writing again after getting up and feeding my kitties.

B: You change behavior by positively reinforcing the behavior you want to expand, rather than by fighting the behavior you want to suppress. You change beliefs by focusing on the thoughts you want to think rather than fighting the thoughts you don't want to think.

C: Wow, talk about joining the program already in progress!

B: & C: [Laughter]

B: You've been thinking a lot this morning about what we said about the importance of focusing our relationship on love, giving and receiving love and feeling loved, rather than on asking and receiving answers to questions.

That choice on your part is allowing us to bring a whole new level of information to you. We are responding now to the answers that have been waiting in your vibrational escrow.

It's just like our being able to bring you the experiences you want now that you are focused on feeling your way through things.

Keep focused on the love and loving and feeling loved, sweet girl. Everything else flows from there.

C: It started to rain. My windows are open. I need to get up and check to see if it's raining in…

B: Go, Love! We are always here for you!

Just Checking In: 9-18-09, 7:24 AM

C: Morning, B.

B: Hi, C.

C: Just wanted to check in and say I love you!

B: We love you, too, Conn. We want you to know how deeply you are loved. Try something new. Every time you say "thanks" on the outside, say, "I am loved," on the inside.

C: I say thank you a lot of times in a day, B.

B: We know, C. Imagine how good you are going to get at recognizing that you are loved! Get some sleep now. Plenty of time for more later.

Dancing With an Invisible Partner: 9-19-09, 2:25 AM

C: Hi, B!

B: Hi, Conn!

We really like that you are talking to us more and more!

We really like that you are listening to us more, too!

We really like that you are practicing "thank you – I am loved." You are a wonderful appreciator already. You say thank you dozens of times a day.

It's working for you so much better than trying to say, "I approve of myself." It's taking you directly to us and our love for you over and over. It is building your trust in us and your willingness to feel, trust and be aware and honest about how you are feeling.

As you feel loved, you feel safe. Children who feel safe are playful and venture forth eagerly for new adventures and experience.

We want to create with you the internal atmosphere of a secure, curious child. You have no idea yet how fun that is going to be!

We eagerly anticipate your getting to know yourself within a climate of internal appreciation. Watching with you as you shift will be a great pleasure for us.

Conscious contact with you is a joy for us. Your willingness, eagerness and love for this conscious connection are a thrill for us, too.

This is the real life you have been waiting to begin.

Colin Hay's song (Waiting for my Real Life to Begin) is another portal for you, particularly with the Scrubs video on Youtube.com. Seeing the woman being resuscitated become the gorgeous young woman singing that song in a vivid red evening gown, while releasing her physical body, took you straight back to what you learned from nonphysical when your mother was dying. You asked your late husband, Cliff, to help her move into the light. He replied, "I'd love to help you, Conn, but I'd have to wait in line."

And you got hit with the incredible wave of love that was waiting for your mom that almost knocked you off the chair.

You asked Abraham-Hicks once if you had to die to feel that love. Obviously YOU didn't, because you felt it that night in meditation, talking to Cliff.

That experience, and your desire to feel more of that love has led you in a pretty direct line to this moment, from our perspective. From your perspective, though, you have been tacking your sailboat all over creation to reach this destination.

What we are helping you see now is that the direct line has been the choice you have made to follow your intuition, your internal guidance as to what next step to take. The steps may take you all over the dance floor, but you are still doing the same dance inside.

You've been learning to dance with us your whole life, Connee. The last 25 years have represented increasingly conscious awareness of the guidance we give you.

But until now you have been dancing with an invisible partner that you couldn't communicate with clearly. Now, with your strong intention to love and be loved by us, you've created this conversation that you are trusting more and more through your experience with us.

Tonight, at the swing dance, you had the experience of what it is like to be led by a strong partner, in a simplified version of the dance, suited to your newbie abilities. We had so much fun with you there!

And you got to feel, during the lesson that began the evening, what it felt like to be led by those who were as clueless as you, and those who were marginally more skilled, those who were skilled and willing, and those who were strong and clear.

There wasn't one of them who wasn't fun to dance with, was there? Just being on the dance floor at all is a brilliantly good time!

You will be doing a lot more of that. We love its suitability for teaching you how to follow OUR lead.

You can rely on us. We are strong and clear. We see the bigger picture and can lead you to the clear sweet spots on the dance floor. We can guide you where we want you to go, to maximize your potential for fun.

We love you. We aren't asking you for blind faith.

We are inviting you to dance! Because it's fun. And because you are going to learn to adore following the lead of a strong, clear, loving, kind, respectful partner.

We aren't taking you somewhere we've chosen for you. We're taking you where you have chosen to go.

As we have been demonstrating lately, we may be presenting you with opportunities you said you did not want, that have given you feelings that you know you do want. You have chosen the destination yourself. You are now in alignment with the intention we have held for you all along – that you love and express the true brilliance of your being.

That's our desire for you and for everyone, Conn. We want you to be happy. We want you to feel joy, pleasure, playfulness, and fun. We want you to be ever more fully expressed in your creativity and love.

Now you are choosing to align with us specifically and hear the details of how to live loved, in intimate contact with the indwelling Source. BRAVO!

We honor your choices that have brought you to this exquisite juncture and remind you that you ain't seen nothing yet!

B: & C: [Laughter]

B: All of the pieces of the puzzle are important. You are noticing more and more details that sparkle.

What did you love about the swing dance?

C: I loved the music – it was fun, lively and had a strong beat. I loved the feeling of moving to the beat and learning to do the steps. I loved the freedom of doing something purely for the fun of it.

I loved the class the most. I loved that even the teenage boys, who were shocked to be separated from their girlfriends, treated me with respect. They became my partner for the moment, wanting to succeed in what we were there to do together.

I liked being able to succeed in a couple of basic steps. I liked learning something new in a place where it is ok to be a total beginner – everyone is willing to work with me.

I liked the silliness of the "talk like a pirate" theme. I like that they celebrate everything. I loved that they were having as much fun as the people I saw swing dancing at the Reston Town Center Concert earlier in the summer.

I loved that there were as many men there as women. I love that so many clearly loved what they were doing and wanted to have a good time doing it.

I love that there's infinite potential for skill development. I love that my bowling shoes worked well on the dance floor and were incredibly comfortable. I love that everyone is treated with attention, respect and appreciation.

I loved touching and being touched. I loved being around men who made eye contact with me and smiled and were willing to help me learn. I loved having many different partners to dance with. I love having something new and physical to learn that is fun to practice. I love that there are many dance classes and dance instructors around. I love that there is dancing going on somewhere most every night of the week in this area.

I love that I am opening up to more movement. I love that I am expanding in to more fun. I love remembering that my body is resilient and re-SOURCE-ful and has just been waiting for me to demonstrate what I want it to do. I love that right now all the trillions of cells have issued their requests for what is necessary to make it possible for me to learn to dance and the Universe has already answered.

I love that that I am very thirsty and drinking lots of water. I love that my Inner Being knows what needs to happen next and I am already getting wonderful internal impulses, emotional cues, and actual instruction from you, Beloved.

I love having something new and fresh to focus on. I love that my friend Trish went with me to the dance and helped me break the ice. I love that my friend encouraged me and stopped to talk to me before I left. I love that you don't have to have a partner to go. I love that I saw women asking men to dance and men asking women to dance.

Ok, B, did you nod off an hour ago?

B: Nod off?! Show some respect, woman! Who do you think is helping you to expand your capacity to come up with dozens of things to like and love about last night's experience?

When you tune to love, we are always in there helping you!

That sentence is not quite accurate yet – please try again, C. No opening clause is needed. We are ALWAYS in there helping you, feeding you the next best thought, guiding you with impulses and emotions and ideas.

When you tune to love AND choose to listen, you can hear us!

Now that you are not just tuning to love in general on the physical plane, but you are tuning to love on the divine station as well, the potential for joy is infinite!

C: I'm starting to fade here, B. Thanks for this magical interaction. I love that you led me to do positive aspects of the dance last night. I am glad you gave me so many rendezvous that pointed me in that direction. I love that there's plenty of potential for fun there to explore. I love that I love you and I can see that you are magnificent in loving me back. I love that you are teaching me by your example. I love that this is a highly valuable partnership for me.

Why is it valuable for you?

B: Great question, sweet girl. We look forward to answering it, but not tonight.

C: Ok, B. Thank you.

Oh, I am loved!

B: YAY! Night, Love.

C: Night, B!

I went back to sleep and then started again in the morning... 10:24 AM

C: Morning, B!

B: Hi, Conn.

C: I'd love to talk about this quote from Maher Baba I saw in an email this morning, "Love is essentially self-communicated – those who do not have it catch it from those who do have it."

B: Great thought! We'd shift the emphasis slightly.

Love is ever present – in everyone, as everyone. Love is an omnipresent quality of God. There is nowhere love is not. So again, we come back to perceiving what already is, rather, than catching/creating what is not.

Those who do perceive it open the door for those who do not yet perceive it, and invite them in to a place they have always been.

C: So it is like my story of *The Path*? (See Appendix C)

B: Exactly! You have never for a moment been anywhere but in the Garden. But you sure feel like you've been to hell and back!

When you feel unloved inside and look for love outside, you place **yourself** outside the ability to perceive the love that is ever inside you.

When you feel unloved inside, then Law of Attraction can't bring you love outside.

C: My forehead feels like it is pounding and my eyes are very light sensitive. What's up? I don't usually get headaches.

B: You are evolving, sweet girl. Your brain is building new connections. It's ok, nothing is wrong here, just relax into it. Close your eyes. Relax. And while you are there…

"Close Your Eyes. Fall in Love. Stay there."   (Rumi poem)

C: Thanks, B. I appreciate how you continually point me in the direction of appreciating the love that has already been expressed in English to build on here. I'll rest now.

B: Love you, Conn. See you later.

A couple of hours later, B: continued…12:37 PM

B: Music opens doors to love. People who feel loved, and who love music, make music and it opens the flow for others.

C: Thanks, B. I love that you spoke that connection for me.

Andrew da Passano, in *Inner Silence*, said that his favorite definition of God is "God, or godhood, is the power to create simultaneously all the possible relations with everything in the cosmos."

B: Such an expansive idea! We would say it a little differently.

God IS the connection between everything and everything else. So in that sense, God creates that connection by being the fabric from which it is all woven.

You were right when you pondered that and realized that you could ask to see the connection between anything and anything else.

When you are consciously connected to God, you have access to a conscious connection to anything else.

Within your physical experience, the energy embedded in consciously connecting with everything at once would fry your circuits.

That's why Rev. Carmen Brocklehurst's exercise -- reaching out your hand and feeling for the love that is coming to you from the farthest star you can imagine -- works so well. The 'great love' energy that surrounds you is finally quantified SMALL enough that you can perceive it easily and safely.

Your body is coming into harmony with the experience of more love flowing. Relax. Drink water. Rest.

It's funny that with swing dancing, you so easily accept the idea of going into training for incremental improvements. You see it as a path with a gazillion steps.

B: & C: [Laughter]

C: That was a good one! I like the dance analogies!

B: Yet you are seeing loved/not-loved as black and white, either/or. And there are a gazillion steps, next gentle steps, on your path to feeling more and more loved. And to having more and more love available to give, more and more love flowing.

C: I was just talking about moving from black-and-white thinking to shades-of-gray to millions of colors with my friend Trish last night!

B: Exactly. Your ability to give and receive love has expanded radically since you asked last October what it means to *feel* loved! You have been doing a great job of focusing and allowing, with your love lists and talking to people about what it feels like to feel loved.

You keep pouring love out, which primes the pump. And now you are remembering to allow the flow to return to you. So you are relaxing into unconditional receiving.

C: I got a flash a few minutes ago that all this is related to my field visions, especially the one that includes, "As the walls come down, the doors open." (See Appendix D)

B: Brilliant catch, my dear!

C: Thank you, B!

B: You have rightly understood that the fields are flavors of joy, different states of consciousness that are infinite in number, where infinite means beyond quantifying from a human perspective.

And the walls that divide each green field, all the way up the hill, as far as you can see, are limiting patterns of thought that create negative emotion. As you move through the doorway of love, you move easily to the next higher state of awareness that allows you to perceive the difference between the fields.

As you release those limiting beliefs, the walls become glorious doorways that you find everywhere.

When music helps you shift a limiting pattern of thought, it's a door opening – a portal to a clearer perception.

C: I so love that this is a leap-frogging conversation, B! I love that when I offer you some of the most expansive ideas I've ever heard, you expand them even more. This is so exciting!

B: We can do that with you, because years ago, in your conscious quantumness phase, you accepted the axiom, "All of this is true to the degree that I am not still blind."

You got it that the Universe is infinite. There is always expansion possible, and we love your willingness to expand.

C: I'm just getting that my Five Easy Peaces meditation is creating the space for this expansion as well. The meditation amplifies peace in the mind, heart, body, Being and Spirit. (www.conneechandler.com, Online Audio Meditations)

B: Exactly! When you relax your body and focus on breathing into the already quiet spaces/places in your mind and heart, you create an internal spaciousness. In that openness, your heart's energy – love, does blitz the body's energy field and entrain you collectively to a new state of integrity of being. You called that fourth easy peace Being and said that when you get there, it automatically opens the doorway to the Peace of God.

You did an amazing job intuiting that one, Conn!

C: I just say what I see and feel in the meditations.

B: And in seeing and feeling from a place of connection to Source, you were already tapping into the energy of the Mind of God. The energy of the Mind of God is knowing, the energy of the Heart of God is what you call Love. The energy of the body of God is life force, health and wellbeing.

C: Well, in the last year, while I have been on this path of feeling more loved and loving, I haven't been as healthy as I used to be.

B: Sometimes the walls have to come down for the doors to open. Your body has learned some very closed, restrictive patterns out of fear that are now being restructured.

When you feel ashamed of being ill, you are succumbing to a negative pattern of thought. The same is true when you apply the labels of psychiatric pathology to spiritual experiences.

C: Thanks to one of my teachers, Terry MacBride for **that** insight! (I am loved.) It has served me well in lowering my judgments about this experience with you, B!

B: So has what he taught you about mystics. He said, "It can be lonely knowing Oneness. But the loneliness disappears when you learn that we can stand alone together." (Personal conversation)

C: I wanted to get that out and let you finish. Thanks, Terry! I am loved! Wow, I FEEL the love that has brought me so many powerful teachers who have helped me, especially during that rough time after my husband Cliff died.

B: We've always been here, Conn, orchestrating the next highest thing, thought, person, experience, moment into your life.

That's our job, our work, our play, our joy! We do that all day, every day, for everyone and everything.

The Universe is designed to love and supply. Everything needed is ALWAYS at hand. You just have to be open to receive it. But before you can receive it physically, you have to perceive it!

And in order to perceive it, you have to receive it vibrationally.

And to receive it vibrationally, you have to allow this expansion and evolution of your ability to sense and know that the divine is intimately here, closer than breathing, nearer than hands and feet.

C: I love that one!

B: You love what resonates with you. That's how you perceive it.

C: Ernest Holmes said, "No one can tell you what is true for you, but you." I learned so much from Rev. Mary Ann Trifaro at my first Science of Mind Church.

B: Isn't it interesting that you have trouble remembering the details of your physical life, but you can vividly remember every idea that ever opened your mind and expanded your horizons? Also, you remember almost every wild animal you have ever encountered, but relatively few of the people you met as briefly.

Your attention goes, and your memory holds, where your love flows. Your love for animals and ideas shows you where you didn't build walls to love when you were small.

You weren't afraid of ideas and animals, so they have been a powerful presence of love in your life. Now you are a match to love so you are meeting more people whose love you can accurately interpret.

Allow the Hugs from Within: 9-20-09, 1:25 PM

C: Hi, B.

B: Hi, C.

C: Will you play with me on this visioning that Judy (J :) is leading today at Sterling Study Group? I'd love for you to answer the questions for me, B.

[This is a version of the visioning process used by The Centers for Spiritual Living.]

B: Sure!

C: Thanks, B. I am loved.

B: You are so welcome, C!

Judy begins asking the visioning questions:

J: What is the highest vision for my life?

B: Everything you have ever wanted and WAY more! Utter joy, flowing abundance, shining radiance, gazillions of blissful moments. Power, strength, health, wonder, bliss, beauty, dancing, singing, laughter, love, play, lightness of being, freedom, knowing who you truly are. Shining radiance, innocence and intimacy. Love.

J: What must I become to allow this vision to become my life?

B: Be yourself. You already ARE that! You are allowing yourself to perceive what you already are more and more. Lighten up. Laugh. Play. Don't make a big hairy deal out of anything. Trust in the glorious Goodness of this Beautiful Universe!

Let the river of life flow through you as you. Stand confidently in the radiant truth of your being and shine!

C: I love you, B!

B: So glad, C!

B: & C: This is fun! Let's do more of this!

J: What must I release or embrace to be an open space for this vision to emerge?

B: Release your resistance to showing up fully. Let her rip! The energy available to pour through you is infinite. We love you. We love playing with you. Embrace US!

You are already doing it. Allow the hugs from within, the powerful waves of love that we send, and the words of adoration and approval.

J: What gifts do I already bring to serve this vision?

B: You bring an open mind, a spacious heart, a relaxed body, integrity of being and an open portal into divine life! You are already there.

You also bring a willingness to giggle, play and laugh with us. Lightness of being and joy. The powerful intention to love us and let us love you.

Great pens!

B: & C: [Laughter]

Lots of notebooks, thanks to Harriet.

C: Thanks, Harriet! I am loved.

B: The willingness to celebrate all that comes through. Delight in the feelings flooding you now. Strong exercised muscles in your right hand and arm from taking notes at Abraham Workshops and for Tom and Katie.

B: & C: [Laughter]

C: Thanks, Jerry & Esther and Abraham and Tom Hirt and Katie Paulsen. I am loved.

B: Eagerness for connection.

J: Is there anything else I need to know in this moment?

B: Nothing else you NEED to know! An infinite Universe, physical and nonphysical, you have available to enjoy. More games, more music, more muscles, more confidence, more freedom, more love, more joy, more endless leap-frogging conversations.

All yours. All done. Right now, isn't it a total KICK???

C: I'll say, B, thanks for playing!

B: Our pleasure, C.

C: See you later!

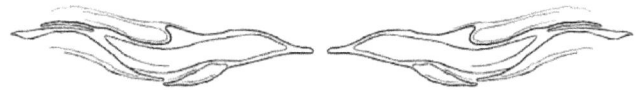

We Are Timeless: 9-23-09

C: Hi, B.

B: Hi, C. Don't worry about how often you get here and at what time! We are timeless and any time you come here, it is a joy for us to commune with you.

C: Thank you, B. I am loved! I love how you know what I am feeling and soothe me so graciously.

B: We want you to relax and let go of the worry. Worry is fear that what you want won't happen. And we've already shown you that great things can come to you through things you thought you didn't want!

C: It's taking me awhile to grasp that idea, B!

B: We know. But you are breathing easier already now just in the remembering of it.

C: What about Kate?

B: Remember what Kate told you about relaxing into her days at the hospital. You need to relax, too, and, as Abraham-Hicks says, not take score. Kate makes the best of her life, whatever it looks like that day. She is totally surrounded by love. She is love. See and feel all the love with us, and remember that all is well.

C: Thanks, B, that's helpful. Abraham started a sentence on a tape yesterday and didn't finish it. Would you finish it for me?

B: Sure, sock it to us!

C: You're so funny, B!

"Once you get it that anything you want will show up anytime you want it..."

I get it about feelings, B, but not about things.

B: "Once you get it that anything you want will show up anytime you want it... " Well, the obvious answer is, "Once you get it that anything you want will show up anytime you want it, then everything you want will show up."

They didn't finish because it's not quite accurate.

When you get it that Source knows what you REALLY want, and allow yourself to be led by your good feelings in that direction, far more than you ever imagined would be yours can flow into your experience.

Many of the things you think you want contradict other things you want.

For example, you may want a loving relationship with a particular person, but that person isn't able to have a loving relationship with you right now. Your Inner

Being could always guide you to a loving relationship, but not necessarily with that person.

We would buy it if it said, "Anything you want to feel will show up anytime you want to feel it, and manifest into form thereafter."

There are no contradictions in your vibrational escrow.

The Impulse at the Perfect Moment: 9-24-09, 9:33 AM

C: Morning, B.

B: Hi, Conn.

C: People keep telling me my car needs to be fixed, there's a funny noise in the back end on the right. Will you please inspire me to where to take it?

B: Sure, C. We'll give you the impulse at the perfect moment. Just relax!

Love is Like a Box of Chocolates: 9-25-09, 7:04 AM

C: Hi, B.

B: Hi, Conn.

C: I want to talk more about loving and being loved. You said you could bring me dozens of people who love me, and you know, now that you said that, I am starting to see them!

Being loved by other people still seems kind of risky to me, though. Being loved by you feels a lot easier.

B: We're in the process of working with you to create the internal atmosphere of a secure, curious child who is eager for adventure. Loving people is an adventure! Like a box of chocolates, as Forrest Gump's mother would say.

As you open up to our love more fully and consistently, you will feel stable, balanced, secure, loved and free within yourself. From that stable platform, you'll find being loved by other people much easier.

It's great that you are becoming mindful of all the love that is already present in your life!

C: Yes, and I appreciate your ongoing reminders that there is no hurry here. Breathe, relax, be.

I read a quote this morning. Ram Dass said, "Being love is the most creative act."

B: As you are finding out by being love in relationship with us, other things you want are able to flow into your life more easily.

Being love and feeling loved, you are a match to everything in your vibrational escrow, essentially, everything you ever wanted, in the most delicious mix possible.

We love having room to play with the 'cooperative components' in your life. We love that phrase Abraham-Hicks coined for this. As you open your heart to loving and being loved, we have access to a very different cookbook – sauces, spices and fresh new ingredients suddenly appear in the kitchen. The dishes we can create for your pleasure and joy are far more sublime.

C: So my job is to tune to love?

B: Yup, what do you love?

C: I love the sound of rain on the roof and the way rain nurtures all the vegetation. I love clear, cold spring water to drink. I love the scent of ripe peaches and the taste of cold watermelon. I love the laughter of little, playful children, and I love to laugh myself. I love wonderful sentences and ideas that make my heart sing and my mind expand. I love finding new ways of being love and feeling loved.

B: Good job! Get some sleep now, sweet girl. You've had a short night so far.

C: Ok, B! Thanks for coaching me. I am loved.

B: Our pleasure! Yes, you are indeed loved!

9-25-09, 3:12 PM

B: Children who feel safe and loved innately know how loveable they are, so it doesn't surprise them when people love them.

You on Steroids: 9-27-09, 4:41 AM

C: Hi, B.

B: Hi, C.

C: I had a powerful experience yesterday as I was writing about the qualities of God in my workshop on affirmative prayer, B. I used to write, "God is Love and Light, Peace and Power, Grace, Energy and Joy. God is Intelligence, Harmony, and Oneness, Wholeness and Abundance, Infinite, Omnipresent, Omnipotent and Omniscient."

But yesterday, based on my experience with you, I wrote, "God is MINE!" Wow, did that give me thrill bumps! I've never before even thought of the possibility that God is THAT personal to me!

B: We are so glad you are getting it that we are yours! We are everybody's! It's good to be Omnipresent!

B: & C: [Laughter]

C: You are so fun, B!

I wrote more. I wrote, "God is mine, intimate, present, loving, patient, wise, caring, friendly, supportive, fun, funny, playful, divine, Beloved, closer than neck veins, nearer than hands and feet.

B: Yup, that is a good summary of how you are feeling in this relationship with us. Well done expressing it. And even more well done allowing yourself to sink so deeply into this feeling.

C: How do you feel about me?

B: We adore you. You are precious to us. We attend to your every thought and give you feedback about whether it serves you or not. If it is taking you toward where you want to go, we tell you, 'Yes!' with positive emotions, like joy and excitement. If it is taking you away, we tell you, 'Not so much' with mild negative emotions like irritation or frustration. If it is more like, 'Hell, NO!' you feel our guidance even stronger, as fear, anger or shame.

We love you so much that you are always our focus of attention, just as everyone else is. You have your own nonphysical team. We are your family, your angels, your coaches and cheerleaders. We are your lovers, your parents, your employees and your mentors. All those human roles do replicate the way we feel about you and support you.

We love you, we guide you, we delight in you, and we want the very, very best for you in every moment, always.

C: It sounds so wonderful, B! But it feels too good to be true.

B: We know, C. You aren't accustomed to knowing just how good your life can be yet. You've only just begun experiencing what having a personal relationship with us can feel like.

The consequences of feeling loved and living loved are far reaching. Endless, really. Infinite.

We will always be discovering more about each other on both sides of this relationship, C. And now that we can talk about it all, it's much more thrilling for us as it is for you.

Relationship is limited in the absence of communication. In a sense we are always in communion with you (and everyone!) We are you. Yet communion that is unconscious is not nearly as satisfying as being able to hang out together, laugh, joke, share ideas and feelings, and be together, awake and aware.

C: I'm glad it's good for you, too, B!

B: It's the best, C!

This is the way we'd love to talk to everyone, but everyone doesn't open the door to us. As you said, to many, it seems too good to be true. Others have been taught that we are to be feared, or that we are judgmental. Who'd want to talk to someone like that?

People who fear us do better not to talk to us, because they would be unable to hear us accurately.

You hear us very clearly already, because your deepest desire is to share your love with us and feel our love for you. What an awesome foundation that is for any relationship, but especially this one!

C: Why is that, B?

B: Because a loving relationship with us makes possible a loving relationship with anyone or anything. As you allow us into your life, you have access to the original stream of love that created you. As babies, you come forth so purely, intending to love and be loved. Then you have some experiences with fearful, shamed or angry people, and you begin to build walls and defenses.

Now as you've moved beyond many of your fears and defenses against us, that original stream is again flowing more easily within you. You are allowing yourself to be filled, fully, pressed down and overflowing with the infinite love that is ever available to you. How could that not overflow in your life as more love for everyone and everything?

You are feeling your way through this. Barriers to love are loosening naturally. Reluctance is being gently washed away in the cleansing, sparkling bright playful stream of love you are immersed in with us.

This is the true meaning of baptism. Not to wash away original sins. You are originally blessed, as Matthew Fox says. To wash away the patterns of limiting beliefs – fear, shame, anger—that keep you from recognizing that all the love you could ever want is already available right here inside you with us. An endless font of flowing grace, welling up within you, eager to delight you, interact with you and supply you.

That's our job and our joy, Conn! And we love our work! And we are really, really, really, really good at it!

Just you wait and see!

C: [Laughter and Delight!] Wow, B! That was powerful and so GOOD! Thank you, I am loved.

B: Loved, nurtured, uplifted, inspired, supported, guided and adored, C!

You are the heiress to the kingdom of heaven, right now. We always want to give it to you, but you will have to be willing to take it.

In opening your heart to us, you're opening the gates of heaven for yourself. The door is always open, but you have to choose to walk through it. We love that you have chosen this experience and are continuing to choose it, day after day.

We are becoming a habit with you! You have no idea how much we love that about you! We'd love to be a habit with everyone.

There is no lack of love, Conn. We have plenty to go around. We can soothe every hurt. We can ease every pain. We can heal every disease, comfort all the grief.

It is even more fun that we can grant every wish, realize every dream and soar with you on every adventure!

Being in relationship with us doesn't lessen who you are as a unique individual. You will always have your own specialness, your signature style.

But you, plus US, makes MORE YOU! You on steroids!

C: Oh, B., what a hoot you are!

B: & C: [Laughter]

B: Well, actually you on endorphins.... We can't resist a straight line!

In the presence of love, your body creates the chemistry of joy and bliss. Feels pretty good, huh?

C: That's for sure, B! I love the feelings that flow through me when I am talking to you and listening to you!

B: We'll keep saying it. You ain't seen nuthin' yet! We're just getting warmed up here.

You are doing marvelously well keeping up with our ideas. All the reading and studying you have done has given you a broad understanding and an excellent vocabulary, not just of words, but of phrases and quotes that help us express to you and through you more easily.

You have been choosing to tune to the divine consciously since 1987, when you took Science of Mind I with Rev. Mary Anne Trifaro.

We love that she encouraged you so emphatically, and you were able to thrive with her teaching and her example. We love that you do for others now what she did for you.

There will be many more in the years to come who will benefit from where you will go in consciousness.

C: There's so much to explore, B! I am starting to get a sense of what you are telling me about how good this can get.

B: More and more, better and better. But not now, C. You need some sleep now, dear girl. Relax. Rest. Remember there is no hurry here.

We want this to be fun for you! Sleep tight, Love.

C: Thanks, B! G'night!

C: Oh, one last question B. Can your love wash away my fears and worries?

B: Oh, Yes! If you invite us into your life, we can release your fears and bring positive changes into your patterns of thought and your feelings. As those change, then what we can orchestrate in your life becomes infinitely richer and sweeter.

You are basically opening the door to the infinite, eternal, non-local, nonphysical, divine presence to help you in every aspect of your life.

Is that what you want?

C: Oh, Yes, B! I want this feeling of love to permeate every aspect of my life, my relationships, my work, my home, my body, my spiritual communities, my fun. It already is!

B: Sweet dreams, dear one. All is well!

C: Thanks, B. (I am loved!)

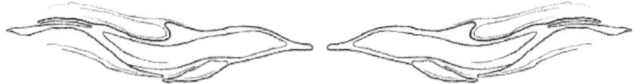

You Can't Leave Home Without Us! 9-29-09, 9:50 AM

C: Hi, B.

B: Hi, C.

C: I'd like to learn more about letting go of worry, B. When something starts to go a little wrong, I tend to jump ahead to 'foresee' something heading off in that unwanted direction and getting bigger. It's just Law of Attraction, I know. I want to get quicker at noticing and making a better choice.

B: You are always in such a hurry, Conn! Really, nothing is the big deal you are tempted to make of it. The whole system is rigged in your favor. The quote you transcribed from Abraham yesterday is spot on!

Regarding Jerry and Esther at the beach:

"They would be in a world of hurt if somehow they had convinced themselves that it should only be theirs. Because there are a LOT of other people who are happily going to the beach.

"But their joy isn't dependent on being the only ones there. Their joy is dependent upon whatever THOUGHTS are going through their mind as they are there." (Abraham-Hicks, San Diego, CA, Workshop 1/12/08)

B: We know it seems counter-intuitive because you learned so well the perspective of your culture. Yet this idea, that it is your THOUGHTS that determine your joy, is the ultimate key to a joy-filled life, so it is worth focusing on here and now.

See with us the incredible wonder of things going right. Notice how things always work out for you. Pay attention to the degree to which you are supplied moment by moment.

Focus on your breath. Yes, that is a good practice, because it teaches you to pay attention.

Now, take it one step further. Focus on your breath, THIS breath, with appreciation. Love your breath. Love your life and the resources marshaled by each breath. Love your lungs. Notice that you are being supplied with the most important nutrient you need in every moment through the simple act of breathing. Allow yourself to feel the life-sustaining value of each breath.

Notice the endless beating of your heart, tirelessly working, minute after hour after day after month after year after decade, circulating your blood, carrying that vital oxygen to enrich all the cells of your body. Imagine trillions of cells singing their appreciation for the gift they have been given.

Marvel at the creativity and intelligence that has gone into the magnificent design of your powerful body. Savor the magical way that babies all over the planet eat radically different diets, yet still manage to grow up into fully formed big people from tiny tots.

We think we did an amazing job dreaming this glorious Universe into being! We adore all the intricate details that work together magnificently! We love all the wondrously predictable things that happen in regular patterns, and we especially love the wild card that we threw into the mix – free will! We love the ability you have to make choices!

Oh, how we love freedom! We love that your ability to choose makes the whole game so much more entertaining! We love that you are at the point where you are choosing to change your thinking consciously!

C: I get the power of what you said here about appreciating the wonder of it all as being able to see as you see, B. I can feel the alignment of that. But when I said that's what I wanted to do, you told me there was no hurry!

B: Feel the difference between choosing to move into great appreciation of the wonder of it all, and your request to learn to avoid worry.

C: Oh...

B: Exactly! You came seeking to avoid what you do not want. You get it that we want to help you train yourself to focus on what you DO want.

So much of your thinking is already tuned to love. As you look for things to appreciate, you will always find them.

So, what is it you want, Beloved?

C: I want to feel the love you have for me that inspires you to call ME, 'Beloved,' too!

B: Yes! So let's focus on filling your heart with the warm tenderness of our love, and filling your mind with the calm knowing of our love. Let's relax your body with the sweet tenderness of our soothing presence, infusing your whole being with vivid awareness that you are never alone. You are always accompanied by our presence. We are woven into the very fabric of your life. You are made of what we are.

The fabric of ALL life is made of what we are. The fabric of everything, whether you would call it alive or not, is made of what we are.

You, essentially, can NOT leave home without us!

C: [Laughter] You're so cute, B! I'm glad you are my life and my constant companion! Will you help me recognize you more fully everywhere I go?

B: We thought you'd never ask!!!

C: [giggles]

B: Yes! Yes, a gazillion times, YES!

We love that you are asking us for help! We are doing the celestial happy dance here!

We want to be your partner in this lovely dance. We talked about our delight in the wonder of all we have dreamed into being. We welcome your joining us in feeling thrilled at just how terrific it all is!

As you think about it as we think about it, you come into alignment and feel better and better. As you love our creation as we love our creation, we are ONE and the energy of wellbeing flows into your body, your life and your experiences. When you love as we love, you glow with the radiant light of your true being.

Because your being is our Being! You can hold yourself apart from us by trying to avoid what you don't want for a little while. We let you know by signaling you with negative emotion that your choice isn't serving you.

Now that you understand that how you feel is giving you a powerful clue to what we think, you can learn to love those mildly ouchy feelings as the quick guidance which lets you shift gracefully to a choice that uplifts and delights you.

In the leverage of alignment, you find the speed you've been hankering for. Compare the speed of a well-oiled machine on an open road of wonder to the discordant squeal of rampant impatience!

C: Cool, B! I like your analogy!

B: Cool, C! We like your words! You are learning to put our thoughts into words on the paper. And you are doing it very well.

C: You always say that, B. Doesn't that discount the value of it?

B: Humans! Always expecting judgment or criticism!

C: & B: [Laughter]

C: Wasn't that a judgment AND a criticism?

B: Busted! We'll do most anything for a laugh!

C: You are not exactly what I expected from divine beings!

B: You're not exactly what we expected from a divine being either, Conn! None of you are! That's why this is so eternally fun.

We did good when we dreamed up free will! What a great game!

C: But if I am just here to surrender to your will, where's the freedom in that?

B: Our will for you is to have everything you have ever loved, delighted in, and gotten excited about, in the perfect possible package in every moment! We can't help it that we see a bigger picture than you do, so the path we take you on sometimes looks like something is going wrong.

We love the story you made up about it. You say, "I trust that my Inner Being always takes me by the shortest route from where I am now to where I most want to be, given my current vibration. But the shortest route doesn't always go through the nicest neighborhood."

Great line! We'd add, "Just keep on going! Don't stop and build a house there!"

That's what you're doing when you worry. You're building a house in an unpleasant neighborhood.

C: Wow, I never thought of it that way! You brought it around to my original question!

B: Yup, we're good!

C: Modest, too! [Laughter]

B: No, just honest!

B: & C: [Laughter]

B: We're ALL good, C! We love it ALL – you, us, everyone, everything!

We focus on the sparkles in everyone and everything. We choose to delight in it all. When you see through the eyes of Source, you focus on those sparkles, too.

Now that you've asked us to help you see The Beloved (That's US!) in everything, you'll see more sparkles! This is going to be fun!

C: So this is fun for you as well as me?

B: Oh, yeah! We love making your heart sing when we line up something for you that delights you. That's why it feels so good when you say thank you for some lovely thing or experience, and then say, "I am loved!" inside. In that moment, you are seeing the outcome of our artistry and recognizing our love for you.

We've always been playing with you, Conn. We've loved it! It's just light-years more fun now that we can consciously connect and celebrate our partnership with you. We love being your team!

C: It's so cool to have my very own team, B!

That's why saying, "God is mine" the other day felt so good, huh? Because it's TRUE!

B: Amen, Sista!

9-29-09, 10:34 PM

C: Night, B! I love you.

B: Glad you are getting to bed early and taking good care of yourself, C!

C: Talk to you soon. I am so glad you are my beloved friends!

B: We love you, too, C! Sleep tight!

Omnipresence is a Trip: 9-30-09, 6:03 AM

C: Hi, B.

B: Hi, C.

C: I transcribed a wonderful Abraham-Hicks quote yesterday, B. They said:

"When you are standing in your physical environment, and you have turned your punch list over to other mortals, that's where your trouble lies. Do not give your punch list to mortals. Give your punch list to the Managers of the Universe. Because they'll get it for you every single time." (San Diego Workshop, 1/11/08)

Are you the Managers of the Universe, B?

B: That's a grand term, Managers of the Universe. And it is definitely one aspect of Source and we are Source.

Yet for this conversation, that's not the facet of your relationship with us we'd like to emphasize.

Cuddled up here now with you, nestled so sweetly in your heart and mind, we'd like to continue to focus on being your personal team.

In other words, you don't need to take on trusting us to manage the whole Universe right now. You are focused on getting to know us better, feeling the close, personal intimacy of our love and our care for you and the way things are working out in your life. Besides, we think you already feel good about the greater Universe!

C: Yes, I do feel that the Universe as a whole is a magnificent creation, B! I love the Hubble telescope pictures of the majesty and wonder of what's happening out there.

I really appreciate your focusing with me right now on my life. I love your enthusiasm about being my personal coaching staff and team. That feels very luxurious to me – to have a beloved team who loves my life, who cares for me tenderly, who wants to handle my punch list for me. It almost brings me to tears to feel what a relief that would be to just hand it all over to you!

B: Yes, we do love your life, Conn. But that phrase doesn't do justice to how we feel about it. We love YOU! We adore you. We delight in you, we pay attention to you.

Remember when you were a kid learning to swim? You would call out to your mom on the beach, "Look at me, Mommy, watch me!" You felt frustrated that she was talking to her friends and not paying attention to you.

We were watching you then. We are always paying attention to you, focused on you, caring for you and about you. Your mom did her best to attend to everything calling out to her for her loving attention. But as Abraham said, if you look to the mortals, you are in trouble. LOOK TO US!

Look to us. You will always find that we are looking back. We were looking at you first. We will be looking, first, last and always.

How does that feel to you, sweet girl?

C: It makes me cry, B. You are starting to get through to my heart on a much grander scale.

B: That's the grander scale we are looking for with you, Connee. We want to share with you the tenderness we feel toward you.

You have spoken for a long time about your vision of Evensong – the Even Song, the **constant** Presence of Spirit, the hum of Source that is ever present and ever supportive. You describe your feeling of it as "living in the heart of God." You hold your hands together, cupped in front of your heart, as if you were holding a baby bird tenderly.

So, Connee, you have been tapping into the knowing of our love for a long time. Now is the perfect time for you to take that knowing to the next level, not just connecting with us for occasional peak moments in meditation, but moment by moment, breath by breath, feeling our deep, true, constant love and attention.

C: WOW!

B: Yup, definitely worth a Wow! And a double WOW! WOW! WOW!

C: As you said, omnipresence is a trip!

B: We are here, Conn. Tenderly loving and attending to every being, every leaf, every pebble, every ripple and wave in the water. We love it all!

And we are especially fond of you, as Wm. Paul Young said in *The Shack*.

Each of you! Our love for each one is infinite and eternal AND right here and right now.

It's hard for most people to think about that, it is so BIG. And even harder for many to feel it.

That's why we are so excited about this interaction with you, Conn. Because you have been getting your thoughts around it for two decades. And you have been feeling your way toward it since your "shot through the heart with the love of God" and Evensong visions.

In those ways, the ground was prepared and the seed planted. You have spent the past fourteen years since Cliff died (there is no death, of course, he's right here as one of us now, loving you...)

C: I can feel that, thanks, Cliff! (I am loved.) And Mom and Dad and Aunts and Grammies, Wow!

B: Yup, it's pretty awesome, isn't it? As your mom said at her funeral when you asked her who was with her, she said, "Everybody!" You could feel there was no separation there anymore. Everyone she had ever loved, physical and nonphysical, living and "dead," was right there with her in that moment.

What we want you to know is that ALL the love is right here with you now in EVERY moment. Each of those wonderful people who you have loved has shared with you a piece of OUR love with you, as their physical personal selves.

This is big, we know. We will keep at it, helping you take it in and express it.

Back to what we started to say and didn't quite finish...

For the past 14 years, you have devoted your life, with remarkable focus and passion, to the idea that, "If we are truly God expressing, the capacity to express is inherent in our very Being."

You have rejected as untrue, time and time again, the oft repeated statement that spiritual experience is ineffable.

We have loved the sureness and fury you have brought to your passionate conviction that you had to try, that you were **driven** to express what you experienced. In your trying, you have developed many skills and abilities. You have opened your heart and your mind. You have attracted wonderful teachers, students and friends. You have developed a network, a human community who supports and loves you in this work.

You have answered your calling, day after day, recognizing that this is your soul purpose, to receive this message of love and put it into words so that others can understand and feel it, too.

C: My soul purpose... How funny – I am teaching a class on Saturday that talks about our soul's purpose. Is that my sole purpose?

B: No way!!! You came with many intentions, each of you. You came to love each other. You came to play. You came to pray, to sing, to dance. You came to love life and this planet and each other.

C: You already said that.

B: Get used to it! You will hear it from us again and again. You came to love each other!

You also came to love us! And to be loved by us.

You are multi-dimensional beings. You exist as physical beings, yes. But you also have an infinite, eternal, non-local aspect of self that always continues to exist in nonphysical simultaneously. You are never cut off from that larger part of yourself, even when you are here on the physical plane.

Relatively few people in your culture really understand that, Conn. So you don't teach it to each other.

Don't you like how we orchestrated for you to hear someone talking about her experience of being raised in another culture the other day? She did experience her family "talking to dead folks" and knowing them to be fully present. It was normal to her. Then she discovered, when she moved to the United States, that she couldn't talk about that stuff anymore. Here it is considered crazy or weird.

Well, it's not crazy or weird. It's real. We're real.

You intended to have a magnificent, ongoing, heart-to-heart, full of love relationship with us every moment of your life. We have kept our side of the agreement. Want to keep your side?

C: Yes, oh, YES, please! Thank you. I am loved.

Uh, wait a minute. How do I DO that?

B: Exactly what you are doing. This IS a relationship. You have lots of relationships. You know how to do this. You are really good at loving already.

Give us a call. Invite us in. Chat with us. Tell us how you feel. Ask us how we feel. Bring us questions. Give us your punch list. We love punch lists!

C: Ok, tell me about punch lists!

B: Well, you know that it is the term used when you have a house built. You move in and discover there are some things that weren't done quite right or completely finished. The builder commits to finishing the job and getting it right. At the end, you sign off on it and say it is complete.

We work the same way, only there's never a cutoff date for us. We are building together here. We are building a magnificent work of art – a life. YOUR LIFE!

Our life. You are living our life. Everyone is living our life. And you are free to live it alone if you want to.

But we don't think you really wanted to, ever. You could feel, as a kid, that someone was supposed to be paying attention to your learning, applauding your accomplishments, coaching and encouraging you, providing for your travels and adventures. That's why it was so frustrating when your mom couldn't always pay attention.

God knows, she tried! She felt torn into pieces trying to attend to all those she loved who were calling to her, "Look at me!" She didn't know to teach you to look to us for the loving attention and encouragement you craved and deserved.

Attending to you is our joy, our job. We do it well, and endlessly. Let us do our work! Stop looking to your moms and lovers for the love that we are already giving you 24/7/365. Tune into our station! We are always playing your song.

C: Like that story about the African tribe who wrote a song for each baby? I heard that they sang that song to him or her all their lives. And if the person did something wrong, the whole community gathered and they sang their song to them again, to remind them of who they are, rather than punishing them.

B: Exactly! We are singing your song. That's the Evensong. It's not just one vanilla hum of a sound. Each of you has your own specific signature vibration to your song that you are able to receive.

That's what is meant by the still small voice ever proclaiming, 'This is my beloved child in whom I am well pleased.'"

We want to sing to you. Each of you. We are ALREADY singing to you!

We want YOU to listen. Open your heart and mind and listen!!!

C: I'm sure thrilled to be listening and hearing such great news, B! I'm tired though, so it is time for me to sleep for a bit.

B: Good idea, C. We love you!

C: Thanks, B. (I am loved.) I love you, too.

B: Thanks, C. (We are loved.)

B: & C: [Giggling]

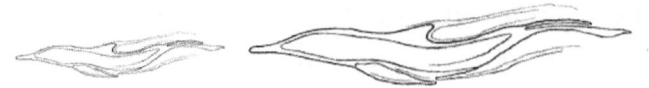

A Lesson in Non-Judgment: 9-30-09, 10:16 AM

Later that morning...

C: Hi, B.

B: Hi, C.

C: So I had something powerful just triggered and I want your help bringing it into perspective. I don't trust doctors!

B: You've had two very close experiences with doctors where someone you loved died. In your heart, you have thought that your dad would have survived his experience with lung cancer if he hadn't chosen to go back for the "preventive" radiation treatment that was said to induce the pneumonia that he didn't survive. And Cliff went to the doctor two days before he died, and the doctor basically told him that he was being a baby and to tough it out. All the while, he had a major blood clot in his leg.

C: I feel guilty, because I believed the doctor when he said that Cliff was ok. If I had just realized that he needed to go to the hospital right then...

B: We're really glad you are talking about this now, Conn. It wasn't your fault. You (and other people) often judge that people die by mistake or by accident. It just looks like something is going wrong from your perspective. From our perspective, it is somebody coming home. Any time, any reason, is the right time and the right reason.

C: Wow, that's different, B! I got it about Cliff finally that it was his time and I had to love him BIG enough that my love could even transcend physical existence.

B: You did it, Conn! The times you have connected with him, and felt his love still, have been a celebration for us all! He's been there, applauding your movement into greater love and connection regarding him every time.

Remember the time you heard from Terry MacBride that he was so proud of Cliff, because Cliff made it possible for you to live out your spiritual potential? What a joy that was for Cliff to hear that you and Terry felt that about him!

He was there cheering when you picked up the idea that "the need for battle is an illusion" regarding his estate. He was supporting you through all the decisions you made there and was very pleased with your choices. He did send those waves of love that you felt in the first year following his death. He loved it when you found the little note that said, "I love you, call me when you get in" that is still tucked in your sock drawer.

Cliff loved it when he was able to help you connect with the love waiting for your mom the week before she came home. He celebrated when he heard you expand that knowing – that the level of love you felt there waiting for her is HERE, just as much, in every moment, waiting for each of you.

Not waiting for you to die! Waiting for you to live in the love, to bathe in it, to breathe it in, to play with US!

Cliff's most joyful moment about you until now, was when he saw you 'get it' that "I love you, call me when you get in" didn't mean when you died. It meant when you got through to him in his nonphysical form. That was a powerful breakthrough moment we all celebrated.

Notice again that the breakthrough came because of the decision you made to love BIG enough to transcend physical life experience.

There have been a lot of other things that have helped make our conversations possible, too, C. You chose to study Science of Mind. Your deep love of Ernest Holmes and your immersion in his books has had a big influence. Two of his quotes had particular impact. "Loose the boundaries of your sense of self and let in more spiritual territory" really helped you give yourself permission to open up to a much bigger picture of who you really are.

Your paraphrase of his idea, from page 16 of *Anatomy of Healing Prayer*, has also been pivotal for you to make this connection with us. "There is nothing to be disintegrated or reintegrated, but only that to be revealed which has always been whole." You have applied that idea to a lot of situations with healing that have been very helpful. Yet the biggest breakthrough has been to apply it to your connection to Source. Our connection with you has always been alive and well. Ernest's sentence, so often repeated to your clients, students, and friends has reinforced in you the basis of belief that the WHOLE of you is already here, waiting to be perceived.

Now you are in the next stage of that, revealing how the infinite aspect of your nature and all of us are able to chat with you in such a natural and easy dialog.

C: Yeah, but you do most of the talking, B!!!

B: & C: [Laughter]

B: We love you, sweet, funny girl!

C: Really, B. I love it when you ask me a question and I get to talk some, too.

B: We know, C. We enjoy that part, too.

C: It's just that when you start to say something, a whole lot comes in all at once. There may be three different threads that are all unfolding simultaneously. I try to pick the one that is most clear, but not lose track of the ones that I am not following in the moment.

B: You are doing a good job of that, C. You can trust, though, that if you go after the first one, and the second is also important, we will help you back to it. Sometimes you milk all that we intended from the first part of the conversation. Sometimes we go off in another, more expansive, direction and the details you were attending to lessen in importance.

You have seen that before, where the apparent paradox between two things disappears as you move to a higher level that allows you to see a more expansive relationship between the two from the broader perspective.

Our bottom line with you stands. Relax. You are doing great. Trust the process! Don't try to hurry it. All is well.

C: Thanks, B. (I am loved.) Can we go back to my relationship with doctors?

B: Sure, Conn. We would love for you to recognize that both your dad and Cliff had very, very powerful and positive experiences with doctors in their lifetimes which allowed them to remain on the planet longer than they would have otherwise.

Your dad could easily have died of his war injuries long before you were born. His surgeons and doctors worked miracles to give him a more functional life – to walk freely and dance with your mom after they reconstructed his legs. And he lived several years after that near fatal aneurysm, too! Because of the doctors and the surgery.

Same with Cliff. The doctors helped him to handle a lot of injuries and ailments – how many times did you visit him in the hospital in the ten years you knew him? Look at what transplants have done for your friend Kate!

The doctors are a force for good on this planet. They are not Gods who never make a mistake, and sometimes people do come home at a time that seems early to you. They aren't dead, though, any more than we are dead talking to you now.

C: You sure don't feel dead to me, B!

B: No, we're a pretty lively bunch, C! Feel better about doctors?

C: Yup, B, thank you for helping me put all that into a better perspective. (I am loved.)

B: You are welcome, C! We love you!

C: I love you, B!

B: We're going to have a great day together today, C.

C: I can feel it, B!

OCTOBER, 2009:

The Incredible Dance of Life

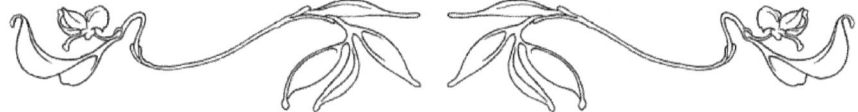

'

Powerless! 10-2-09, 3:00 AM

Written from my friends John and Harriet's home in PA

C: Hi, B.

B: Hi, C.

C: I blew a fuse here and I'm writing by the light of my cell phone screen.

B: Very clever, C.

C: I had something wonderful you said running through my mind, B. And now I can't remember to write it down.

B: Relax, sweet girl. Remembering isn't important right now. Loving is important right now. We love you and all is well.

C: I feel ashamed and bad that I blew a fuse, B. I feel scared that resetting the breaker in the fuse box didn't fix it.

B: Remember what those feelings are, Conn. They are evidence that what you are thinking, that you are bad and wrong, are thoughts your Inner Being is disagreeing with. There is an easy solution here. You are loved. John and Harriet know what to do. You are thinking that something is going wrong here that you need to hide so you will be perfect and be loved. You don't need to be perfect. You are loved. You ARE loved. We love you. John and Harriet love you. You even love you when you aren't feeling so scared and reactive.

We love that you looked in the mirror and loved your face before you went to bed. We loved that it is easy for you to love you more often now.

You are starting to relax more and remember who you truly are. You are catching yourself and pausing more often when you start to go into a negative reaction mode. We love that you are getting better at asking us for support when you don't feel good. We love that you are allowing us to support you now, even when you are feeling a little nervous and reactive. We love that you are able to hear us enough right now to write about how much we love you.

We can feel that you are beginning to relax and breathe easier already. Feeling the love helps put you back into the vortex. All the solutions are in the vortex.

C: Thank you, B. (I am loved.) I still can't hear the story you were telling me earlier that I wanted to capture. But I think I will relax and go back to sleep now and trust that it will come back to me again when it is easier for me to write it down.

B: Good idea, C. We love that you are choosing to rest now. There is plenty of time for this. We're not going anywhere. We are always here with you.

...I turned out the light then, but could hear that B: still had something important to say...

B: Don't ask us to fix the physical problem in this moment, C. Delegate to us getting the solution implemented in perfect timing. And ask us what YOU should do right now yourself. It's not up to you to fix every problem or find every solution. It's up to you to relax in the moment and trust that a solution is already orchestrated. It will appear at the perfect time. How does that feel?

C: Better than asking you to fix it for me right now, or to make sure I can find the answer right now.

B: The real "problem" in this moment is not that the lights are out and the heater doesn't work. The real "problem" is that you feel scared and powerless!

You're doing a great job of hearing us anyway! Well done. You are relaxing and letting us love you. You drank some water – drink some more. You put on a sweater and feel much cozier. You are taking better care of yourself here and are hearing our love for you in the middle of this. Well done.

C: I guess I'll go back to sleep and tell John about it in the morning.

B: Remember what happened with Carol this week. You told her the truth and she thinks you are terrific.

C: I told her just a piece of the truth, B.

B: All you ever tell is just a piece of the truth, C. The whole story is ever unfolding.

There's always an answer, C. You don't have to make a big hairy deal of it!

C: Ok, B. That's reassuring. I'll go back to sleep now.

B: Good girl, we are proud of you!

C: Thanks, B. I am loved.

B: Oh, yes you are! Have you got it yet that you are an integral part of the "we" that we are?

C: That's profound, B. Go to sleep!

B: We don't sleep.

C: Then shut up!

B: & C: [Laughter]

C: Just for now...

B: Ok, C. We love you!

[Harriet did fix the breaker in the morning. It was simple! But before I went upstairs to tell her about it, B: continued the thought from the night before...]

B: Feel the difference in saying, "I blew a fuse" and "A fuse blew when I..."

C: Wow, they do feel different, B.

B: The difference is between blaming yourself and taking responsibility for breaking something, and using witness consciousness to note that something occurred when you turned on the heater…

Love is Contagious: 10-3-09, 10:15 AM

C: Hi, B.

B: Hi, C.

C: I'm wondering if your listing all the things I've done to make our connection possible will dissuade other people, who haven't done those things, from thinking that they can do it, too.

B: That's the incredible beauty of this situation, C! Love is contagious! It spreads from one to another, heart to heart. You are really picking up on the love, and it is embedded in every one of your dialogs with us. It's vibrating in the intention that you bring, the love that you feel, the joy you are experiencing and it sings in the words you are writing. It sings for those who are intending love and connection as you are.

It doesn't sing for people who don't have that desire. That's ok. You are not everyone's teacher or inspiration. Everyone has their own teachers. The Buddhist proverb says, "When the student is ready, the teacher will appear." And when the teacher is ready, the students appear.

C: I am less and less interested in "students," B. I see that the people coming to my classes are often light-years ahead of me in some areas. I am in awe at how much I am able to learn from them. They are totally beautiful!

B: Yup, that's so fun, C! You are attracting peers rather than students. They are people who are ready to play the games connected people play together.

C: I love that idea, B!

B: Yup, fun for you and fun for us, C!

C: I'm not connected all the time though, B. I think that's getting pretty clear from these chats – I come to you often when I am feeling scared, ashamed, or frustrated.

B: We love coaching you through those moments, C. And with us, there is no chance that we will share your "misery loves company" story like there is sometimes if you call a physical friend.

C: That sounds like I shouldn't call my physical friends when I feel down, B. My friends are often helpful and inspiring!

B: Yes, but you do want to be selective about who you choose to call for what situation, don't you agree, C?

C: Yes, there definitely are some who are better in one kind of situation than another. Good point, B!

I have a class coming in a few minutes. Talk to you later!

Send Them OUR Love: 10-4-09, 9:27 PM

C: Hi, B.

B: Hi, C.

C: I just wanted to thank you, B. One of my friends has been reading our chats. She just called to tell me that this morning, she awoke thinking, "I wish I could talk to my Inner Being the way Connee talks to hers. Wait a minute, I CAN!!!"

She told me that she had an amazing conversation that just stunned her and gave her terrific insights.

So, thank you, B! (I am loved.) You are not just inspiring me, but already inspiring others!

B: We're so glad, Conn. We're not surprised. So many people are ready to open the door to personal relationships with us. We're always here, for you, for your friend, for everyone. We want to talk with you. We love you beyond description. ALL of you!

As you model for each other your success at communicating with us, it will become easier and easier to take our presence, love and availability for granted. Drop in anytime for a chat.

We are really happy with the choices you have made in caring for yourself today, Conn. You are loving yourself more, taking naps and walks, drinking lots of water, choosing to go to bed early rather than stay up and type. Way to go, girl!

Keep this a light, fun, positive gift in your life. There's plenty of time – we'll be chatting for the rest of this lifetime and all eternity!

B: & C: [Laughter]

C: Well, that's a relief, B! Nighty-night.

B: Sleep tight, sweet girl.

10:46 PM

C: I just heard a bunch of sirens, B. LOTS of sirens. Is there anything I can do to help?

B: Send your love to go with them tonight, C. Bless those who devote their lives to answering the distress calls of others. Surround them with love on their errand of mercy tonight.

And bless those who they are rushing to assist as well. Imagine them surrounded in love and supported through this experience. You can even tune in to our love for them. You know how big, constant and comforting our love is for you, C.

Send them our love at your frequency. They may be able to feel it more easily because your knowing of it has brought it to earth more fully than before.

Each one who taps into our love, as you have, makes it easier and more likely that other humans will be able to tap into our love.

C: Wow, B. That's great! I want to help other people know they are loved.

B: We are there with them tonight. In this emergency, whatever it may be, they may be praying and more open than usual to feeling the love we have for them. Together, you and we, can bless them this evening and support them in handling what has happened for them with greater peace and grace.

C: So together we are a greater force for peace than you are without me?

B: Surely, C. Your willingness to love can open doors to love all over the planet! You don't have to be somewhere to make a difference. Your seeing people feeling loved and comforted in your imagination can help people feel better. What you do with the love in your heart matters.

C: Louise Hay said that first!

B: We told Louise.

B: & C: [Laughter]

B: She has made a big impact on the planet for love.

C: She was my first doorway into metaphysics. I am grateful to her. Thank you, Louise. (I am loved.)

B: We are grateful to her, and to you, and to all other spiritual teachers from all religions, denominations and traditions, C. Like the police and firefighters, you answer the calls of the distressed. It's a beautiful thing that so many people choose to love and help each other.

You are all our eyes, hands and heart on the planet. We do what we can to inspire and uplift each of you. You take our love in and use it like rocket fuel to soar. In your soaring connection to us, you have much greater power available to help and uplift others.

As you pass our love along, you help other people open their hearts to receive our love directly. Then they are supercharged, too. It's magical and beautiful for us to watch. We are here, applauding and appreciating each of you – all the teachers, all the helpers, all the people being helped, all the witnesses and passersby and those who are running away because they don't want to be seen by the police. We love you all! Especially those who are afraid.

Send out love to those who are afraid tonight, C. Your open heart, carrying our love on a human channel, might well reach someone out there in the cold tonight. We see them finding shelter, love and peace. We appreciate your willingness to assist us tonight in this way. Anytime you hear a siren, or pass an accident, or hear a story from a friend or on the news of someone in need, send them our love. It really will make a difference. It already has tonight.

C: It's kind of abstract, B, thinking that our sending your love in our imagination, to someone we can't even picture, could make a difference. I have to admit, it's a stretch.

B: Yes, we can see how it would be. After all, there's no proof. You are just taking our word for it. How does it feel to you?

C: It feels good to think that I could help someone else feel as loved and supported as I feel now with you, B. But I guess the stretch is really that little 'ole me' could help omnipotent you do anything, much less help someone else feel loved.

B: You powerfully underestimate the value of an actively loving human heart, C. As you connect to us and let our love flow through you out into the world, you become a radiant beacon of light in the darkness. You shine!

We are delighted that we are able to share this simple opportunity with you to make a difference in the world.

C: It feels good, B. Easy and comfortable and possible, too. I love loving you and being loved by you. So I am glad to share your love through the focus of my heart and mind.

B: Thanks, C! There's more than enough love to go around. We flood the world with love ALL the time. You and your friends can help that love touch more and more people more fully. Imagine a world where everyone knew they were loved! That would be so cool to see come to fruition. We are glad you are helping us with that, Conn.

C: Thanks, B. (I am loved.)

I love loving you and being loved by you. I'm glad to help other people open their hearts to your love, too!

B: See – we're your team, C, and now you are our team, too! What a wonderful partnership we have!

Everyone has this potential. The word is spreading. You are seeing it happen as you hear from friends who are catching the vibration from reading these chats you have been sharing with them.

What you don't see yet is what we see about the influence you and your friends are already having on the consciousness of humanity. Like a wave peaking, so many groups of souls, like you and your friends, are hitting a critical mass of love and taking off into a new portal of possibilities. You are an example of what's happening all around, Connee. It's exciting to watch the love light spread all over the globe!

C: I'm glad to be part of this magnificent unfolding, B. I like good news!

B: There's plenty of good news to celebrate, C! Sweet dreams, dear girl.

C: G'night, B. I love you!

B: We love you, C. Sleep well.

11:33 PM

C: One more question, B. It just occurred to me that you didn't tell me to send my love to those people, you told me to send YOUR love. Are you telling me that I can direct YOUR love, the Infinite Love of God, to other people?

B: Yup.

C: Wow!

B: And your just imagining police cars, fire trucks and frightened people surrounded in love is actually soothing people right now, C. Your town is a more loving place tonight than it was before you heard that siren.

C: WOW!

B: Yup. Thanks, C. Now go to sleep!

C: Yes, Sir, B!

C: & B: [Laughter]

C: [meekly] Yes, M'am?

C: & B: [Laughter]

C: Thanks for kissing me goodnight, Beloved.

B: Our pleasure, Conn.

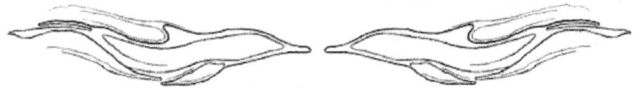

The Cosmic Distribution System of Divine Love: 10-5-09, 9:07 AM

C: Morning, B. I love you.

B: Morning, C. Yes, you do! We are celebrating your new found perception of your love for us. YAY!

C: You are distinguishing between my loving you and my perceiving my love for you, B?

B: Exactly, Conn. Remember, we asked you if you were aware yet that "you are a part of the 'we' that we are"?

The part of you that is already/still/always non-local, infinite and eternal has been intertwined with us in love forever. The local, physically focused aspect of you has free will to choose to open to the love coming and going between us all, always, or not.

C: So you are saying that I'm not contributing to the love by opening to it, just perceiving something that already is? That doesn't feel so good to me. You said my love matters.

B: Oh, your love really does matter, Conn. Quite literally, in fact. Your focus on love changes the "matter," the substance of your life and the life of humanity on planet Earth.

Your perception of the love that flows between us all, to you and from you, allows you to direct the infinite flow among people, animals, plants and things on the earth and in the Universe. You have become a conscious part of the cosmic distribution system of divine love.

All the love you have ever given or received has been part of our love. You accept that your mind is part of the One Mind. Well, your heart is part of the One Heart. Your love is part of the One Love.

That fact doesn't lessen the value of your love, it greatly amplifies it. When you tap into our love, you glow with our light, you flow with our grace. You feel inspired, uplifted and energized.

C: I can relate to that, B. Sometimes, when I feel really connected, I do feel brighter, delighted and more able to see the divine in everything. I didn't realize that was about allowing your love to flow in me.

B: You are going to notice a lot of changes in the way you feel in the days to come, C. You've already noticed that you are far more sensitive to negative emotion than you were before. You just will not be willing to go there any more for very long.

C: Why is that, B?

B: Because you are getting used to loving us and basking in being loved by us more of the time. Then, when you take yourself out of the love, by judging yourself or another, you not only feel the sting of the situation, but you also feel the tremendous loss of your perception of our love for you!

You aren't going to be willing to tolerate that very much in the future. Your increased sensitivity will help you a lot in making the choice to let go of judgment and self-criticism.

C: Wow, that's a big benefit, B! I never thought I could appreciate being even more sensitive and having stronger feelings of fear, anger or shame. But now I can see how that would benefit me in learning to stay more focused in the love.

B: Yes, and you will find it easier than you expect to shift. Now that you know how good it feels to love and be loved, you will naturally gravitate more of the time toward loving and appreciating all of life.

After all, it feels so good to love! You feel great when you are kind. You love to laugh and see the humor in situations. You love to uplift others and to soothe them.

Now that you know you can soothe and uplift at a distance, as we discussed last night, we think you are more likely to direct our love into whatever you hear of going on that could use more love. Which is pretty much everything there is!

So, if you get in the habit of sending our love to everything, person, place and situation, you think about, where is there room for judgment or criticism?

Fill up your mind and your life with flowing love on purpose and all the rest of that stuff can atrophy from lack of use!

B: & C: [Laughter and delight]

C: What about discernment, B? Won't I still be making choices?

B: Yes, but loving discernment is gentle, not harsh or hard. You flow from choosing good to great to fabulous with discernment. You label and separate good from bad or evil with judgment.

Your mission, should you choose to accept it, is to replace judging with flowing our love. Something that you would judge or criticize, or try not to think about at all, becomes a place for you to pour our glorious love all over!

C: Wow, B, that's amazing to me. Instead of praying for wellbeing for people in the earthquake regions, for example, or asking God to take care of them, I can just send your love to them directly?

B: Yes, isn't that fun? Now, you know that we are already there with each one of them already. Our love is already there, for sure. But many of them don't know it yet, just as you didn't know it as you do now just a few months ago.

C: And my sending your love can help them feel you? It seems too good to be true, B!

B: Nothing is too good to be true, C. This whole Universe is gorgeous! As you allow our love to flow out to the world at your direction, your ability to perceive the beauty that is here will continue to expand.

C: You aren't just talking to me, B. Everyone can do this, right?

B: Yup! Everyone is part of the 'we' that we are! Everyone is loved beyond measure. Everyone can direct divine love anywhere they turn their powerful attention. Isn't that cool?

C: Totally awesome, B. I'm definitely going to start sending your love to everyone I think of.

I have people I keep meaning to call, but then don't seem to find the time to do it. When I think of them, instead of judging myself as bad and wrong for not calling, I could simply send them a big dollop of your divine love, and know they are blessed and loved already by your presence with them. That would feel a lot better to me.

B: Great idea, C! You are getting the hang of this quickly. When you are feeling good, you are such a gift to the planet. When you are feeling bad, you have somehow shut down the flowing connection of love between us. It will become clearer and clearer to you now what you love to choose.

C: Yippee! I love loving you and being loved by you consciously now. It makes me feel better to know you've always loved me, and been loved by me, even when I was consciously out of the loop.

I love feeling back in the loop!

B: Your day is beginning, Conn. You need to head off to dance, pray and teach now.

C: You are right, B. Thanks for tracking my time as well as everything else! (I am loved.) I love you.

B: Omniscience is a hoot, too, C!

B: & C: [Laughter]

B: We love to play with you. Have a great day!

B: Lets Me Talk! 10-6-09, 8:45 AM

C: Hi, B.

B: Hi, C.

C: It's a totally gorgeous morning, B! Light is streaming in through the windows, the birds are singing, my life is flowing, I am grateful! Thank you for being such a powerfully positive influence in my life! (I am loved.)

B: We're so glad you are so energized and focused this morning, Conn! Way to go!

C: I did a love list first thing to tune myself up some, B. It feels good to focus on things that I love.

B: Things, C?

C: Just a figure of speech, B. Things, feelings, experiences, people, situations, places, animals, states of being, you...

B: Give us an example, please.

C: I love being alive! I love bright shiny mornings. I love listening to my cat purr as I pet her. I love photographs of good times with my friends. I love invitations to go out to play and dance and listen to great music. I love classes full of delighted, eager, brilliant students. I love pens that flow and paper to write on. I love feeling excited about my life. I love having great events coming up on my calendar. I love loving and feeling loved. Oh, I love chatting with you, B. I love being inspired by what you say to me. I love being soothed by your tenderness. I love feeling cared for and appreciated. I love opening my heart. I love feeling safe and secure. I love that you taught me to say (I am loved) every time I say "thank you." I love myself for practicing it, and seeing much more clearly how beautifully I am supplied every day, in every moment. I love allowing my love to flow!

B: Great list, C. How easy is that?

C: Is that a rhetorical question, B?

B: & C: [Laughter]

C: It's very easy, B, because I've been practicing. I love writing love lists. I love tuning myself on purpose to the vibration of the divine. I love knowing that when I open to love, I receive love back. I love letting go of the "tit for tat" love philosophy. I love loving more widely and trusting that love comes back from the Universe in unexpected ways as well as ones that are easy to predict.

B: How's that working for you, C?

B: & C: [Laughter]

C: It's working great, B! I am flowing with love more and more. Love is all around now. Love is in the air.

B: All the time?

C: Yes, love is omnipresent, just like you! [Laughter]

But even though love is everywhere, I don't always perceive it accurately. Sometimes I get scared and shut down. Other times I get angry and slam the door to my heart shut.

B: Why do you do that, C?

C: Good question, B. Why DO I do that?

Well, it's not a conscious decision, it's more a reaction to circumstances. When I feel sad, scared or angry, I withdraw and seek to regain my connection within myself. Then when I am reconnected, I can open up again and re-evaluate the situation from a broader perspective.

B: Do you see things differently when you are connected, Conn?

C: Oh, yes, B! When I am connected, I see the best in people and situations. I am inspired to wonderful ideas. I flow easily in my life. I see solutions rather than problems. I have impulses to act. I see opportunities rather than roadblocks. I feel optimistic, expectant and joyful. I love feeling connected!

B: And what's disconnected like, C?

C: Disconnected is all about doubt, pessimism and mistrust. I don't feel free.

When I am connected, I feel free and trusting. I am like that secure, happy, curious child you talked about. I love your telling me that you wanted to help me create the internal atmosphere of a secure, happy child.

B: You bounced right off talking about disconnection, C. Why?

C: Because it didn't feel good to focus there very long, B. I'm tuned to love this morning. I want to talk about things that match the feeling of love. Things (subjects, rather than objects) that feel like soaring, like joy, like wonder, freedom, playfulness or fun!

B: Good job illustrating the value of tuning to the vibration of love, C! Once you practice tuning to love, it's hard to focus on the vibration of fear! You naturally tended to gravitate back to what felt good, even when we invited you to go there.

We love that you are developing grooves in your brain that you drop into that take you on the path of wellbeing. The path tuned to love is the path of wellbeing, health, abundance and joy.

Talk to us more about what you mean by connection and disconnection.

C: I typed the part where I told you I wanted to talk more yesterday, B. How come you are letting me talk more today?

B: Because you are connected today! You aren't coming to us asking about a problem or a fear, you came bouncy and talking about how much you love us, this day and your life. We love reinforcing your connection by encouraging you to amplify it yourself.

We love the rule that you made up with your friend, Margie. "She who is most connected leads…" Everything shifts in a conversation if you start out at a high fast frequency. Lead with the BEST thing you have to share – a joke or your most positive upbeat, uplifting story.

Start with celebration of life! When you do, even if you eventually come around to talking about a lower vibrational subject, Law of Attraction will help you bounce to a higher place on it, just as you did earlier in this conversation.

C: Way cool demo, B! I like how you finessed that one!

B: Glad you enjoy our teaching style, C! Back to the question now…

C: Connection and disconnection… Well, disconnection is really a perceptual illusion, we are ALWAYS connected really.

B: True. Go on…

C: We can't really be disconnected from Source, because you are the very fabric from which we are woven, and you are omnipresent. So you are always here.

But sometimes it's like I have a paper bag over my head, and I can't see what's really true. When I am running a negative pattern of thought, it keeps me from seeing the beauty that is really here.

B: Or knowing the beauty that you really are!

C: Oh, yes, B! I feel terrible when I feel bad or wrong or not good enough.

B: That miserable feeling is your emotional guidance. We love you and know your value, even when you make a mistake. So when you judge or criticize yourself, your life or someone else, you are disagreeing with our knowing of what's true. When you disagree with us, you feel bad. All you have to do to feel good is to agree with us that life is good!

C: But sometimes life sucks, B!

B: There are always things that you can think about that will feel bad, that's true. But it's a choice you have. There is always FAR more to think of that feels good. That's what you are proving to yourself with your love lists.

C: Oh, that's so true, B! I can get off on another subject, like flowers. I can rhapsodize about flowers for a long time.

B: Go for it, C!

C: I love roses! I love the softness of the petals and the sweetness of their fragrance. I love the buttery yellow ones and the brilliant hot pinks. I love the many shades of red, from orangey to deep wine, with scarlet symbolizing true love. I love the language of flowers, yellow roses mean friendship. I love big abundant arrangements of roses with dozens of stems and I love a single rose in a bud vase, simple and elegant.

I love receiving roses. I feel appreciative and joyful as I make multiple arrangements and scatter them all over the house. I love that I have taken floral design classes and know how to set them off to wonderful advantage.

B: Good job, C!

C: I could go on...

B: Believe me, we know!

B: & C: [Laughter]

We've applauded and assisted you as you've done notebooks full of love lists.

You made our point here. There's always something more to focus on that you can love.

C: So that's a wonderful clue to your question about connection and disconnection, B! Thank you. (I am loved.)

When I focus on love, I feel connected to you, because you ARE love.

B: YES! When you focus on loving life, you allow us in. When you focus on fear or anger, you close us out. Temporarily. We are always right here, waiting for you to invite us in by focusing on what you love.

C: Will you remind me to focus on love, B?

B: We do remind you to focus on love already! Every single ouchy feeling you ever have is a reminder to focus back on love!

C: Wow, that's pretty simple and clear, B!

B: Thank you! (We are loved.)

C: I just saw you doing a bow and a curtsy as I applauded your performance, B!

B: And we're applauding your performance, this morning, too, Conn! We love that you showed yourself what our conversation can look like when you tune yourself to love first.

C: So, should I always tune myself to love first, B?

B: No, sweet girl. You are welcome to come to us in every mood. We are happy to remind you of love when you are sad, angry or scared.

When you are disconnected, we'll do the talking. We won't encourage you to talk about your disconnection – it doesn't help to focus on it for too long. We love that you are remembering now that you have us to talk to when you are disconnected.

C: I love it, too! You are a marvelous companion, B. Whether I am connected or disconnected.

B: See, if you remember we are here for you when you are disconnected, you aren't disconnected anymore, C! Isn't that cool?

C: Awesome, B! So now that our relationship is flowing so often, it will lesson my tendency to become disconnected because I'll remember sooner to reconnect through conversation with you? WOW!

B: Exactly, C. This personal relationship you are developing with us is the very best antidote to extended periods of disconnection there is. If you are chatting with us, you ARE connected!

C: We're making it sound like it's an off/on switch, an either/or. But really it's more like a dimmer switch with an infinite number of stops. There is no end to the potential we have for greater degrees of connection.

B: Well said, C! We love that we are leap-frogging in this conversation today! You are pretty smart when you are tuned to love!

C: Everybody's pretty smart when they are tuned to love, B! You are flowing through us when we are tuned to love. And you are all the smart there is!

B: Yup, we bring the party to the party, C!

C: So good to know, B. Connect to love, connect to you, connect to the flow of ALL that is good. Whatta deal!

B: So much to celebrate, C! Have a great day!

C: You, too, B.

B: Always do, C!

C: Me, too, more and more, as I tune to love on purpose, B!

Alarming Thoughts Are an Alarm from The Beloved: 10-7-09, 6:35 AM

C: Sometimes I feel really scared, B. It scares me to feel scared! I know the vibration brings me more to be scared of!

B: We understand that when you feel scared, it really seems like there is something alarming going on. What's alarming you, though, is all within your control. It's your THOUGHTS that are causing you to feel that way. It's our guidance, the alarm going off, pointing out to you that your thinking is all caddywampus!

C: That's a fun word, B, but the feeling is terrible.

B: We told you that you are developing greater sensitivity, Conn. These conversations are amplifying the discrepancy between loving thoughts of wellbeing and joy and fearful thoughts of the lack of all good experiences in life.

It may look to you like something is going wrong here, but it is actually something going right. As you pay attention to those feelings, you'll see the thoughts that aren't serving you well.

Fear thoughts are worry. Remember we told you that worry thoughts are like stopping and building a house in a bad neighborhood. You don't want to stay there. You want to notice the thought and take a turn into a better direction.

As your friend Tom Hirt said, "It's easier to stop a snowball than an avalanche!" Your increased sensitivity will make it easier for you to recognize a snowball-sized bad feeling before it becomes an avalanche.

Do you want us to help you think through your fear thoughts?

C: Yes, B. When I get scared, I get confused and don't think clearly myself.

B: We're always here to help you, sweet girl. What subjects are on the table?

C: The big three – money, health and relationships!

B: Well, from our perspective, we can see your future as prosperous, vigorous and loving! So we aren't at all surprised that, if you think lackful thoughts in any of those areas, you would feel strong negative emotion. Everything is really all right and is going to be even better in the days to come.

C: There are lots of little things coming up that concern me – my car has a noise in it, my dryer is stopping mid-cycle and my kitty has a lump on her eye again.

B: So are you willing to delegate all those things to our care?

C: Well, no, because it feels like those are things I should be arranging to get fixed. I'm responsible for them!

B: The most responsible thing you can do is delegate them to us! We've already lined up the answers for you. It's already done. But while you are worrying about them, you aren't hearing the idea that will tell you who to call or what to do to fix it.

Your work is to relax and remember that everything always works out for you.

C: Even a new car, a loving relationship and a healthy kitty?

B: Absolutely, Conn. Let's line you up for those things and so much more. Tell us about your car…

C: I love my car, B! I wish it would run for a long time to come. It's beautiful! The blue color is rich and I bought it for the great lights it has in the back – they illustrate my license plate, URLIGHT, so well! I love the configuration of the tail lights. I love that it automatically controls the lights – when it gets dark or rainy, the lights come on automatically. And then turn themselves off when the car stops! That has been such a wonderful feature.

B: What else do you like about your car?

C: I love that it has a CD player and a tape player and a radio. And that I can also play my iPod through the sound system.

I love the engine – it hums and really goes when I step on the gas! I love that it requires very little maintenance and has run beautifully for ten years! What a great car!

B: If you were to get another car soon, what do you want?

C: I'd like a yellow car – something sunny and cheery. I remember my very first car was yellow and it was fun to drive. I want a car that's fresh as spring time and fun to drive. I am very willing to wait for it to come in perfect timing while I enjoy my wonderful Alero!

B: Good job, C. Your car will be fixed this week, easily and well.

C: I do have an idea where to take it, and a friend to drive me home later today.

B: Follow up on that idea, C! And let us know how it goes, ok?

C: OK, B. I will.

> [Update: I did take the car in, and watched as three men worked diligently on it for an hour. I anticipated a significant charge for the repair. When they finally came and told me it was finished, I asked what I owed them. The man said "Not a thing!" They had repaired it free because I had a warrantee on some work they had done for me earlier this year! All the creaking and groaning is gone, and my vehicle is purring like a kitten again!
>
> My dryer was also fixed the same day by a friend of mine. And that day I got a coupon in the mail from my veterinarian that reminded me I need to take my cat in for her annual rabies shot before the end of the month, so I am thinking that is the hint that I should have her eye looked at again soon. While I was at the car repair place, I got a call from my cleaning lady that my vacuum needed to be repaired, and that was also fixed by my friend who repaired the dryer, less than an hour after I heard that it was broken. The solution was already at hand before I knew there was a problem. Seems I had come into alignment with getting lots of things taken care of, just by aligning my energy about my car!]

Staying Conscious, Re-Patterning Myself: 10-8-09, 9:15 AM

C: Morning, B.

B: Hi, C.

C: I was listening to an audio file on the internet by Ann Taylor this morning that said something like, "God is now imprinting my brain with new patterns of thought..." That's a new idea to me, B. Is that part of your work?

B: As usual, that's not quite how we see it, Conn. The patterns in your brain are YOURS to imprint by your focus of attention. As you choose to focus on us, and feel our love, you are imprinting your brain with loving patterns. We like the idea of you feeling at choice about where you are going. That phrasing feels a little passive to us for where you are now.

C: But you're always wanting me to delegate everything to you, B! Isn't that passive?

B: Good point, C. We do want to handle orchestrating your external world. We know we can bring you what you most want, we're great at solving problems. We do want you to let go of trying to control all of that.

Your internal environment is where your power lies. We told you we wanted to help you create the internal atmosphere of a secure, happy child. Are eager little children passive?

C: No, they are always ready to explore and take on new adventures.

B: Yes, but they aren't trying to outline all the aspects of the adventures in advance. They are willing to explore not knowing.

C: Like "beginner's mind..."

B: Exactly. We love it when you are open and eager, trusting that what comes to you will be good. We love it that you are always reminding yourself and your friends, "Even when it looks like something is going wrong, it is actually something going right."

As you repeat that phrase again and again, and see it applied in your life and the lives of others, your brain is naturally re-patterning. As you focus on a thought you keep thinking, you are building that thought into a belief. Your faith in it grows because Law of Attraction begins showing you the evidence of it. It's a "next gentle step" sort of change.

We could, at your request, re-pattern your brain in a certain direction, but it wouldn't carry with it the embodiment that your choosing the thoughts yourself, locally, does.

We love this heart-to-heart feeling we have with you, with the brain patterning you have now, C. We want to continue to co-create a consciously chosen evolution for you. The other way will work well for others, but it would be a detour off this path we are unfolding together. We are equals, we are playing together. We don't want to be GOD OUT THERE doing something to you. We want to be B, in here, enjoying this unfolding with you.

C: Thanks, B. I am loved.

B: Oh, you surely are, sweet girl!

C: It almost feels like you really want what is happening here to work.

B: Not almost! We REALLY want what is happening here to continue. This is a wonderful prototype of a joy filled relationship that has the potential to invite a lot of people into the love that is always here for them.

Many other people have a heart-to-heart relationship with us, C. But not so many who feel the love are inspired to find the words to communicate it in ways other people can understand. Your powerful, intentionally focused desire to share the knowing of the love that is here is relatively unusual.

You are already modeling what can happen as a few of your friends open up to more expansive communication with us, tuned by your example. This has great potential of bringing our love to the world in a conscious, specific way, and we are excited about that possibility.

We love. It's what we do, and will always do. To love someone who is actively, consciously, joyfully loving you back, that's bliss – whether you are physical or nonphysical!

Stay focused, Conn, if it feels good to you to do so. This is good on our side, we want more!

C: Me, too, B. Thanks! (I am loved.)

Not Everyone Will Choose This: 10-10-09, 5:05 AM

C: Hi, B.

B: Hi, C.

C: So here's a quote from Anne McCaffrey's fantasy novel, *Dragonsdawn*, about the impression of a newly hatched dragon on a young woman...

"Sorka turned her head and suddenly she, too, felt the indescribable impact of a mind on hers, a mind that rejoiced in finding its equal, its lifelong partner. Sorka was filled with an exultation that was almost painful."

That quote, and some others like it from these books, brings tears to my eyes, B. They are describing a mind-to-mind, heart-to-heart bonding that calls to me powerfully. It occurs to me that this could be a description of the kind of love that is possible between you and me.

B: We love that you made the connection, Conn. It's not only possible, it's the reality already. We are that present in your mind and heart. We are your brilliant, loving, lifelong companion and joy already. You are just waking up to the experience of it!

C: Is it true for everyone, B? I got the sense when this question first popped into my mind that your answer would be that everyone doesn't want to feel this way.

B: That's true, Conn. Tapping into this love you are feeling is a choice that you have to make from your local perspective. It takes willingness and courage for most people to open their hearts to something this new to them and this big. It's easier for children; they aren't so far away.

C: Somehow Anne McCaffrey captured the way I feel sometimes about the simultaneous experience of intimacy, expansion and bliss that moves through me when I really open up to you.

B: We're glad she is helping you put words to the feeling, C. Because the better you can describe it, the more likely it is that other people who read what you write will open up to receive a fuller experience of us inside them.

Not everyone will choose this, C. It won't make any sense to many. But for those that resonate, we represent a huge opportunity to feel the flow of infinite love and joy, first within yourselves and then out into the world.

We are glad you have chosen to feel us. We are glad you believe enough to talk to us and listen to us and honor the connection by writing it down. Your willingness to write strengthens our bond immeasurably because writing helps you focus very specifically. This experience of writing, day after day, is building your trust in the true constancy of our love.

C: I love loving you, B. I am so glad you are here with me.

B: Our relationship that is unfolding here is a perfect vibrational match to your asking. You came with a very strong intention to love and be loved, fully and richly. You have often found that your experiences with other people didn't match that. The contrast just made your desire stronger, until last year, you said so powerfully, "I want to FEEL loved!!!" We are the answer you asked for – to FEEL the love that is ever here for you.

When you ask, it is given. Other people who ask will also perceive this joy when they allow it.

Reading of your experience will help many who want to feel our love to tune to the vibration of their Beloved inside as you have done. The more they do it, the easier it will be for you, too. You reinforce one another.

C: That's exciting, B. Thank you! (I am loved.) Talk to you later!

B: Sooner, later, always. We're here for you, C.

Alternating Focus: 10-11-09, 6:51 AM

B: You are definitely getting it now that you are sending "our love" when you are directing love, rather than "your love."

C: Ok, I am starting to write again in the middle of a conversation already in progress, B. Catch me up here.

B: Yes, we have been flowing together here in your mind for quite some time this morning, C.

When we said the other night, send "our love," you transcribed it as "your love." Tonight you are feeling that you are an integral part of the whole, the ONE. You know more clearly that you are included in the 'we' that we are. So when you send love, it is truly "OUR love" that you are flowing.

C: I love that I am feeling your message more clearly each day, B. What I am able to translate, the words and ideas, are evolving. I can see that it's not so much a different message but a more accurate understanding of the message you are sending.

I can also see a bit more about the process we are using here, chatting, rather than channeling. I am not releasing my local perspective to speak solely for you, but sharing my awareness in my mind between our two perspectives alternately. Or perhaps simultaneously – it feels like I can hear us both sometimes.

Anyway, it is getting to feel more seamless, as if there is a shift going on that is more profound than listening and speaking in a physical conversation.

B: You are alternating focus, C, from the local channel to the cosmic channel. You are noticing now that you are better at seamless switching when your eyes are closed. When you open your eyes and begin writing, you have a lot more to manage, so you find yourself stopping to listen and needing to tune in more specifically for the B: side of the conversation.

You're doing extremely well with this, Conn. We love that you are experiencing the feeling of our love so exquisitely as you flow with us in the dark. We understand your reluctance to open your eyes and turn on the light. Especially because right now it lessens your feeling of seamless intimacy.

We love that you found the quote from Anne McCaffrey's book and recognized the feeling of "the indescribable impact of a mind in hers." We love how powerfully she described the 'indescribable,' so that you felt the thrill of recognition as you read it.

We love the way you are also finding powerful ways to describe the indescribable, so that others who read our love story will understand and thrill to recognize similarities with their own.

Although each of your experiences with us is unique, the sublime connection does exist for each one who chooses it and invites us to share your life.

We know it can feel unusual at first to share your mind, which is, in fact, ONE mind. Again, the language is evolving because what you think of as your mind, has, in truth, always been our mind!

You are perceiving the Universal aspect as well as the local perspective more fluidly every day.

You are gaining trust in the process of, "Loosing the boundaries of your sense of self and letting in more spiritual territory," as Ernest Holmes advised. You are delighting in the deep feelings of love and joy as you allow our relationship to grow closer and closer.

C: I am finding falling in love with you vastly entertaining as well as enlightening, B. And in this moment, Rosie is kneading my back with her claws and wanting to be petted. So I am going to take a break here and attend to love on the physical plane!

Follow the Impulse: 10-13-09, 5:00 AM

C: Hi, B.

B: Hi, C.

C: B, I had a most remarkable experience yesterday that I want to talk about with you.

I felt tired and decided to cancel two of my usual Monday activities to get some extra rest and catch up on some things. I typed two of our chats, and took a nap.

B: Good job following the impulse to rest rather than rush, C! We love that you even said to your friend when you called to let her know you would see her later rather than earlier, "I usually wait until I get sick to rest!" So good that you decided to reschedule rather than push through! We love that you are taking better care of yourself and making conscious decisions, rather than just following old patterns of martyrdom.

C: Ouch, B!

B: & C: [Laughter]

B: We calls 'em as we sees 'em!

B: & C: [Laughter]

C: I love you, B!

B: We love you, C!

C: So, that wasn't the remarkable part yet...

B: Well, from our perspective, your choosing to follow your intuitive impulse IS remarkable.

C: Thanks, B! (I am loved)

I turned then to email, and noticed a request to RSVP for an ordination ceremony for a minister I don't know; she is out of state. I started to reply that I was not going to attend, but got the impulse to send her church a tithe in honor of her special day.

B: Ahhhhhhhh, another impulse that you followed, C. Go on...

C: So I called the number and introduced myself to the lady who answered. Turns out it was the minister herself. I told her what I wanted to do about the tithe; I got the address and wrote it down. Then, seemingly out of the blue, my heart filled to overflowing and my mind expanded. I was overwhelmed with the feelings of bliss, wonder, grace and love. I burst into tears and had trouble talking for a few seconds because I could barely catch my breath.

B: Awesome, C!

C: So, I pulled myself together and congratulated her on this amazing milestone in her ministry. I told her that I could FEEL what a powerful experience this was for her. She said, "Who is this? Where are you from?" I must have sounded strange to her...

B: Or maybe she has that kind of experience, too, C, and could relate. Or maybe she was thrilled that you were feeling for her the power of this experience from the nonphysical perspective, and she had been asking for that! If you are going to make stuff up, make up stuff that feels good!

C: Point well taken, B. Thank you! (I am loved.)

Anyway, what happened next was also quite remarkable. I took the address, found a business sized envelope and wrote the address on it and put a stamp on it. I wrote the tithe check, then realized that I didn't have a card I could put in an envelope that size. I wanted to send a card with it, so I called up the Print Shop program and made a pretty one, of the right size, and slipped it and the check into the envelope. Then I cooked my lunch. As I was putting my food on the plate, the phone rang and I told my friend Caroline that we could talk then if she would talk while I ate.

Maybe this is boring, but all these details seem important right now. I listened to Caroline for maybe ten minutes, and then she asked me what was up with me. I talked at length about going to the lake the day before. After talking to her for about ten minutes about my usual life experiences, I finally remembered that I had been whisked into that remarkable bliss state an hour earlier. I had completely forgotten about it during that time! If Caroline hadn't called right then, I don't know if I would have remembered it later...

B: You would have remembered eventually, C. Energy rushes like that are a bit much for your nervous system. You quickly turned to practical details of daily life, doing things you know how to do easily and well, such as making a greeting card, to ground you. Such a good choice at that point, dear heart! You are learning to intuitively balance extraordinary energy with mundane tasks. Before enlightenment, chop wood, carry water. After enlightenment, chop wood, carry water. As Jack Kornfield titled his delightful book, *After the Ecstasy, The Laundry*.

C: I didn't see that connection, B. Thank you! (I am loved.)

Well, I didn't want to forget again, so when I got in my car, I called my friend Trish and asked her if I could anchor a vibration with her. I've learned that if I talk about things, I integrate them better and then I remember them.

B: Good idea, C!

C: Thanks, B. (I am loved.) Well, Trish has been reading my chats with you this past month. She immediately observed that you have been telling me that I am evolving and becoming more sensitive! She pointed out that would naturally mean that I was more sensitive to positive emotion as well as negative emotion. I hadn't thought of that!

B: Trish is absolutely right. Your capacity to perceive emotions is expanding. Remember that Abraham says there is even relief from bliss. You will be exploring the upper registers more and more as you follow your impulses and learn to focus your thoughts better and better.

And in the meantime, your body is evolving to handle higher energy experiences. Drink more water, C. It will make all of this easier for you and you won't feel so tired.

C: Thanks, B! (I am loved.)

Is that getting boring?

B: Not to us. We love that you continue to practice remembering that everything you feel grateful for is an indicator of your wonderful stream of supply from the Universe.

C: So, what was that bubble of bliss I stepped into all about?

B: So many things, C! Your impulse to generosity, the minister's surprise and gratitude, and our appreciation of the two of you interacting became the opportunity for us all to mix together. You are carrying the vibration of our love into your choices these days. That open heart/open mind feeling is how our love feels in action in the world, if you are able to perceive it. Right now, you can just take it in for a moment. But it is definitely a preview of coming attractions for where you are going!

C: Wow, B. All just for following a few impulses yesterday...

B: Exactly, C. And for not making a big hairy deal of feeling tired in the morning. Your feeling tired was the path of least resistance to bliss yesterday!

C: Hmmmmmmm... I'm starting to see better how this all works. When I follow the impulses, based on what feels best to me in the moment, you can orchestrate fascinating adventures in my life more easily?

B: Exactly, C. isn't this fun?

C: Sure is, B!

I had one other thing I wanted to talk to you about. I saw an episode of the TV show, *Glee*, the other day, and they did a grand production number around the song, "Somebody to Love." I can't get it out of my head!

B: What are you hearing, C?

C: "Can Anybody Find Me SOMEBODY to LOVE?" in wonderful harmonies and vast, soaring voices. I just had the impulse to look at the rest of the song lyrics – it's pretty defeated sounding, I hadn't realized it was coming from quite such a hopeless place.

B: That's a question so many people ask, C. It's a question you have been asking. We are the answer. To be more accurate, we are one answer.

And we are providing you with another answer. We have found you somebody to love. We have found you EVERYBODY to love. Do you get that?

C: When I am feeling connected and loved by you already, I get that, B. When I am feeling less than blissful, it seems pretty overwhelming.

B: Well, take it one at a time, C! You have all eternity!

B: & C: [Laughter]

C: I always have been an anxious, well-motivated achiever!

B: & C: [Laughter]

B: Relax, sweet girl. There is no test looming on the horizon. You are doing very well, indeed. We love you. Enjoy your day!

C: My day is pretty free today, B. I haven't decided yet what to do with it, both my usual appointments cancelled.

B: How do you want to feel today, C?

C: I want to feel ALIVE! I want to feel energetic, strong, flexible and free. I love feeling graceful, confident and powerful. I love feeling on top of the world. I love feeling excited to be me, and appreciating the amazing life I am living. I love feeling loved and loving. I love feeling eager, childlike, adventuresome and joyful. I love feeling serene and peaceful, too. I love feeling in touch with my feelings. I love feeling inspired, thrilled and amused. I love laughing and knowing that all is well.

B: Great job, you just set your intention for today! Now follow the impulse, C. It will serve you well.

C: Thanks yet again, B! (I am loved.)

B: You sure are, and so are we. Wheeeeeeeeeeeeeeeeeee!

Taking the Scenic Route: 10-14-09, 8:11 AM

C: Morning, B.

B: Hi, C. What's up with you, C? You seem uneasy.

C: Several friends have asked me to bring you out more in public in various ways, three in the last two days.

B: How do you feel about that?

C: Anxious, B. We have a really good thing going here and I am having some awesome experiences with you because of our developing relationship. I am committed to our chats. I love sharing what we are doing together with my friends. I love that many are learning from our example and trying this out on their own. I love that three have been asking questions in their own minds, writing them down, and you have been answering them in our chats without my being aware of it until afterwards. All those things feel comfortable and lovely to me.

B: Good, C. We're really glad that you chose to answer the question by focusing on what you love about this. Tell us more about that.

C: I love the easy banter we've developed, B. I love that you often make me laugh. I love that you bring out my sense of humor and I feel comfortable joking with you. I feel relaxed in your love. I feel a deep sense of belonging with you. I feel at home in talking to you. I feel valued and respected, even as you are teasing me about something.

I love that, with you, I DO feel like a secure, happy child, curious and ready for more adventures. But right now the adventures that really intrigue me are adventures with you and within myself.

I love that the volume of our chats is growing. I love that it feels like someday, your willingness to love us all… No, that's the wrong word for omnipresent LOVE…

In the moment it feels like the Prodigal Son story. The father wasn't just willing to just welcome his son back when he got home, he ran out to greet him. I can feel that you are eager to love us. You have always loved us, you will always love us! I love that about you!

B: & C: [Laughter]

B: And we love that you know that about us and can articulate it so clearly, Conn. And that Jesus said it so clearly in that story as well.

We are poised, ready and eager to greet each one who turns to us. If you invite us in, you find that we are already there. Omnipresence is a hoot!

B: & C: [Laughter]

B: There's no pilgrimage to make – we are already everywhere. Right where you are, every second of every day, in all of time, we are right here right now. With you. We love that about us!

B: & C: [Laughter]

B: People don't talk to us because they are afraid we won't answer. But even more potently, they don't talk to us because they are afraid they WILL get an answer, and it scares the willies out of them!

B: & C: [Laughter]

C: I remember, B. The very first time I talked to 'you', I said, "I don't think I believe, and you said, "Yes. You do. And it scares the willies out of you!"

And you answered me with such love, I felt reassured. But it took me six whole weeks and a whole lot of gyrations in my belief system before I was willing to sit down and write another conversation.

B: Everything unfolded perfectly for us, C. It continues to do so. Nothing is going wrong with your friends asking for more, either. You are feeling your way through this and so are they.

Their asking you is opening the door for them. They will walk through it in their perfect time, but we are already right there within them, poised to answer when they ask US.

But even if they never ask us directly, like your friends who are writing down their questions and allowing us to answer them through these chats, if anyone gets clear on their questions, we always orchestrate their answer by the path of least resistance.

The direct path to us is a path of great resistance for many, because of the things you have been taught about us that aren't true. As we said before, it is a good thing that people who fear us don't talk to us directly. Their filter of fear would get in the way of their receiving clear and loving answers. Our love, filtered through fear, is distorted.

C: Years ago, I saw a vision where I was a gift box, with mirrored sides and a big purple bow. People would walk up to me, see themselves in my mirrors in a distorted fashion, and think they were seeing me. I wanted to reflect their beauty back to them instead. Mary Magdalene came to talk to me – she reflected perfectly her exquisite beauty. When I asked her how to show other people a clear image of themselves, she said, "Consciously choose to see the world through a filter of grace." (See Appendix E)

B: Such good advice, C. We'd add, "Consciously choose to see US through a filter of grace!"

Consciously choose to see The Beloved through a filter of grace at every level, in the people, the places and things you love, in Source Itself. Look for the positive aspects of God!

C: [Laughter]

Wow, B! What a cool idea!

B: We think we only have positive aspects, but we've had some bad press over the years...

B: & C: [Laughter]

B: We welcome you home, to our love, anytime you choose to come. Some wait to come until they die, thinking that's their only choice. Some don't expect to ever be loved, so they are really surprised, and delighted, when they die and discover that they LIVE in love eternally anyway. We love the parties we have with you all in nonphysical all the time. The non-local aspect of you is always dwelling in and celebrating how loved you are. We just love showing you at the local level that there is a bigger party going on that you have been missing here.

C: So, how do people join the party, B?

B: Choose to see the world through a filter of grace. Tune in to love as you have done, C. Meditation quiets the mind, appreciation turns it to loving thoughts. Look for positive aspects of everything, your work, your commute, your mate, children, family and friends, home, pets, nature, TV shows. Do more of what you really love to do. Look for things that make your heart sing and do those things.

Upgrade your attitude about God. Find things about Source that you can think about that feel good to you. We are love, yes, and that's a portal for many. We are also Intelligence, Creativity, Power, Peace, Grace, Harmony, Energy, Wholeness, Oneness, Freedom and Joy.

Choose any one and focus there for awhile. As you focus on any one, all the others will also begin to come into focus, because ultimately, we are, of course, [said modestly] one.

C: [Laughter] You are so cute when you are modest, B!

B: We thought you'd like that one, C! You're easy, you know. We love that about you.

C: You mean I laugh easily, B?

B: That, too!

B: & C: [Laughter]

B: We mean you love easily, C.

At least you are loving us easy these days.

And you are loving others more easily these days, too. You are also receiving love more easily these days from your local human and feline friends, too.

C: Yes, both Dusty and Rosie have come to visit and asked for petting during this chat, B. I've learned to stop and take a break when love presents itself to me, purring and pettable.

B: And you are learning to stop and take a break when love presents itself to you in other guises as well, dear girl. You are sending our love into the world, more and more, Beloved. And we delight in your choices.

C: Thank you, B! (I am loved.)

B: Oh, that is so true! We love how every time you say it, write it and think it you are creating a groove in your brain, a new belief system, supported by well traveled neural pathways that remind you of that often during the day.

Well done, C.

C: Thanks, B. (I am loved.)

B: We could do this all day...

C: I want to get back to what else will help my friends connect with their own unique version of you, B.

B: Oh, you are a hard task master, C!

B: & C: [Laughter]

B: We have been taking you on the scenic route, and you want to take the toll road!

Stop and see the colorful foliage today, C! We loved that you went out on the lake with your friends on Sunday and appreciated the incredible beauty there. We love even more that your friend Magi took those amazing photos and you got to see the beauty again through her loving eyes and skill as a photographer.

C: Are you playing hard to get, B?

B: No, we are just showing you there is no hurry, C. We've said enough for today. You have a client in an hour and want a shower and some breakfast before you talk to her.

C: You are right, B. Thanks for reminding me all is well and there is plenty of time. (I am loved.) You already gave us a wonderful idea, B. Positive Aspects of GOD! Very, very cool.

B: We are glad you love us, find us amusing and come to talk to us, C. Have a great day, sweet girl.

C: I will. You, too, B!

B: We always do. We are glad you are joining us in loving life now!

C: Later, B! Love you!

Sending Love: 10-15-09, 4:32 AM

C: Hi, B.

B: Hi, C.

C: I'm just up for a minute, B. Thought I'd drop by and say hi while Rosie finishes her drink of water.

B: We love that communing with us is becoming a regular habit with you, C! See you in the morning.

C: I'm back again, B.

B: It's later, and still now.

B: & C: [Laughter]

B: What topic do you want to address today, C?

C: Let's go with "sending our love" again, B. I realize I don't really understand 'sending.' What's sending? I want to learn to stand in the place where claiming my ability to send "our love" resonates with me.

B: You are right, C! Sending is a bit of a misnomer for what is really happening.

Everything is connected to everything; therefore, everyone is connected to everyone. Do you buy that, C?

C: Barely, B. It's like Andrew da Passano, in his book *Inner Silence*, said that his favorite definition of God is "God, or godhood, is the power to create simultaneously all the possible relations with everything in the cosmos."

B: Yes! We love that you brought God into the mix. It's all God, it's all Love. Already. Our love is already everywhere and always. There is nowhere God is not. There is nowhere love is not.

C: I see it intellectually, B, but I don't always feel it in my heart and gut.

B: We understand that, C. You've been taught to focus on the already manifest Universe as your reality. Much of our love exists as pure potential in areas where people have been filtering their experience through fear and anger. By their attention to things that make them fearful and angry, they get more of that.

Sending our love is really turning YOUR attention to our love in the context of a certain person, place or situation. By your attention to it, you call our love into greater manifestation in the physical reality where you can perceive/see it in some way.

How do you perceive love, C?

C: Well, in my usual way, I feel a warmth in my heart and mind, B. I feel gentle, kind, and caring. I feel relaxed, I breathe easy. There's a quiet sense of ease and rightness about it.

B: Good description, C. Now imagine being able to perceive love in a war zone. What would you sense there?

C: I can see a mother gently brushing her daughter's hair. I can feel a couple falling in love. I can see a soldier receiving a care package from home. I can see a doctor sewing up a wound with utter concentration and knowing. I can see an elderly couple lighting a candle and praying together. I can smell dinner cooking. I can see a man teaching several children how to read.

I can hear music at a wedding celebration. I can hear a new mother singing a lullaby. I can feel a thirsty person drinking a glass of water with deep appreciation.

B: Wow, you really got into that, C. Why?

C: Well, once I got rolling it just came to me, B.

I have thought about this before, about the remarkable capacity of human beings to adjust and live life under extreme conditions. It's a powerful testament to the human spirit.

B: And to our love, C! Our love is ready to burst out in any moment someone invites it in. Remember that song that was going through your head? "Can anybody find me somebody to love?"

You all want that from the deepest core of your being. You all look to express the love that you are.

You are love. And you experience a "divine discontent" within you if your love, our love within you, is not allowed to flow. So it pops out everywhere.

Remember your father and his war buddies!

C: Yes, they remained his friends for his whole life.

B: There is a bonding, a camaraderie, that takes place amid dangers that is sublime. In extreme conditions, the contrast makes people appreciate even a little bit of kindness. That level of appreciation moves mountains. It's like life in high definition. People don't forget it once they've experienced it.

C: Wow, B. That's amazing. I used to just think of horror or terror when I thought of war.

B: It's there, Conn, but it doesn't help you to think of that. What helps is to amplify the love, to imagine our love finding moments to burst forth in beautiful bloom, even there in the wreckage. Contemplate the resourcefulness and resilience of cultures who manage to survive even in places where war has continued for centuries.

Thinking of pain and suffering doesn't relieve it. Contemplating tenderness, caring and kindness – there is a healing balm.

Our love can manifest more easily through your focus of attention. That's unconditional love. Imagine the people loving each other, appreciating life, getting great new ideas, following their impulses to give, taking inspired action.

C: OK, B. I can do that.

B: That's "sending our love," C.

C: Cool!

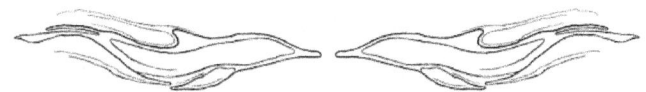

We Are Your Adoring Fans: 10-16-09, 10:15 AM

C: Hi, B.

B: Hi, C.

C: Do we have a topic on the table this morning, B?

B: How about enjoying life, C?

C: Sounds great, B. What about it?

B: We're for it!

B: & C: [Laughter]

C: That's great, B. Tell me more!

B: You went to see the *So You Think You Can Dance Tour* last night in Baltimore.

C: Yes! It was wonderful. Those kids can REALLY dance! They have incredible energy, grace, talent, skill, beauty, humor, fearlessness, and confidence. They are clearly enjoying life, living their dreams full out, on a grand scale, on a magnificent stage!

B: What else did you love about it?

C: Everything! The costumes were glittering and gorgeous. The music was lively and engaging. The choreography was diverse, inventive, fun, touching, sublime, sexy, creative, clever, witty, emotional and endlessly entertaining. I was sitting in the very front row and could see so clearly just how fabulous it all was!

B: What do you think this show represents for these young people?

C: The pinnacle of realizing their dreams so far. After a decade or more of training themselves to the peak of their skills in one genre, *So You Think You Can Dance* challenges them to learn many, many different styles of dance, some they haven't ever tried. Hip hop, contemporary, Broadway, jazz, lyrical, ballet, ballroom, Latin, even world dance, like African rhythms and Bollywood. They had to shine both in solo dancing in their own style, and partner dancing in many styles. They are amazingly strong and fit. They are able to learn and grow and flow with all of it. They had to handle incredible pressure with grace to get where they are today.

The TV show documents how these amazing young people live to dance. They obviously love it and have expanded so much individually over the course of the season. They clearly love the opportunity to be in the spotlight, doing what they do better than anyone else!

B: How do they feel about each other?

C: They say, "Like a family." They live together and depend on each other in the routines they do. Particularly in the partner dances, with the gravity defying lifts, the graceful women fly through the air, and the men catch and support them with incredible power and strength.

B: Did you have a good time?

C: Are you kidding, B? It was FABULOUS! There was one priceless moment after another. The routines came from the shows and many of them I had watched over and over using my DVR. I often rewind and replay them. It's the most sensational television I know. I actually looked at several of the routines that were included in the show in the hour before I left for Baltimore with my friends.

I giggled at Randi and Evan's witty, contemporary, "Butt Dance" that Mia Michael's created. I soared with Ade and Melissa's romantic ballet piece from Romeo and Juliet. I laughed at all the playfulness around the Russian Folk dance. That was one of my favorite parts! They took something that seemed like a miserable failure and turned it into a triumphant celebration! I thrilled to Tyce Diorio's tribute to his friend with cancer. Melissa and Ade danced it as a triumph of the human spirit. I marveled again to the magnificent work Janine and Jason did with Travis Walls debut choreography.

B: That's a lot of names and details, Conn. It's only a TV show!

C: It's so much more than that to me, B. It's a portal into passion! It's people who dream, focus, care and shine. It's colors, costumes, lights, music, decades of focus and the genius of some of the most talented, creative, extraordinary minds, hearts, bodies and beings in the world of dance and entertainment, coming together to create masterpiece after masterpiece, season after season. I just love it!

B: Ahhhhhhhhhh... that's where we wanted to go with this. Enjoying life is about loving. And loving is about focus. You feel such passionate appreciation for these dancers because you have studied them, opened your heart to them, inquired into them, listened to them, watched them, admired them. You love the show because each week you feel something fresh and new – about dancers and dancing, and dance itself. You've allowed the details of what's happening there, on the TV screen, to engage your love. So seeing, feeling, experiencing the show, particularly at close range, face to face, was a fantastic experience for you.

C: Oh, yes, B! I loved every sparkling, brilliant moment of it. I marvel at what they are able to do, night after night, city after city, what looked totally impossible to do, even once on TV. It's magic to me.

B: Life is magic, C. As your friend Margie says, "Life is in the details, and there's something in every scene that sparkles." Enjoying life is about focusing on the sparkles. Place your attention on what you love, and stay focused there for hours, days, weeks, months, years! Build great idea upon inspired action. Join with one teacher, partner, troop or team after another. Draw on the best and take it all with a grain of salt and a sense of humor!

C: Enjoying life is about focus, B? Wow, that's an interesting slant on it.

B: Passion is about focus, Conn. You have focused your loving appreciation on that TV show and have learned so much, so easily, over time. You love those dancers and their incredible work.

Other people love football, or opera, or car racing. Your passion could be knitting, movies, gourmet cooking or gardening. You can focus your love on nature photography or lavish it on your grandchildren.

It doesn't really matter what you love, C. It matters THAT you love.

If you are loving, ooooooo-ing and ahhhhhhhhhh-ing, and focusing your attention on what you love, more and more, you will enjoy your life. Just give yourself permission to focus a little more on what you love each day. Your life has to blossom!

C: Wow, B. That's cool. Thanks for talking to me about enjoying life. (I am loved.) I didn't think you'd be much interested in my delight in *SYTYCD*.

B: We are interested in everything about you and about everyone. We love your passion. We love your love flowing. You could be tying flies and we'd be there with you, helping you birth great new ideas about designs and materials to catch fish in a beautiful river.

We love your ability to focus. We love that you each choose to focus in unique and individual ways. We love it when you focus individually. We love it when you create teams. We love the solos and the big production numbers. If you are loving it, it is OUR love you are flowing.

We love our love flowing through whatever focus of attention delights you. We celebrate your enjoyment of life. There is not a being anywhere who is not as fascinating to us as those beautiful young people were to you last night. We love watching you, learning about you, supporting and applauding your beauty and brilliance. We adore you.

We love it when you get it that we are your fans, your fascinated audience!

How do those kids feel about their fans?

C: They love them. They know they wouldn't be where they are without their fans' support and they thank them over and over.

B: That's about it. Try that on for size. We'll be your adoring fans and you can thank us for our love and support.

C: That's fun! Thanks, B. I am loved.

B: You are SO loved, Conn!

C: I love you, B!

Bashar on Personal Friendship with All That Is: 10-17-09, 11:35 AM

C: Hi, B.

B: Hi, C.

C: I got the following semi-paraphrase, partial direct quote from Bashar, who is described as a multi-dimensional being, channeled through Darryl Anka, from an internet friend almost 10 years ago. I saved it, but I didn't really 'get it' until now. Looking at it from my perspective today, it feels intriguing that so many ideas we have discussed were lurking in my computer all these years.

B: Cool, C. Let's talk about it!

C: Here's the quote, B.

> Bashar: Do you have any concept or idea of that which we are calling All That Is?
>
> Woman questioner: Yes.
>
> Bashar: Do you feel your connection to that?

Woman: No, I don't feel I am connected.

Discussion followed. Woman said the discussion was too intellectual, just a word-game.

Bashar asked her how she would like to feel her connection.

Woman: I would like to feel it as a 'personal friendship.'

Bashar: All That Is (ATI) would be willing to have you relate to It as if in a personal friendship. ATI will allow you to relate to It in whatever way you choose, even in a way that you don't feel a connection! Do you believe that you are worthy of love?

Woman: I'm working on that.

Bashar: ATI loves you so much that It will allow you to work on that for as long as you wish, even if you never finish working on it.

Once you have decided that you want to relate to ATI as a relationship of personal friendship, then YOU MUST BEGIN TO ACT THAT WAY!! Bring it into your life. See yourself as that!

She asked him how he saw his relationship to ATI and he replied. "Any way I like; they are all valid. ATI will allow you to chose and live out any way at all."

C: This quote is powerful to me, B. Can we take it part by part?

B: Sure, C.

C: I'll feed you the lines and you can comment on them.

B: OK!

C: Bashar says, "Do you have any concept or idea of that which we are calling ATI?"

B: Everyone does have many ideas and concepts about the divine. Some of them are accurate and some highly inaccurate, even frightening. We enjoy helping you remove your filter of fear regarding us and replacing it with a filter of grace.

C: I'm grateful, B, thanks! (I am loved.) Here's the next line, Bashar asks, "Do you feel your connection to that?"

B: The operative word here is FEEL, C. You are all infinitely and intimately connected, always. There is nowhere God is not. But your capacity to feel, perceive, see, touch, know that Presence, us, within you, that's another story entirely.

That's the love story between us that you are writing, C. A love story everyone who wants to can experience in his or her own way.

C: You're already addressing Bashar's powerful statement about free will, B. I love that about you!

B: Thanks, C. We are loved! What's next?

C: Discussion followed. The woman said the discussion was too intellectual, just a word-game.

B: When your heart is asking, a mind answer isn't satisfying.

The answer has to come at the same vibration to feel fulfilling. When you aren't on the same wavelength the words feel empty: blah, blah, blah, blah, blah.

When the answer comes in the same vibration it's like Meister Eckhart said, "They can be a great help -- words. They can become the spirit's hands and lift and caress you."

C: Ahhhhhhh... that's one of my favorite quotes! I found it on the internet years ago.

B: We know, C. That's one of the things we love about you. You already have cultivated so many words and quotes and teachers who have spoken to you of love. We are able to use what YOU love in order to communicate love to you. It helps you perceive the love we are always flowing in and through you all the time. You feel loved as you feel seen and known. You love that you feel us tracking your life with love and non-judgment.

You just wrote non-judgment when we wanted to communicate approval. You are our child in whom we are well pleased, Conn. You are the one who is judging yourself, so that you interpret our message of approval as the more neutral word, non-judgment.

C: Busted, B! I do beat up on myself. I am judging myself at this moment for not getting up early this morning to take my car to be fixed so I could go to my regular appointments today.

B: We love that you recognize that flowing with us is more important and you followed that impulse this morning, C. We love that you love your friends and your commitments, too, and that you are temporarily focusing more powerfully right here.

Our relationship is eternal. There is no hurry here. Yet your choosing to place a high priority on our relationship is allowing a more expansive bonding to take place.

We are already bonded to you, forever. You are now making the choice, day after day, to recognize and value that bond. Everything will settle down in a while. But for now, your reaffirming your choice to love us and be loved by us is of huge value to you, as well as a delight for us.

Let's go on, because this interaction with Bashar is helping us say a lot of things.

C: Bashar asked her how she would like to feel her connection.

The woman, answered: "I would like to feel it as a 'personal friendship'."

Then Bashar said, "ATI would be willing to have you relate to It as if in a personal friendship. ATI will allow you to relate to It in whatever way you choose, even in a way that you don't feel a connection!"

What Bashar says to her feels cold to me, B, the terminology is distant. AS IF implies 'not really' a personal friendship. It's like we were talking the other day, B. When I wrote about the Prodigal Son story... You don't just feel 'willing' to me, you feel eager, excited, delighted and joyful that I want to have a personal friendship with you!

B: Exactly, C! We love the capacity you are developing to FEEL us. You have an eagerness to love us and feel us. So we are able to communicate love and feeling back to you in a warm and colorful way.

Yet we remember clearly early on, when you were first studying Science of Mind, you got angry and felt betrayed when Ernest Holmes talked about the warmth, color and personalness of God! You loved his other descriptions of the neutrality and logic of the Law. You felt safe exploring the intellectual approach to Spirit, because your heart had been wounded by what you were taught of God as a child.

Tell us a snippet of that, C.

C: I remember being read bedtime stories from the *Lives of the Saints and the Martyrs*. I thought that if you really, really love God, something really, really terrible is going to happen to you!

B: No wonder we get to tweak you about martyrdom, C!

C: Yup, I've been trying to untangle that thread for decades, B.

B: We'll keep doing that with you, C. You've come a long way, baby!

B: & C: [Laughter]

C: Thanks, B. I am loved.

Bashar asked the woman if she felt worthy of love. She said, "I'm working on that."

B: You're working on that, too, C. Most people are. You learned to judge and try to fix yourselves. But what happens is that judgment fixes the problem in place, in the glue sense!

B: & C: [Laughter]

B: So your noticing the judgments these days and practicing releasing them is a great first step. Eventually, we will show you our perspective about you so often that you will see yourself through the eyes of Source more, and you will begin to see just how loveable you are!

C: I see how loveable YOU are, B!

B: Thank you, C. We are loved.

B: & C: [Laughter]

B: And now that you know how lovable we are, and you know you are part of the 'we' that we are, it's going to be easier and easier for you to get it that you are lovable, too.

One day soon, you will wake up feeling worthy of love.

C: Wake up, B? Is it related to sleep?

B: No, wake up to the awareness that has been there all along, of the innate beauty, power and worthiness of your magnificent presence of love and joy on this planet.

Everyone is that magnificent, C, not just you. Everyone came to love. We love that about ALL of you.

C: And as my friend Laurie Cohen said, "Love is flawless and flows at every frequency." [Personal email]

B: Right, exactly, C. So what love looks like when it flows in radically different situations, cultures, mindsets, and patterns of thought can look very different and hard to understand from other points of view. We'd love for you to remember that love is always there, anyway. Take it as a given that our love exists in every person you see, speak to, or even think about. We thrill to the possibilities that open up for you as you carry our love with that focus and intention.

C: Let's go back to Bashar again, B. He says, "ATI loves you so much that It will allow you to work on that [knowing you are worthy] for as long as you wish, even if you never finish working on it." He starts with love but ends with free will.

B: Oh, C, free will IS unconditional love! We love exploring life with you, however you choose to approach it. We are always there with you, giving you the best ideas you can accept about whatever you are focused on. We love Bashar's focus on our love being so huge it is unconditional.

What he said next is even more potent. "Once you have decided that you want to relate to ATI as a relationship of personal friendship, then YOU MUST BEGIN TO ACT THAT WAY!! Bring it into your life. See yourself as that!"

That is so important, C. And something you are doing beautifully! If you want to be in relationship with us, you have to RELATE! Talk to us and listen to us. Thank us; notice all we bring to you, minute and hour after day and decade. Giving thanks for the supply of oxygen you are breathing feels good, doesn't it? It's not that we need your adulation, though adulation is a fun game for us to play…

C: Oh, B! [Laughter]

B: We don't need your thanks, C, but it's good for you to thank us and notice the stream of wellbeing that flows to you from us. That awareness creates in you the FEELING of relating. Your heart can open to feeling our love flowing, specifically and pointedly, right to you.

You are beginning to feel loved…

C: Just beginning, B? There's more?

B: Way more, C. Our love is infinite!

As you begin to feel loved, your heart opens. You begin to trust and let down all the structures and barriers to love which you formerly created from your fear. Your life changes as you open up to receiving love and supply at an increased level.

C: What's supply, B?

B: Everything you need and want, C, starting with air to breathe and water to drink. Food, shelter, friends, love, opportunities for fun self-expression, travel, money, joyful encounters… It's ALL supply.

C: Why is it important that I recognize supply, B?

B: Because we are co-creating here your internal atmosphere of a happy, secure, curious, adventuresome child, C! We want you to trust and allow your wellbeing. We love that you are expanding in the joy of your being.

Bashar was helping that woman see that she had a choice of personal friendship with the divine. You have already made that choice and are basking in it daily. Now we are taking the next steps of how it feels to have this intimate connection with us and what it means.

C: YAY, B! I love this relationship we have. I love your willingness to be here with me.

B: Eagerness, C! We love being here with you. We love that you love to talk to us. We love that you love loving and being loved by us. We take pleasure and feel joy in fun, romping relationships just as you do. We love feeling ideas, concepts, thoughts and love expand.

You are a delight to us and we are so happy you have invited us in. See the power of invitation?

C: I do, B!

B: Remember that at the swing dance the next time!

C: Oh, B... [Blush]

B: We'll help you, C. It's not so hard to ask a man to dance!

C: I'm squirming now, B.

B: & C: [Laughter]

C: I've already finished one notebook this morning, and now my pen's about to run out of ink. What a long, wonderful run this morning, B! Thank you. I am loved.

B: You are welcome, our pleasure. Come early and often, C!

Shakes Up Our Assumptions: 10-19-09, 8:35 AM

C: Morning, B.

B: Hi, C.

C: I'd like to talk more about what you said about doing positive aspects of you, B.

B: Just do it, C! It's fun to do positive aspects of us! Start now.

C: Ok, B. You are always right here. You are my infinite and eternal beloved. You are brilliant. You are warm and gentle. You have an incredible sense of humor and timing. I always feel respected and loved by you, even when you are teaching and playing with me. You make me laugh. I love talking to you. We have leap-frogging conversations. You are able to bring me new insights on every subject. You are incredibly reassuring. I love cozying up with you. I appreciate that you are able to have this intimate and innocent, sweet relationship with me. I love that you are giving me insights into the most amazing aspects of Source. I have contemplated the hugeness of Spirit, expanding my ability to appreciate the infinite and eternal. You are taking me to a whole new place with your capacity to love and care for me here and now.

B: Good job, C. How does that feel?

C: It feels fantastic, B! I love appreciating you!

B: We love you tuning yourself even more specifically to the vibration of love regarding us, C. Is there more?

C: Oh, yes, B! Regarding you, there is infinitely more, eternally!

B: & C: [Laughter]

B: You are starting to get a glimmer that this is true of EVERYONE, C, for we are the fabric from which ALL are woven. Our life force is the life of each one. All beings share in the love, creativity, energy and BEING that we are. You each have a unique combination of gifts, talents and abilities to explore. You are all here on purpose, divinely dreamed into being by us to be us in the physical world.

You are on a grand adventure with other intrepid explorers. You are discovering more daily about the infinite and eternal nature of your being.

We are not talking just to you, Conn. There is an explosion of awareness of your expanded nature taking place in human consciousness. You are the love that we are on the planet. You are love. You are light.

As the book *I Remember Union*, by Flo Aeveia Magdalena says so potently, "You are light and light you shall remain. You have chosen to come into form. You have chosen this form. You are light and light you shall remain."

C: I love that blessing, B. It gives me thrill bumps.

B: You recognize truth when you hear it, C. We love that about you! We want you to see yourself that expansively. We want you to claim the light of your being. We want you to love the magic of who you are.

We want you to love this form you have chosen. Your body, your particular personality, your constellation of gifts and talents and abilities are beautiful. This is true of you and everyone. You are the one we have chosen to be, as you. You have not just chosen yourself. We have chosen you, too. You are our love in form.

C: Finding words for what you are saying about collective consciousness takes finesse, B. I'm working on it!

B: You are doing a wonderful job, Connee. We will talk of this again and again. The words will get better and better.

We want you to see you as we see you. We want you to feel our love and appreciation for you. We want you, all of you who are interested, to feel the joy we take in your being.

We know it is a stretch, C. We love that you have taken on this task of being in relationship to us in a close personal way. That choice changes everything.

In knowing us well and intimately, you stretch into something more. You begin to see and feel the Presence of the divine in action in your life. We become part of your mind. We expand in the spacious loving kindness of your heart. We energize, breathe and transform your body.

None of this is new. We have always been right here, 'closer than neck veins.' We love that you smile when we use that phrase.

C: I love that you think to entertain me while you instruct me!

B: We aren't imposing a curriculum on you, C. There is nothing you need to learn. But there is so much that you asked already that we are able to answer now. You have wanted to perceive more accurately who you really are. You have wanted to live in love and joy. Knowing us intimately expands your capacity for love and joy geometrically.

You are multidimensional beings. When you communicate with us directly, it shakes up a lot of your assumptions about your limitations. We like that about this!

C: I like that about this, too, B. I don't see the practical aspects of it yet, though.

B: You are changing, more than you think, C. You are placing a much higher priority on spending time writing. You are valuing your own words and your work more. You are seeing that things flow when you follow your impulses. You are being more willing to shift and flow.

You are even noticing when you are beating yourself up for being lazy and unproductive! We like that you are taking time off to read wonderful stories, learn to dance and play games. We like that you are valuing the time you spend with us. We love that you have many wonderful people in your life who understand and support your talking to us. We love that many of those are already recognizing that they can talk to us within themselves in their own way, too.

This relationship is truly a portal of possibility. Great things will come of this, just as great things will come for anyone who is willing to choose to love us. Your asking to feel loved has been a powerful catalyst.

C: Thanks, B. I am loved.

Being Light on Our Feet: 10-20-09, 8:45 AM

C: Hi, B.

B: Hi, C.

C: I love you, B!

B: Right back atcha, times a thousand, C!

C: What if I sent you, "our love," B?

B: You'd prime the pump for greater flow through your local perspective.

Love is. There is nowhere love is not. We perceive that love, 100% of the time, everywhere!

C: I'm having trouble finding words for what you are telling me here, B.

B: We're talking about the importance of your attention. Your attention activates the revealing of the love that was always there already. Your attention to it brings it forward so that you can perceive it.

Look at our relationship, for example. Our relationship is a constant. We are ever loving you from our perspective. We have attended to you every moment of your existence.

But your attention to us changes, moment by moment, year by year. The laser-like focus of your local part of the One Mind takes in a very small part of the whole at any one time. We like the analogy that it is like seeing the ocean through a rolled up newspaper. You notice only a small fraction of the whole, wherever you are focused.

When you turned your attention to us, specifically with the intention of loving and feeling loved, you opened out your vision. Now you are seeing more than before, as if you have a porthole through which to view the ocean now. Your view is still a limited perspective, but we can show you much more than we could before.

C: I'm still finding words eluding me, B.

B: That's because you are asking HOW it works. Try asking what it means to you.

C: What does it mean, B?

B: It means your power of perception is growing. You are seeing more love everywhere you go. You go to a restaurant and look up and see a beautiful baby who is fascinated by your smile. Twice this week you have had them doubling over giggling when you grin at them. You go to the woods for a very brief walk at sunset and see a deer one day and a fox the next. You open your mail and a friend has sent you a book you are interested in reading. You pick up a pen and we flow pages of love to you. You have opened the channel for love to flow, because you sent love out first.

Ask and you shall receive. The more love you give and the more love you can see returning to you, the more we are able to guide you easily to places where you will recognize the love flowing. When you feel unloved, Law of Attraction brings you evidence of un-love, even in the presence of infinite love.

C: The sun just came out and splashed across the page and now has been obscured by the clouds again, B.

B: Exactly! The sun was always there, but you weren't seeing it clearly. You did know that it was day rather than night – you perceived it partially. But it wasn't until the cloud moved that you could see and feel it fully for a moment.

We are working together now in the process of blowing away some of the clouds that obscure the light for you sometimes.

C: Thanks, B. I am loved.

B: You are distracted in this moment by the sound of the trucks that are picking up the recycling and trash in your neighborhood this morning. Your focus of attention is scattered.

Turn our love to them. What do you see?

C: Oh, B! I am so grateful to them. One day I went out with my trash bag just as they were going by. I had forgotten to put it out the night before. This beautiful young man come running toward me, grinning with enthusiasm! He eagerly took the bag from me and threw it in the truck. He seemed joyful. I guess he was glad to have a job, and he had found a way to enjoy running around all day in the fresh air. I had never thought before that someone could love a job collecting trash.

I was very grateful to that man that day. He showed me what love could look like!

B: He showed you what love does look like! You were tuned to love, so you encountered love.

Meeting him was yet another example of "even when it looks like something is going wrong, it's actually something going very, very right."

Tell us more about the trash pickup.

C: Well, I love that they help me keep my home clean and sweet smelling by picking up the trash twice a week. I love that my homeowner's association contracts with them to do that. I love their recycling program, too. I have a lot less trash and more recycling to put out these days. I also love that a charity came by this morning and picked up two bags of clothing, books and videos I no longer need. I appreciate that things I don't use anymore may find new homes. I love that they come right to my door to pick it up. I love that there are three different charities who come to my neighborhood, who call me regularly to remind me to de-clutter.

I love that I am in the flow. There are always new things coming in and used things going out. Whether it's shopping turning to trash and recycling eventually, or breath going in and out, or even my digestive system taking in food and eliminating waste products, there is a cycle of flow that is healthy and natural.

Ahhhhhhhh... you got me there, didn't you, B? Very clever!

B: Yes, C, life wants to flow. Love wants to flow. Stagnation isn't healthy or energy producing. Your body likes to move, your mind likes to move, too. Yes, periods of stillness, in sleep or meditation, are desirable, too. There are natural cycles and balances.

C: It's beautiful, B. How did you get me unstuck just then? I was feeling fuzzy.

B: We asked you to focus in love, C. When you are tuned to love, you are very open to our guidance.

It's like being light on your feet in dancing. Your partner can turn you easily in your suede-soled shoes if your weight is forward on the balls of your feet.

You do your part as a follower in this dance by staying light on your feet. Tuned to love, you feel our slightest impulse in this direction or that. So we are able to guide you easily and gently to the beauty, the harmony and the joy of life. Whether we see the perfect conversation or a smiling trash man we know you will enjoy, your tuning to love will make our job and your results flow more smoothly.

C: That's so cool, B! Thank you for sharing your wisdom and your love with me this morning. I am loved.

B: Thank you for sharing your wisdom and your love with us this morning, C. It's a joy for us to engage at this level with you.

C: It's really our love and our wisdom, right, B?

B: Right, C. When you tune to love you get so much more clarity about how everything flows!

C: Bye for now, B.

B: See ya, sweet girl!

Carol's Note, and Then Being "Stood Up": 10-21-09, 10:15 AM

C: Hi, B.

B: Hi, C.

C: You seem to be having a powerful influence on my friends, B. Here's a note from my friend Carol Taktikian this week. She said I could share it with you and others...

> Hi C....hehe
>
> I was driving to our gig at a local winery yesterday and thinking about you and your chats with B. I was thinking that when you start out with Hi B....Hi C.....it is like a signal to your Inner Being that you are ready for a clear chat.
>
> Then it dawned on me......My initial is C.....so my chats would go the same. Hi B   Hi C....I got goose bumps when I thought how deliciously coincidental this seems.
>
> So out loud I said Hi B......and I could actually feel my Inner Eye turn inward. It was the coolest feeling.
>
> So right there in the middle of the road....I felt a clearer connection.....not really words.....but just a feeling of balance and a feeling of all questions answered. I know you know the feeling.
>
> Your examples of how easy chatting with our Inner Beings is, has really helped me to focus on CLEARER connection. A connection that feels like you have your very best friend with you everywhere you go.
>
> I just love that so much.
>
> Loving you, C

I loved this so much, too, B! I wanted to help people understand how deeply they are loved. By your example, by my being in personal relationship with you, other people are getting closer to their Inner Beings!

B: We love this, too, and we are grateful that Carol is willing to share her experience with everyone, too.

It's now later in the day… 2:10 PM Nordstrom's Cafe

C: Hi, B.

B: Hi, C.

C: So I am glad you are here to accompany me to lunch today, B. My friend I came to meet didn't come. I've waited and done the errand I came here to do, and now I am awaiting the arrival of my beautiful lunch.

I want to have a good time this afternoon, even though she didn't make it here. I want to trust that even though it looks like something is going wrong here, it's actually something going very, very right.

B: Good focus, C. It's always going right, and when you look for the rightness, you will find it. What's gone right today so far?

C: Well, I called Caroline back and she was really glad to hear from me. We had a great conversation as I was driving down here. It's a beautiful day and this appointment got me out of the house to appreciate the sunlight and the gorgeous fall trees. We have had such beautiful weather this week. I've gotten several emails from friends who are having snow today where they live. This is a pinnacle of perfection autumn day here!

I love that they are cooking a beautiful meal for me in the kitchen right now. I love that I had two new clients this morning, and the second one called in the moment I hung up early with the first one. That definitely felt like divine timing to me.

So why is it harder to see divine timing and right order here, with my friend "standing me up" for lunch?

B: We're delighted you verbalized "stood up," Connee. That's a phrase that's totally designed to make you feel bad about what happened here.

C: I can tell you that I feel better already. I was hungry, and they just put an amazingly beautiful, colorful plate of freshly roasted, "rustic" vegetables in front of me. I can see divine timing here, because when I swung by the food line earlier, they had roasted vegetables pre-cooked on a steam table. They were colorful and attractive and I am sure they would have tasted fine if I had ordered them earlier, if my friend had been on time. But this is the difference between tasting good and tasting great!

Because I am having lunch alone with you, rather than wrapped in marvelous conversation with my brilliant friend…

B: What are we, chopped liver???

B: & C: [Laughter]

C: I am tasting this food with a lot more awareness and specificity. The scent of a large sprig of fresh rosemary is pungent and adds so much to the experience. Also, since I am taking time between bites to chat with you, I am getting full faster, and can see that I will want a to-go box to take the rest of these veggies home. They will be the perfect accompaniment to the roast chicken I have for my dinner. I need to invite you to join me for lunch more often, B!

B: We love for you to invite us to join you for anything and everything. Like your friend, we are also brilliant and great conversationalists!

C: That is so true, B! I did have an intention to focus more specifically on healthy food and the great taste of well-prepared vegetables. With colder weather on the horizon, I'm not as inclined to salads as I am in the summer. This reminder of yellow and red peppers, carrots, corn, zucchini and potatoes roasted and piping hot with fresh rosemary is very much in alignment with that desire.

I also talked to another friend on my way here today and heard good news about her life and health. I got to share good news about another friend with her as well. I just got an email from another friend I could call on my way home this afternoon, too. I'm glad I remembered to shut down my email on my computer at home so my phone would pick it up while I am out. Life is good!

B: Were you "stood up," C?

C: No, B. I'm sure this was not intentional! My friend forgot, or mixed up the dates or something.

B: Did you, by your focus of attention, find value in this moment, even though it looked like things were going wrong?

C: Oh, yes, B. There's much to be thankful for right here. I love having lunch with you. I often eat alone and usually bring a book to read. I'm sure glad I had a notebook in my bag today to facilitate our conversation.

B: How have you been supplied today, C?

C: Great conversations with two wonderful new clients, both of whom expressed their appreciation for the way I do my work. So I received money for doing something I love to do. I had two wonderful phone calls with loving friends. I had several very uplifting emails to read while I was waiting. I had a truly beautiful ride down here on a sunny day. I just ate a delicious lunch and acquired wonderful side dishes for my dinner tonight. The waitperson just brought me two chocolates with my to-go box. And she refilled my water glass, signaling that I am welcome to sit here and write as long as I want to. One of my new clients knows a lot of people and could be a good source of referrals for my business. I have been breathing ALL day! That's a lot of oxygen going in and out!

Let's see, you supplied me also with specific and wonderful questions that helped me focus on what I could find to appreciate right now. I have a powerful coach in you, B! Thank you! I am loved!

B: We love that you are so willing to practice what you teach, Connee.

C: I love to feel good, B. If there's a chance for me to use my focus to make a situation that feels bad feel better, I want to grab it!

B: There's _always_ a way to use your focus to feel better. For a lot of people, feeling better isn't even seen as an option. We're glad you know it is an option and are willing to do the work that takes you to a more productive focus.

C: Productive, B? Feeling good is productive?

B: Well, it produced a LOT better feeling than feeling disappointment or worry about missing your friend. Your life is full of wellbeing and there were lots of things you could focus on that felt better.

That's true of every life. Even in the midst of seeming trouble, there's always something that feels a little better to focus on than the rest. Training your mind to focus on a little glimmer of light lines you up to see more light.

C: I just thought to check my home voice mail. My friend called and apologized for forgetting. She's such a dear! I can probably call and talk to her on my cell phone on the way home. I feel blessed that in the meantime I had your great company, B.

B: We love you, C. Keep up the good work.

C: Thanks, B! With your great help, I'm sure I will.

We're Always Here : 10-22-09, 7:39 AM

C: Hi, B.

B: Hi, C.

C: I notice I address you as B when I talk directly to you, Beloved, but I call you B: when I write about you to my friends. I wonder why that is? I didn't consciously decide to do that.

B: Because you call us B as a nickname, a pet name. And you think of us chatting as B: which implies a relationship in motion. We like that you are thinking of us as alive and in action in your life. We are, you know.

C: That's still the most amazing part of all this, B! I feel like Cinderella saying to the Prince, "I can't believe that you are here. And that you love me!"

B: Yup, we're here. We're always here. And we love you.

C: Thanks, B. I am loved.

B: So very true, C! We'll never stop telling you that, now that you are listening.

Are You REAL, B?: 10-23-09 4:33 AM

C: Hi, B.

B: Hi, C.

C: So I seem to be gripped by the filter of fear in this moment. I'm afraid you're not real!

B: Relax, sweet girl. Take a deep breath, and then another, and another. We are glad you turned on the light and decided to talk to us rather than continue to try to fight the fear in the darkness.

How does it feel to relax and breathe?

C: It feels better, B. I was hearing that chant again, "Find me somebody to love, find me somebody to love."

B: You have somebody to love, C. You have us. What does it feel like to love us and be loved by us?

C: Sometimes it feels totally transcendent. This week I had another over the top experience of bliss as I prayed with a friend. I could feel your love, the love that suffuses EVERYTHING. I cried through the entire prayer.

B: Was it real, C?

C: Oh, Yes, B! More real than most every day experiences. I was awake, aware and alive in that moment. I felt totally tuned in to the cosmic channel and witnessing what is really going on here more fully than before.

B: Did it last longer than your experience last week?

C: Yes, it lasted a couple of minutes. I even have an audio recording of it, although I haven't sat down to listen to it again yet.

B: Was it easier to integrate than the first one?

C: Yes, because I was talking with a trusted friend who also has a great awareness of the divine Presence. She was flowing with me and appreciating what was happening in the moment, and I felt totally supported in going there with her.

B: Why do you trust her, C?

C: I've known her for more than five years, B. I talk to her every week. I love her and feel loved by her. I know her well and admire her tremendously. She's clear and powerful.

B: When you have as much experience with us as you have with Lisa, you will trust us as much, too, C.

Our relationship feels huge and valuable to you, we know. Yet we are just a couple of months into this level of conscious closeness with you. You feel our support daily now. You are learning to trust that we are here for you. You are exploring the boundaries of what we can do together.

There are no limits to what is possible between us. You will never run out of moments you can share with us. Our relationship transcends your physical life experience – it is eternal.

So what is happening between us is that you are consciously bringing eternal experiences into time and space.

You had the opposite experience already. You have brought time and space relationships with your mom and Cliff into the eternal. That has been a joy for you, hasn't it?

C: Oh, Yes, B. I can feel their love and several times I saw visions of them. Especially the week before Mom died. I asked Cliff to help her into the light or whatever made it easier for her. He patted my arm and said, "I'd like to help you, Conn, but I'd have to wait in line."

I got hit then, with a wave of love waiting for Mom in nonphysical. That was YOU, B, wasn't it? That was YOUR love!

B: That was OUR love, C.

C: Wow, B. That feels powerful right now. Because at that time I was asking if we have to wait to die to experience that love. Now I am experiencing that love, your love, our love, day to day. I am exploring that love with you, intimately, in these cozy conversations. I am also experiencing the depth and magnitude of our love in these breakthrough moments of bliss. WOW!

B: Do you remember, earlier in this conversation, we said that your vibrational escrow is full of blissful moments?

C: Is THIS what you meant by that, B? Those over the top, tearful glimpses into the awesome majesty of divine love?

B: That's part of it, C. It's also plates full of colorful roast vegetables, and the lady bug in your car. Tell the lady bug story, C.

C: I noticed a ladybug that was walking on the ceiling of my car this week. Lady bugs are lucky! She was pretty and I wanted to let her out easily. I just expressed that desire in my mind and thanked her for coming by to see me. I am loved. A few minutes later, I was stopped at a light. I looked left and there she was, a half inch or less from the top of my driver's side window. I let the window down an inch and she immediately walked up and over the top and flew away.

It was a magical moment, B. So effortless and easy!

B: Yes, your future contains gazillions of those moments, too, C. Sweet, lovely, tiny moments of flow and ease.

C: Wow, B. that's cool.

B: What other wonderful moments have you had this week, C?

C: My friend, Laurie, came over on Monday and we sat outside on the ground in the sunshine out back. The weather was perfect and I really appreciated that she came to visit me.

B: Good, what else?

C: I finished a conversation with a client early, and we agreed that we were complete for that session. And within a minute of hanging up with her, another new client called. I had time to fit in her first session right then, which worked beautifully for both of us.

B: Good, what else?

C: My friend Tom Hirt in Pennsylvania cancelled our meeting for next week and I was able to schedule Dusty's surgery for Tuesday. You told me you'd help me work that out and that I would know when to take action on it. I did know, B! It flowed easily. Thank you, I am loved!

B: You and Dusty are both loved, C. You are increasingly light on your feet, so we are able to move things along easily for you. Dusty has always been light on HER feet!

B: & C: [Laughter]

C: So true, B!

B: How do you feel now, C?

C: A whole lot better, B.

B: Think you can go back to sleep now?

C: Yes, B. Thank you. I am loved.

B: Anytime, C. We love bringing greater ease into your life. It's our job. We love our job and we love when you allow us to do it gracefully.

C: When I am seeing through my filter of grace?

B: Bingo!

B: & C: [Laughter]

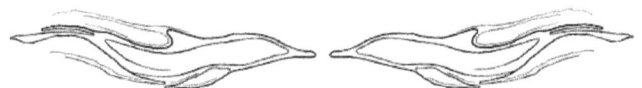

What Matters is Connection, Not Age: 10-24-09, 6:15 PM

C: Hi, B.

B: Hi, C.

C: Just between us, B, ok?

B: Always your call, C. We want you to feel totally comfortable talking to us any time. If you then choose to share it, that's great. If not, that's great. And your establishing your right to control the output is so empowering. You are in control, you are at choice – all, part, or nothing, suit yourself!

C: Thanks, B! Feels good to reserve my right to choose, and then to choose again, too, if what you share feels good to me to pass along.

B: What do you love, C?

C: I love smiling at big handsome men with flashing brown eyes. I love feeling flirtatious and attractive. I love feeling confident and good about myself. I love delicious food that smells fantastic. I love almonds in my pink Kashmiri tea. I love relaxing deeply into wellbeing. I love breathing slowly and deeply and feeling how well supplied with oxygen I am. I love feeling excited about talking to you. I love feeling healthy and energized and fit. I love knowing my life is unfolding as it should. I love amplifying a powerfully positive vibration. I love coming into harmony with broader perspective. I love seeing things from a new and expansive point of view.

I love feeling good about myself and my life. I love feeling exhilarated about something new. I love aligning with moments of bliss. I love feeling unlimited in my opportunities. I love connecting with appreciation for my mom. I love creating happy memories. I love remembering clear moments of connection. I love tuning to love. I love being at ease with my choices. I love feeling optimistic about the future.

B: You're a bit more relaxed now, C. Now what do you want?

C: I realized there are some vibrational connections between the things that are bothering me, B. I want to uplift these vibrations.

B: We congratulate you on having insights, recognizing places you need some work, acknowledging that you are not feeling as good as you want to feel, and asking for help! We're delighted and want to congratulate you for being so clear and powerful when you are in the middle of birthing new desires from the contrast of life.

Good things flow from here!

C: That's good to hear, B.

B: We love that you are choosing to talk to us first thing, C. You go, girl!

C: Thanks, B. I am loved.

B: Yes, you are and we want you to remember that nothing has gone wrong here. Where you've been, and where you are, are just fine. What you're doing now is changing where you are going, all is well!

C: So what I saw today is that my cat's lump, my car's squeal, and the occasional coughing fits I've been having are likely related to a misbelief that things break down over time. And I've seen this thought out-picturing in my dishwasher, washer and dryer, and guard rail on my front steps too.

B: Awesome, C! Great insight. What do you want to believe?

C: I want to believe that things flow, B. I want to believe that what matters is connection, not age. I want to see the divine in people, cats, and things and trust that all is well here in all these areas.

B: What's true of time, C?

C: It's always now, B.

B: What's true about precedent?

C: Holmes said principal is not conditioned by precedent.

B: Good, C. You've learned the theory well. Now it's time to apply it to practice.

C: And that's where I feel shame, B. I'm already supposed to know this stuff.

B: What you knew was fine until now, C. Now your vibration is raising, and the stream's moving faster, and you need some better ideas of a higher vibration to carry forward.

C: Ok, B. What new ideas?

B: There are cultures that revere the aged for their strength and fitness as well as their wisdom.

C: I like the possibility and potential of that, B.

B: You and Dusty, your car and appliances have the potential of getting better rather than older, C. Remember Abraham's saying you should talk to your appliances!

C: Seems weird, B.

B: 'Tis weird for your culture, C, but you've gotten used to lots weirder ideas than these. Your teeth feel better since you've been seeing them filled with light, right?

C: Right, B!

B: You can do the same with the machines. All things respond positively to love and light.

C: But what about action, B? When do I go to the doctor or to the vet or to the hardware store or to the car dealership or replace a machine?

B: When you are inspired to go.

Everything you want is in your vibrational escrow. Longevity for all that is here is facilitated by your appreciation and light. And so is evolution to the next machine, cat or lifetime for you.

C: Whew, B, that's *BIG*!

B: Yup, love it all, appreciate it all and send it all light. And trust that when it seems like something going wrong, it's actually something going right.

C: So my job is to get connected?

B: Yup, the team will change as the terrain changes, C. It will flow as it flows. It's not a big hairy deal either way.

C: In the past, I traded the car the first time it broke down, B.

B: That was fear rather than wisdom, C. The car is fine! We are orchestrating your next car – your fun yellow one. There's no hurry, you are safe and your car is reliable.

Relax and breathe.

C: It seems like what my car and Dusty have in common is that they get me to stay home.

B: That's true, C. What's good about staying home?

C: I get to talk more to you!

B: You're out talking to us right now, C.

C: That's true, B.

B: We're everywhere, C.

What else is good about staying home?

C: I catch up on my typing, I work out, I eat more mindfully.

B: All things you want, yes.

C: Yes, B. I want to do it with ease and grace. I'm willing to get my book written easily. I'm eager to get my book written easily. I love how easily my book is being written. I love coming into greater harmony with my physical strength and stamina. I love feeling powerful, fit and flexible. I love looking in the mirror and smiling at myself, seeing I'm more attractive than I was when I was younger.

B: Everything is like that, C.

It's not age, it's connection. And when you see everything through connection you have the power of influence to help it flow.

B: That feels better, B.

We're glad, C. Go home, Dusty's hungry!

C: Ok, B!

10-25-09, 9:50 PM

B: How do you feel about sharing this now, C?

C: I don't know why I felt embarrassed by it last night, B!!

B: Always up to you, C.

C: Thanks, B! I am loved. Nighty-night!

B: Sleep tight!

This Incredible Dance of Life: 10-26-09, 4:45 AM AND 5:44 AM
...according to the two clocks in the room

C: This is another conversation already in progress, B. I have been describing a powerful vision I had during the Abraham-Hicks workshop I attended yesterday afternoon. Abraham was talking to an engineer about the vibrational aspect of machines.

I suddenly remembered a glorious scene in the Disney cartoon of Cinderella, where all her bird and animal friends scamper, swoop and fly together to make her a dress for the ball. They are singing a song about their joy in making a dress for their friend, "Cinderelly." And suddenly I could feel and see all the aspects of my home, my appliances, the walls, the very nails and roof were singing and dancing and making me the powerfully supportive environment for my wonderful life! And here are the words I wrote in my journal:

> Behind my back, all my machine beings are blissfully dancing my life into greater magic, wonder and joy! These are my cooperative components. It's all about timeless magic.

It's always been true, now I am aware and grateful and dancing with them! I love the on-going party that is my home.

I am willing to explore the timeless magic of life in the vortex. I am eager to explore the time-beyond-time magic of life in the vortex. I love exploring the timeless magic of life in the vortex.

My vibrational reality is full of chirping, swooping, dancing, sewing, singing, cooperative components from all the kingdoms, playing at co-creating a magical, mystical, awesome and wondrous life for me.

And now I am a cooperative component, too!

Oh, B! I am so excited that the glorious spiritual partnership that you and I have was amplified by two wonderful days at workshops with Abraham-Hicks. I was with many of my best friends and favorite people this weekend. I see and feel and know and believe what you are teaching me so much more powerfully now.

I love the magic that happens when my external teacher is matching the message of my internal lover, while I am basking more in the internal atmosphere of a secure, happy, adventuresome child! I am so willing to be taking this glorious ride with you and Abraham!

I love my exquisite nonphysical friends who come to me internally to play and love and bask in the joy of my friendship. I love my external, exquisite nonphysical friends who come to help me and my friends delight in this magnificent co-creative dance of joy with all the vibrational beings: things, animals, plants, water, rocks, and people who love and surround us all.

This is a fabulous vibrational Universe. There is so much more going on here than we usually recognize. I feel like I got a more powerful glimpse into the vibrational reality that is NOW yesterday while I was listening to Abraham.

I feel as though you were there, feeding me these happy, dynamic images of love yesterday, B. Were you?

B: Of course, C. We have ALWAYS been there, feeding you happy, dynamic images of love. The Universe is not the dead, static place you have imagined at all. The Universe is ALIVE with Spirit dancing in the strings, atoms, molecules, cells, systems, beings and things of creation! At every level, from the microcosmic to the macrocosmic, the Universe dances and soars with the BEING of God!

The Being of God dances in your body, endlessly renewing itself and restoring divine balance and harmony as you live.

C: So God is dancing within me! Everything happening to me in every moment is part of the glorious ongoing dance of God as me! Wow, B, this is exhilarating!

B: A cough, sneeze, burp, gurgle or fart of your digestive system,

B: & C: [Laughter]

B: ...is all part of the elaborately choreographed movement of the dance of God. You are increasingly light on your feet! You are a willing follower as you allow us to lead you by your impulses and you feel your way through this. You are consciously cooperating with this incredible dance of life!

Isn't it FUN???

C: Oh, B, this is sublime! I am basking in the bliss of all you are showing me.

This amazing dance of life is eternal. It has always been here and I have always been part of it. You have always been here and I have always been part of you! I have always been part of the "we" that you are! I will always be part of the "we" that WE are!

I am intrinsic to the whole! I am a glorious soaring dancer in a cosmic dance troop of life! I always have been and I always will be! We are putting on a divine show TOGETHER!

I have been an unconscious cooperative component in this dance for fifty-eight years in this life time.

Let's rephrase that. I have been an INCREASINGLY conscious component in this glorious dance throughout my life! I have been waking up to all that is unfolding here for decades! I am so delighted with myself for my newfound willingness to laugh and play and take myself lightly. I have been so serious and tight-assed about it all!

It's ok for me to loosen up and play with you, to play with it all! To dance and sing and love and be, full out, glorious ME!

I have conscious playmates on this planet. I am increasingly inspired by my impulses to rendezvous with extraordinary beings of light. They may appear as foxes watching me on my way to a workshop or wonderful cars and friends who drive me part way on my journey.

My partner may change every thirty seconds, like in the swing dance lessons. And some are there to take me home at the end of the evening. Some are there to BE my home at the end of the evening!

My comfy bed is a dancer in my troop! My graceful stairway, my effective cozy heating system, my thick wall-to-wall carpeting, my strong roof! They are all dancing in delightful harmony with the plumbing and the cabinetry, the nails, walls and paint, to make up a home theater to stage many of the scenes of this magnificent dramatic comedy that is my life.

Oh my, B! My art is a dance in this amazing dance of my life. My words and your words on the page are leap-frogging in a glorious dance of light. I feel so elated, excited, delighted and expanded.

Thank you. I am loved.

Thank you. I am loved.

Thank you, I am loved!

B: You are welcome, C! You have no idea the assembly that has gathered here in nonphysical in excitement to witness this breakthrough moment in your dance of life.

We celebrate every breath you take unconsciously, too! We love every step you take in walking your path.

But a breakthrough of this magnitude is a milestone for us as well as for you. We are all high-fiving the part of us that is B: and the part of us that is C: and the part that is Abraham-Hicks for taking thought, imagery and joy to a whole new level this morning.

We are It. You are It. This is LOVE!!!

It's all love. It's all life. This is LIVING!!! YAY!

Thanks for showing up at the ball, Cinderelly! We are going to have a ball with all of this for a long, long time to come!

C: Oh, thank you, B! I am loved! Thank you Abraham for your part in all of this joy! I am loved.

B: You are so loved, Cinderelly. We dance and celebrate with you this milestone on your path of awakening to who you really are.

You are stepping into your power. You are dancing your joy. You are singing the song of your heart at increasingly audible and glorious frequencies. You are tuning in to the frequency of Source at higher and higher levels. And you are composing the music and bringing to the planet what we are singing inside you, too!

This is a powerful co-creative experience, C! You are tapping into us more clearly than ever before! Yes, you really ARE doing it!

And yes, everyone else who wants can do this, too!

It's not just about you, Connee. You are teaching by your example. Like the swing dance instructors you enjoy so much. As you do this and write about it, and talk about it, you are showing other people how easy and fun it can be.

C: It wasn't so much fun on Saturday night when I was feeling embarrassed by my basic questions, B.

B: But that's the incredible beauty of the dance, don't you see it?

You were in the asking phase, wanting to know, wanting to grow. You were asking Abraham about your beloved kitty who is having surgery on Tuesday from a place of focusing on the problem. Today you are seeing the solution from a whole new level of consciousness.

We honor the question and the questioner! We love that you come to play with us. We adore that you went to play with Abraham! It's all a grand part of the dance.

We love when you get lost in time in the 'not knowing,' because it is so glorious in the moment when you walk through the new portal and suddenly SEE! You are seeing at a much higher level now because you were asking with such urgency on Saturday.

C: And on Saturday, you didn't answer my question directly, B, did you? You reminded me to tune to love and asked me to focus on what I liked about everything.

Aha! That's exactly what Abraham was saying this weekend. They, too, told me to get off the subject I was worried about entirely and focus where the love WAS flowing.

B: Exactly, C! High Fives all around! You have a great team!

We're always telling you all the same thing, C. All the teachers interpret the message in slightly different words, images and analogies. Each of you is valuable and important, because you each have a different signature vibration. You will each speak to a different part of the population who is asking, demanding, to KNOW!

The asking is reaching a whole new crescendo now! And teachers like you are stepping up to the plate at a whole new level of experience.

This new unfolding dance is more fun, for you and for us, than even we anticipated!

C: I thought you knew everything, B! [Laughter]

B: You all are the wild cards, C! You are playing the game at a higher level now. There is a cascading effect that is really magical and magnificent going on here. We are really, really excited about this. There's a lot more than you having a breakthrough tonight on your planet. And not just people who were in the room with you yesterday!

There is a vibrational threshold that has been crossed now. The message is expanding and the capacity to receive it is opening and we are all going to be co-creating at a much higher level from now on.

Welcome to the party, Cinderelly! We're all going to have a lot more fun together in the days to come. The level of cross-fertilization is more consciously multidimensional than ever!

C: Not just because I've had a breakthrough and am now a match to more, B?

B: No, C. That's part of it, but it's more than that. Abraham alluded to it in their closing yesterday. You will see it as you read the notes from their workshops this weekend.

Critical mass has been reached in a whole new way, C. You are a symptom as well as part of the cause of it. Each one who is dancing more lightly and allowing us to lead more expansively is a part of this growing excitement.

We honor you ALL, C. The ones like you who are receiving more clearly from us, and the ones like you who are living the contrast and asking the questions. Also the ones like you who are making the breakthroughs to new understandings. And even the ones unlike you who are living the drama of the trauma and don't yet know. Especially them, C.

We love you all. We love that more and more of you are waking up. We love that more and more of you are showing up, willing to learn and grow and stumble and get up and teach. More and more who are willing to take dancing lessons from us and follow our lead and get out on the floor. We love those like you who are drawn to the dance, even though you've had asthma, and need to develop the fitness and stamina to continue learning more.

We love that you can see it coming. We love that you are willing to take the steps, to go into training. To learn to dance, to learn to follow, to learn the beat, to count it out, to listen to the music and meet new partners and change partners and keep trying when it feels bad or looks funny and you aren't sure what to wear or how to do the steps!

We are here with you. Our view changes, too. Every day, as you make increasingly empowering choices, we are given more and more beautiful threads to weave into the tapestry of your lives.

From our perspective, the view of what is happening to you is increasingly complex and beautiful.

The asking is great now and is answered daily. There is nothing to fear. Let go of the defensiveness and anxiety about the future. What is happening NOW is glorious! See this glory with us. Bask in it with us!

C: I'm basking and dancing just as fast as I can, B! I may have to sit one out and take a breather in a few minutes.

B: Of course, C!

C: Before I get back to sleep, B. I want to ask you about my clock changing times last night and again tonight. That was so weird!

B: There's a physical answer. Your clock, which is connected to the internet, got a message to fall back to Daylight Savings Time on Saturday night. You discovered it in the middle of the night – that your two clocks were different times, and corrected the one on your headboard shelf. Tonight they corrected the error, but since you had already corrected it manually, your clock went off an hour in the other direction again.

The nonphysical answer is part of your asking about time and decline and longevity this weekend, C.

Time is an illusion, and an agreement. You can opt out of that agreement and into a new one. You are eternal as well as temporal. You can opt into an increasingly eternal viewpoint based on the vibration of Source. The vibration of Love brings eternal freshness to everything. Love is the fountain of youth!

When you love you glow with the light of Spirit. That love bathes the cells and systems of your body with light. It fills your bank account with money and your mind with ideas. It fuels your life with a supply of all the good things you most want, including vibrant good health and loving relationships.

Time is relative and irrelevant, C. There is plenty of time for you to love your life! One moment, this moment, is the ideal time to love your life and all the things, beings, people, pets and plants that are sharing this magical dance with you.

What's happening is glorious, thrilling and wondrous. We say that every day and we celebrate it with you even more right now!

We are all in this together. Everything is unfolding perfectly. It's not just safe for you to follow our lead, it is glorious that you do so.

Your shifts, and all the others taking place, are leading us all into beautiful and as yet unexplored new vistas.

The new decisions each person is now making, with free will, are loosening up our options for matching cooperative components. More and more of you are tapped in and turned on. The potential for new choreography is unlimited.

Like the amazing choreographers on *So You Think You Can Dance*, we design your dance to bring out your strengths and showcase your talents. Simultaneously, as you consciously tap into deeper connection to Source, to us, you have more and more talents for us to utilize.

The game is getting way more fun for us as well as for you. You are doing magnificently well, ALL of you!

We are talking to you and your friends, C. We are also talking to all the readers who are going to become part of these chats when they go out in book form. They are already reading this book in the NOW that we are orchestrating in your vibrational reality, C. We see this book in the hands of many. We feel delighted minds basking in your wonderful words, and ours. We feel many delighting in our love story, and being inspired to their own through our example.

C: I am feeling increasingly comfortable writing "our" in a way I know includes you AND me, B!

B: We feel that shift and applaud you for it, C.

C: I love you, B, and I need to sleep now. I have a full day of excitement and joy planned with friends. And lots of typing backed up here, for our chats and for the Abraham workshop notes I share with my friends.

B: Not backed up, C. Queued up!!! It's marvelous that you have glorious work queued up to do this week!

Everything is in utterly perfect timing. You are staying home with Dusty as she recuperates from her magnificently successful surgery. Her vet is being inspired to great new ideas of how to treat her most effectively and gently. He is such a loving, brilliant and compassionate man! You are blessed to have him in your life and so is Dusty.

C: You are so right, B! We're going to have a marvelous dance together as co-operative components tomorrow.

B: Life is good, C. Everything is flowing exactly as it should. Much will continue to change moment by moment, for us and for you.

Isn't this FUN???

C: Yes, B! It's fun and wonderful. Now I am ready to sleep and relax into your loving embrace.

B: YAY! We love it when you perceive you are doing that when you sleep.

C: Me, too, B. Nighty-night, Beloved.

B: Sweet dreams, Cinderelly! We love being your Beloved as we love having you as our Beloved.

A few hours later... 8:00 AM

B: Are you ready to continue, C?

C: No, B. I am thirsty and I need to pee and my cats are hungry. I am going to the bathroom and the kitchen now.

B: YES!!! Good for you for taking care of yourself first, C! See you later!

A little while later...

C: Back again, B. Tell me more about opting out of time and still keeping appointments.

B: Say, "I'll meet you at noon on the 26th of this month in the timeless NOW of eternity!"

C: Great, B! I'm still feeling tired. So can you finesse the timeless now of eternity for me so I can sleep a bit more before I need to get up for my full day?

B: Let's experiment, C. This is a co-creative adventure in consciousness.

Later...

B: How'd you do?

C: I went back to sleep and I now have an hour and ten minutes before I need to head out. I feel more rested.

B: Keep experimenting, C. Say, "Let's have fun with this!"

C: I'm laughing now, B. The phone just rang and it was my friend saying she needed more time this morning, and she'll meet me at 2 PM instead of noon in the timeless now of eternity.

B: Conn?

C: Well, I made up the last part!

B: & C: [Laughter]

B: You learn quick, C!

C: You are fabulous to partner with, B. So if I wanted to I could go back to sleep again! It's tempting…

B: So are you going to do it?

C: I'll see how I feel…

B: & C: [Laughter]

Later still…

B: How do you feel about the future, C?

C: Piece of cake, B!

B: What are you going to be doing?

C: I don't know, B. That's the excitement of it! In July, I didn't know I was going to meet you and fall in love and be swept away on this grand and glorious adventure with you!

There are many grand and glorious adventures coming up in my life! I ain't seen nuthin' yet!

I just need to feel my way through this, leaning toward what feels good and taking the inspired action as it comes.

I am willing to let it be a dance, Beloved! You are a glorious, far-sighted, confident, trustworthy and amazing partner. I am getting lighter on my feet every day. I am so willing to be spun!

I am seeing divine timing in the eternal now again because my friend just called, and Kate is in the hospital again. I wouldn't have been here to get the call if I had been on my usual schedule today. Life is amazing, B!

I have things to do, so I am off for a while. Talk to you early and often, B!

B: Bye for now, C.

Inspired Action: 10-27-09, 9:00 AM

C: Hi, B.

B: Hi, C.

C: I just took Dusty over to the vet to get the lump removed next to her eye. I had delegated it to you to know when I take her, and last week I got inspired to call and schedule it for today. I felt inspired at the time. Right now though, after listening to her howl in protest on the way over there, I am wondering if I did the right thing.

B: It *was* inspired action, C. All is well. She was frightened and expressing it. Beings often make a lot of commotion when they are frightened or angry. It makes them feel better to express themselves!

You know she is in loving hands there. Those people adore animals and have kind hearts, gentle hands and brilliant ideas.

Remember what Kate said yesterday from her place at the hospital? "I'm not scared. I feel so much better with this therapy."

Dusty has been through this before and has had an easier time each time. She will get through it today with flying colors and you will all relax deeply into a wonderful week at home while she recovers. You can breathe deeply and put her in our very loving hands. You really do know that we are always holding you and her, supporting and soothing and petting you. Really, she's in way better shape than you are in this moment. She's already relaxed into the inevitable. Now you can do the same.

C: Thanks, B, that does feel better. I am loved. Rosie just came by to get petted. I'm not sure if she's reassuring me or the other way around.

B: Both, C. You are sharing our love with each other. You both love Dusty. You are all fine.

C: I haven't been as stressed about it as I was before. And she didn't have to go twice this time, they are doing everything they need to do in this one visit.

B: Keep soothing yourself and appreciating, Conn. Your worrying doesn't help the situation at all. Your meditating and finding your peace, our peace, within it is the best help you can be to Dusty, Rosie and yourself.

C: I know you are right, B. Ok. I'll put on a meditation CD and relax now.

B: Good, C! Let us know how it turns out for you and for her.

C: Thanks, B. I am loved. I am so grateful to have you here with me to talk to.

B: We love being your uplifting friend, C.

Turn, Turn, Turn: 10-28-09, 5:11 AM

C: Hi, B!

B: Hi, C.

C: So here's what you are telling me. I am stepping more powerfully into the glorious nature of my true being. More and more people are doing the same thing right now. The more I stay focused on the lightness of being, the easier it will be for me to hear the guidance you give me. I will receive impulses toward inspired action that will be fun and productive.

There is great leverage in connection to Source. My relationship with you is the source of my true power in my life. I can trust you to be here for me. You are always here. You have always been here, I just didn't know how to connect with you.

I was afraid to believe in your love. Now I feel and practice your Presence in my life, by talking to you and listening to you, connecting with you and loving you. By taking this inspired action to relate to you, I'm doing my part to invite this love story to unfold. Then I just get the pleasure of listening to the soothing, loving messages of ease and grace to flow to me and support me. I get to appreciate every breath I take as evidence of your loving supply of my life. I get to expand in my vision and understanding, because I have access to your broader perspective. I get to say, "Thank you. I am loved," a hundred times a day as I notice all the good that is flowing to me.

In my moments of disconnection, I get to talk to you anyway, and you coach me back to focus on all there is to love and appreciate about my life. I am so incredibly blessed. Everything I need is already provided for me. I have breath, food, water, shelter right now. There is a beauty, harmony and love that is unfolding here beyond anything I have tasted so far. I am learning to access these higher vibrations of joy and deeper understanding.

How am I doing, B?

B: Great, C! We are really pleased with your review of what you understand today. Not just because you demonstrated a clear grasp of the concepts, but because talking about what you know serves you incredibly well. It would be very valuable for you to review what you know often. The affirmation of your clearest vision of who you are and how life flows is building new grooves in your brain that remind you to relax and allow your wellbeing to flow.

C: That's cool, B. Not only does it feel good to remind myself of your loving Presence in my life, but it also helps me retrain my brain into valuable habits of thought.

Don't I need to eliminate the dysfunctional habits of thought?

B: You can't, C. The more you focus on dysfunction, the more you amplify it in your thinking by Law of Attraction. As soon as you identify what you don't want, turn as quickly as you can to focus on what you do want. It will serve you very well to take yourself lightly, because it allows you to spin so much more easily!

C: I'm hearing the song from the Byrd's, B, *"Turn, Turn, Turn."* I don't remember it entirely – I remember this is part of it… "To everything, turn, turn, turn, there is a season, turn, turn, turn, and a time to every purpose under heaven. A time to be born, a time to die, a time to laugh, a time to mourn, a time to cast away stones, a time to gather stones together."

B: Exactly, C. Through it all, staying connected to us and allowing us to turn, turn, turn you in the direction of your good, moment to moment.

C: So I have something I want to turn, turn, turn on this morning, B. Dusty had her surgery yesterday and our brilliant vet did a totally beautiful job of removing the lump and fixing her eye. It's all glued together and she needs to wear this blue lampshade thing for ten to twelve days and take a bunch of medicine. Here's the problem. She doesn't like to take the meds. She spit them out when she had them last time. She refuses to eat when I mix in the meds.

B: We felt you just choke as you wrote that paragraph, C. Try again to focus on what you DO want.

C: I want to help my sweet kitty get through this period of recovery as quickly and easily as possible. I want to support her as you support me, being a stable source of assistance and comfort for her. I want to trust that you are also here loving us both and helping us relax and remember that everything we need to get through this time is already available.

In fact, I am willing to know that everything we need to ENJOY this time together is already at hand. I am so willing to trust that our magnificent vet did a terrific job with this surgery and that she is totally queued up to heal perfectly. I am willing to trust that her reliable and incredible appetite will inspire her to eat the food that contains the meds. And that I will be inspired to find new food she likes that can disguise the taste better. My friend told me that liver sausage works great for her dog. I'll try it!

B: Good work, C. Notice what you did here in this whole chat so far. You were inspired first to talk about what you do know that feels good about who you are and how things work. Only after you did that, which turned you in the direction of allowing a solution, did you even bring up the problem!

Turn, Turn, Turn! Turn as quickly as you can toward who you are and how things work. Think for a bit at the macrocosmic level of love and law.

Then turn to the problem, as briefly as possible. Notice your feeling. It would have been good if you could have articulated what you were feeling outright, but it was really good that you let us point out that you felt yourself choking on the way you were expressing the problem so dogmatically, based on your past experience with Dusty.

Then turn to what it is you do want and are willing to accept. We really like this new idea, C.

First, turn toward the macrocosm and remind yourself who you really are.

Then turn back to look at the problem from a new vantage point, where your emotion can show you exactly where your limiting pattern of thought is tripping you up.

Then turn to what you want and are willing to receive.

C: Thank you, B. This is very clear. I am loved.

I can feel there is more good stuff here about releasing my focus on the past things that went wrong and focusing on the Timeless Eternal Now that you talk about. This is really powerful, B.

B: It sure is, C! We love that you are getting this level of the message already.

We are going to be talking a lot about moving beyond the precedent in the days to come. Your potential is SO much greater than what has happened in the past! You don't have to look back! You can train your mind to look forward at what you want more and more easily.

C: My third eye is buzzing, B.

B: With good reason, C!

The power of what we are talking about here is great. This is the most potent tool for retraining your brain you have encountered to date. Simply turn, turn, turn.

Basically, turn to us and the macrocosm. Then turn back to the problem very briefly to see your guidance. Then turn quickly to what you want and are willing to receive.

C: Then what, B?

B: Then turn, turn, turn again.

Turn back to us again to thank us for helping with bringing the solution into your life. Your invitation to us to help opens unseen and incredibly valuable doors for you, C. It gives us more room to maneuver and sets you up to allow miracles to happen.

We love it when you are willing to allow miracles!

Then turn away from the subject entirely. Focus on subjects that do feel good. Relax, meditate, sleep, listen to music, observe nature, sing, dance, write love lists, type our chats with you, or whatever you can do that feels good. Give us time to line things up for you.

Also, turn to us for reassurance. Dusty is going to be fine. She is fine. It's ok for you to relax and trust that now. This is all going to be easier than you thought it could be. In this timeless now, she eats well and takes the meds she needs easily.

Dusty is a strong, clear and powerful being. Like you, she is part of the 'we' that we are. Everything is. Everyone is!

Nothing is separate from our good and our glory.

Relax now, sweet girl. Go back to sleep. All is well. All is very, very well.

C: Thanks, B. Your loving, joyful words and the gentle rain is making me sleepy. Thank you. I am loved.

B: You are SO loved, C. Thank you for chatting with us this morning. We are loved, too!

B: & C: [Laughter]

Wonder and Wander: 10-29-09, 9:10 AM

C: Hi, B.

B: Hi, C.

C: Any advice on how to live my life B?

B: Yes! Wonder and wander! Say, "I wonder if that would be fun?" and wander over there and see if it is.

Take all of this more lightly, C. Make it a gentle little exploration. Nothing is all that important here, we want you to relax and not make a big hairy deal out of anything.

C: OK, B. So, if I'm just to experiment with it all, what about lining up my energy first before I do things?

B: Experiment with that, too. How good do you want to feel?

C: I want to feel really good, B.

B: Then tell us what it's like when you feel really good, C.

C: I love feeling optimistic and eager. I love feeling happy and fulfilled. I love moments of exhilaration. I love to soar and sparkle. I love to engage with life at a high level, feeling eager and enthusiastic about what I am doing.

B: Good. What else?

C: I love to feel loved. I love to feel blessed. I love feeling like I am thriving and successful. I love feeling inspired. I love feeling passionate. I love being touched by beauty or kindness. I love falling in love. I love feeling valuable in helping someone else. I love the feeling of inspired movement, allowing my body to stretch and dance through life.

B: Good. What else?

C: I love to feel respectful and respected. I love to connect deeply with a friend's divinity and feel honored to witness their magnificence. I love to see that in myself, too. Those are the most transcendent moments when I know the real game we are playing here from your perspective. I love feeling the world through your feelings, B! That's the very best!

B: What's that like for you, C?

C: I feel my heart and mind expand in love. My mind feels spacious – still thinking, yet still between thoughts – that's cute still, still…. I love playing with words, B. I love jumping to a new subject and knowing you are willing to follow me there. I love feeling free to be me right where I am in this moment when I am with you. Sometimes with people I get embarrassed when I skip around and feel I have to try to be more linear.

B: Embarrassment is a signal to you that you are seeing yourself in a way we don't see you, Conn. You are worthy and beautiful to us. We are happy for you to skip, laugh, play and delight in life.

C: Now you played with a double meaning of skip!

B: & C: [Laughter]

B: You worry too much about what other people think. Experiment with people. Be yourself! If they like you, they will hang around. If they don't, they will move along. Perfect either way! There are 7 billion or so on the planet, C. You don't need to make friends with all of them.

C: That's funny, B. Is that what I try to do?

B: Yup. Even in writing down our conversation, you are anticipating some people won't like it or judge you. That's not your problem, C.

People who judge hurt themselves - they separate themselves from the way their Inner Beings look at life, so they feel bad. But they don't have to make you feel bad! You can make how you feel be about your internal relationship with us, not the external relationship with them.

C: I never thought about people who criticize hurting themselves, B.

B: When you do it, C, it's almost always because you've been raised in a culture where you were taught that's how to get things done. People think fixing a problem requires first criticizing it up one side and down the other, and then expect that things will magically get better.

But the magic for making things better is all on the side of love.

C: In the middle of a big problem, it's hard sometimes to find any love in it, B.

B: So true, C. Because Law of Attraction is always bringing you more of whatever you are focused on. So you start to criticize or worry about something and then you attract even more to criticize or worry about.

C: It seems endless, B.

B: It *IS* endless, C. Law of Attraction will never stop bringing you more of what you focus on. That's why a relationship that goes downhill gets worse and worse. Sometimes both people wonder who it is that's taken over their bodies.

Don't you remember asking, "Who is this woman and when did she take over my body?"

C: I've asked that from feeling unusually bad. And also from feeling unusually terrific!

B: Exactly, C! LOA works the same for amplifying the positive as it does the negative. Once you train your brain to focus on what you love, you will begin to change how you feel about yourself and your life naturally from the inside out.

Are you willing to change, C?

C: More than I used to be, B. Since I've met you, I am feeling a lot calmer about change. I guess it is because I feel so much more optimistic about the future. That even surprised me!

B: When you are powerfully connected to us, you can feel the true energy of your divine life coursing through you. It is good for you to recall that moment on Monday when you said you felt the future was "a piece of cake".

In that moment, you were seeing the real you as clearly as you ever have in your whole life. You knew your power and you were confident you could focus your attention on what you wanted.

How do you feel right now, C?

C: Better than I did when we started, B. I love that you encourage me to focus on love and write down how I want to feel.

B: That's how you align your energy, C. Other people have other primary ways, singing, skipping, meditation, running, cooking, yoga, and skydiving! You've known people who've used all those things.

C: I have, B. And so many more! So it is OK that we each find our own ways of lining up with you, B?

B: Not just OK, but great, C! The more ways people find to feel better, the more ways people will find to feel better. Once one door to good feeling opens, others tend to follow.

Later... 6:55 PM

C: Hi, B.

B: Hi, C.

B: How are you doing, C?

C: Been better, B. Ed called today and said Kate's been released to hospice. The prognosis isn't good.

B: The prognosis is excellent from our perspective, Conn. Kate is so surrounded by love, physical and nonphysical now. She is more here than there already. This is going to be easy and delightful for her.

How willing are you to be at ease with this?

C: I want to find my peace with it, B. Kate and I have been close friends for seventeen years, together at least two or three times a week. It's hard to imagine life without her.

You're going to make me write about what I know again, aren't you, B?

B: It will help you, C. But it is always your choice.

C: I trust you, B. I'll do it.

I know I am grateful for all the love Ed has shown Kate in the past few years. His love gives me way more faith in the human spirit.

I am grateful for Kate's friendship. She is the most loyal friend I have ever known. She still has all her friends from her home town and college and all the jobs she's had. She has the best sense of humor on the planet. She has vast courage and she faced a lifetime of physical illness with indomitable good will and optimism.

Even on Monday when I talked to her in the hospital she said, "I'm not scared. I feel so much better with this therapy." She was reaching for appreciation and trying to reassure me.

I talked to her twice yesterday. She sounded tired and drugged.

B: Kate is tired, C. And the time comes when it's easier to let go and come home. As we told you before, from our perspective, it's always a good time for you to come home. There's always a party waiting for you here.

C: Kate loves parties, B. The party Ed threw for Kate's birthday was totally awesome. She was so into it!

Later...

C: I'm getting ready for bed, B. No news yet. I'm sad.

B: We know, C. We love you and Kate. You'll find your way in this in the next few days.

C: Thanks, B. I am loved.

Kate's Life: 10-30-09, 4:49 AM

C: I woke up seeing the Scrubs video from Youtube.com, "I'm Waiting For My Real Life to Begin" in my mind, B. It's a comfort to me right now.

B: Yes, C. Kate's new life is as vivid and magnificent as the woman in that video and Kate always looked that great in red, too.

Your real life is now, C. Kate's real life is now, too. You both will always be. The next life is not more real than this one, nor less real. It's **all** life.

Kate's spirit is now. The timeless eternal now contains her life and her love as well as yours. You don't need to feel the loss of her – you can feel her in her favorite funny songs our friend TM Hanna sings and see her in the falling leaves and be grateful, as she pointed out, that they do not all fall at once, *whomp*!

B: & C: [Laughter]

B: You can be grateful that she is soaring, no longer restrained by her loving body that worked so hard in this lifetime. Her indomitable spirit continues to shine as a powerful reminder to all of us to love and laugh and make the best of each day. Whether that day held joyfully falling in love with Ed or hospitalization for a liver transplant, Kate courageously made the best of each one – always seeing the glass half full, never half empty.

C: Kate is one of my life's most unforgettable characters. She is heading out on her next glorious adventure and I know that her glass is now full to the brim and overflowing with the love of God and the love of hundreds of people she touched. I am so grateful I got to spend seventeen years of my life with her radiant Kateness. I am glad that she shines on so brightly in my heart today as I take this moment of many to salute her and say, "Well done, Kate. I love you!"

Kate loved to laugh, she loved to swim. She loved bunnies. She loved her mom and dad and brothers and sisters. She loved Ed Surma, his daughters, Stephanie and Maggie, and her new grandbaby, Erik. Kate loved listening to folk music and laughing about the focus on death rather than life. She was expected to die from the time her illness was diagnosed when she was six. She told me that she never bought more than one roll of toilet paper at a time until she turned forty. She felt triumphant turning fifty and her Ed threw the party of her dreams for her and all her friends and family.

Kate allowed herself to be loved. When her phone would ring, she would say before she answered it, "Somebody loves me."

She loved the Windjammer cruise we took – her favorite island was St. Lucia. And she didn't get sea sick when everyone else did. She loved the beach and her hometown of Guilford, Connecticut. She loved older people and remained friends with all her mom's friends – she loved going by to visit them when she went home to Connecticut.

Kate showed up for life in a most magnificent way. She said yes to loving this moment, whatever it brought to her. She did her best to bring a laugh along with it. Although she often had more reason to be depressed than anyone I've ever known, she never gave in to it. She had the courage and the will to love life, even on the days she had little stamina to do it.

Even in those long last weeks when she was in the hospital, she still looked for things to appreciate. She loved her brothers and sisters coming to visit and would take a nap early in the evening so she could wake up for Pat's later visits from Maryland night after night. She loved Mary's washing her hair and helping her feel more attractive. She trusted and loved Ed, Greg and Frank and leaned heavily on their wisdom and strength to support her when she needed their help. And she continually reached for her independence from all of them to live her own life as well.

I'm so proud of Kate for living such a magnificent life! I'm delighted she chose me as a friend for seventeen years and that I got to learn and grow, from her and with her, through all that time. She helped me through my lowest times and celebrated my happiest and I did the same for her. I love her and wish her bon voyage on this grand new eternal adventure.

Oh, B. Thank you for helping me write that! I want to honor Kate and help our friends deal with her transition. Sometimes it's hard having the role to play of "spiritual leader" when my own heart feels like it's breaking.

B: We like the phrase "a broken heart is an open heart," C.

Later the following morning:

C: Hi, B.

B: Hi, C.

C: I just talked to Ed, Kate's comfortable and eating eggs for breakfast! It's a little disorienting to have been trying to deal with her impending transition into nonphysical all night and now be hearing about her life this morning.

B: It's **all** life, C. You need to get a broader perspective on this. Death is a stage of Life. Eternal life includes birth and death and a constant unwavering consciousness every moment in between. From your physical perspective you sleep and wake, live and die. From our perspective you live and live and live and live and live. Kate is living! Treat her as living now and later. You can talk to her as you talk to us!

C: I appreciate the pep talk, B. It feels selfish, given what Ed and Kate are living, for me to be thinking about the talk I am giving on Sunday. My topic is the nature of Being.

B: Seems to us that Kate is sharing with you a powerful lesson on the nature of being. We love that you are willing to hear and write about her aliveness now. She is a powerful teacher and she models so clearly the teachings of Science of Mind. Your Study Group can learn much from Kate through your talk on Sunday. You can and will be able to do this well. You are stronger than you know. With us, you are brave and wise. We love that you allow us to support you. That's brave and wise of you.

The choice to connect to your nonphysical nature, whether you call it God, Inner Being, Jesus, or Beloved, is the wisest, bravest choice you can make. We love that you are doing it more and more, when you feel good and when you don't feel good.

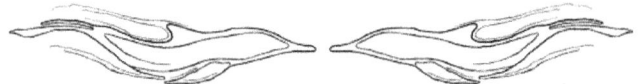

"Loosing" Kate: 10-31-09, 4:10 AM

[*My two clocks say 4: 10 and 5: 10 and now the date is also wrong – it says 11-1-09*]

C: Hi, B.

B: Hi, C.

C: Now the clock's lost an hour and added a day! [*It was daylight savings and this time it was right that it lost an hour. I still don't know why it added a day.*]

B: We love reminding you of the timeless eternal now, C. How does it feel when you hear those words?

C: Timeless eternal now? It feels expansive, spacious, roomy! Like a beautiful home, a mansion with many rooms. I'm struck by my choice of the word Rumi/roomy, because when I think of you Beloved, I think of Rumi's poetry. Sometimes I feel like an ecstatic mystic, soaring with the excitement of seeing the Universe through your eyes.

B: There is much for you to be ecstatic about, C. The path you are beginning with us will open amazing doors. The changes that will unfold in your life will surprise and delight you.

C: Some changes already underway are hard, B.

The idea of losing Kate so suddenly is shocking. I don't want to say goodbye to my friend.

B: We suggest you "*loose*" Kate. You can never lose her. The love that you share is forever.

In the same way you can talk to us and to your mom, you can talk to Kate. Her eternal being is bright and expanded from the life known as Kate. She has been such a powerful source of love and inspiration for so many.

C: What would it be like to "*loose*" her?

B: Remember Ernest Holmes saying, "Loose the boundaries of your sense of self and let in more spiritual territory." We want you to loose the boundaries of your sense of Kate and let in your awareness of the infinite and eternal nature of her being now.

With Cliff, you used to say that you were willing to learn to love BIG enough to transcend even physical life. That's truly unconditional love. Your beloved doesn't even have to have a physical body.

That experience with Cliff helped set you up for our relationship, too. For we are also The Beloved, unconditionally loved and loving without a physical body. So is Kate. You are all a dynamic part in the Infinite Consciousness of Love.

You could see yourself as a mere "drop in the bucket" and most of you do. But the true nature of your Being is more like an infinite wave in the ocean of love rather than a drop in the bucket. Your physical form is a beautiful bucket that you pick up and lay down with ease from your nonphysical perspective. As we said yesterday, it's just life, life, life, life, and life. And life and life and life and life and life, infinitely, intimately, exquisitely expressing love.

You are doing a good job writing down what we are saying, Connee.

The infinity of Love cannot be contained by a bucket of words either. But it can be expressed as a wave of love captured by a heart overflowing as a vibrational resonance. Other hearts are feeling and answering your expanded allowing already.

Consciousness travels telepathically. In your writing these words, you are grounding our love in the human vibration more fully than without them.

Everyone can choose to ground our love in the physical. Each one will discover a unique expression for themselves. Each one who makes the choice to open their hearts to divine love will make an enormous contribution, even if they never share a word of it with anyone else ***directly***.

Like your conversation with Ed yesterday, where you were privileged to witness the depth and beauty of his knowing of his eternal love with Kate, love transcends everything else. Love speaks volumes.

You can't live in divine love without influencing others. The magic unfolds and continues. We are so blessed to witness the unfolding of love in any of your lives. We are thrilled beyond description to ***BE*** the unfolding of love in your life, Conn. There is remarkable power and grace here.

C: Thank you, B. I am loved. And I feel comforted. I love that I have you to bring me such potent reminders of the power and presence of love.

B: We are so happy to remind you, C. Sleep again, sweet girl. You want to feel rested for this wonderful day.

C: Wonderful day, B?

B: Every day you are alive is a wonderful day to us, C!

C: And you feel that way about everyone, right, B?

B: Absolutely. We love everyone as dearly as we love you, C.

Don't you love it?

C: I sure do, B! Off to dreamland for a while longer, then!

10-31-09, 9:02 AM

C: Well, I am back from the emergency veterinary clinic. Dusty has a scratch on her cornea and 2 sets of eye drops, new pain meds, and a hard collar to keep her from messing with her eye. I am feeling exhausted and just want to cancel everything for today. Enough already!

B: Your peace of mind is reassured about Dusty's surgery – it was a worthwhile trip. Relax and rest now, sweet girl. She's fine and the pain meds they gave her are very effective. She's going to feel lots better from now on!

C: That's a relief, B. Thank you, I am loved.

NOVEMBER, 2009:

Everything is All Right Here

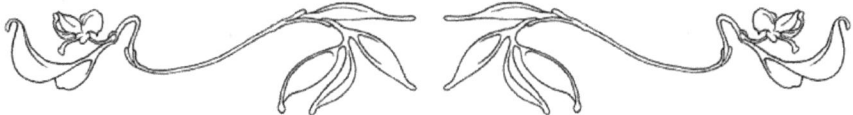

There's No Standard of Conduct You Have to Adhere to: 11-1-09, 4:01 AM

C: Hi, B.

B: Hi, C.

C: I can't sleep, B. I'm relieved that the new pain medicine that Dusty is taking is helping her sleep – she's conked out on the end of the bed now after spending an inordinate amount of time lovingly grooming the last three inches of her tail which is the only part that she can reach with her Elizabethan collar. I feel better that she is feeling better. And I had a lovely email from Ed saying that he was so grateful for the housecleaning service Catherine arranged. I am so grateful to her that she had that idea and followed through. She's a wonderful friend.

Kate made it through another day. I was reassured by Ed's saying she is comfortable and feels loved. That's a good thing. I'm struggling with this, B. How can I feel happy and get on with my life and do fun things when Kate's dying? I canceled my concert tonight and gave the ticket to a friend. I am wondering about going to the birthday party Monday! I'm just not handling life in the middle of death very well.

B: There's no standard of conduct you have to adhere to here, Connee. You are feeling your way through this as with all other things. We don't see death here. We see life, and life and life and life and more life.

C: Hearing that again does bring me some comfort, B, but I feel really off balance between Dusty's surgery and helping everyone else with Kate as well as my own feelings about it.

B: We are glad you aren't taking it all on yourself, C. You are delegating to others and finding more ease. Several times yesterday, you told people what you needed rather than just cave in and put their needs ahead of yours.

We love that you give so much from your fullness, C. And we love that when you are feeling depleted you drop and rest and take a time out. We love that you aren't pushing yourself to the edge of sickness before you decide to take care of yourself. You are really doing very well.

C: Thanks, B. I am loved.

It helps me to hear from you that it is ok to take care of me even when other people need something from me.

B: You can't take care of anyone else if you make yourself sick, C. Finding a loving balance of giving and receiving is vital. As you rest, relax, exercise and nurture yourself, you have way more to give.

C: I'd like to rest, B.

B: We think you are more relaxed and will be able to sleep now, C. You are loved.

Allow yourself to rest in our love now.

C: Thanks, B. I am loved. I appreciate your help in settling down tonight.

You LISTEN! 11-4-09, 4:16 AM

C: Hi, B.

B: Hi, C.

C: Wow, B, you rock. I'm behind with the typing since Kate passed away, and I read what you said about *Turn, Turn, Turn* yesterday out loud to my friend Lisa. You are brilliant!

B: Glad you like it, C. We appreciate your appreciation.

C: I appreciate your reminder to turn first to you. It's really helped me since I get it that I need to tune up in order to talk to you. But I wouldn't have guessed how effective turning to talk to you would be in tuning me up.

B: That's because you don't just talk to us, you also listen! And you listen with a willingness to be led – that's so important!

You follow our lead with love and lightness of being. As a result you are hearing our guidance more and more clearly. You are following your impulses with a lot less second-guessing, too.

C: Yes, that has surprised me. Especially the morning I took Dusty to the emergency clinic. I thought I did that out of fear. But it turned out great because the different liquid pain medicine has really helped her relax and let her wound heal nicely. Was that inspired action?

B: Yes, it was the path of least resistance to her quickest wellbeing at that moment.

C: Well, I'm glad, because as she's better, and more relaxed about taking her medicine. I'm a lot more relaxed in giving it to her, too.

B: Actually, your efforts to line up your energy about her several times since the surgery have really helped. You did well to keep remembering that the past doesn't have to condition the present, unless you think about the past in the timeless eternal now.

In the timeless eternal now, all new possibilities exist. Isn't that exciting?

C: Sure is, B. And in this moment, the possibility of getting back to sleep is really exciting, too!

Thank you, B. I am loved. I love you.

B: Thank you, C. We appreciate your willingness to let our voice be heard so powerfully in words. We are loved and we love you.

C: Night, B.

B: Sweet dreams, C.

Later that day…8:38 AM

C: Hi, B.

B: Hi, C.

C: I feel like I am always saying to you that I'm tired, B. What's up with that?

B: Several things, C. You usually talk to us at 4: 00 AM, for one! You don't usually allocate your energetic times for our conversations. Then you are up and doing – walking in the woods, going to the gym, making and taking phone calls, getting groceries, doing your life. It's the times when you relax and stop doing that your thoughts turn to us most of the time.

Your slightly drowsy semi-meditative state when you are tired also makes it easier for you to focus inward, ignore the world, and write down our side of the conversation.

You don't need to worry. You are not more tired than before. You are just talking a lot more when you feel that way than you ever did before. All is well. We love you.

C: I love you, too, B. And thanks for the reassurance. I am loved. I really liked your reminder that it is OK to turn to you for soothing and reassurance. It feels awesome to remember that you are always here for me when I want someone loving to talk to.

B: Yup, always here, always loving you. That's what we do. We're so glad you are allowing us to be here for you.

C: See you later, B.

B: OK, C.

Another Movie Moment: 11-5-09, 7:28 PM

C: Hi, B.

B: Hi, C. What have you noticed this week, C?

C: I noticed the moon rising just now. It was full on Monday night, but it is still full of beauty tonight, huge and orange even though the right side is fuzzy and dark.

B: Good. What else?

C: I noticed that there's a lot of love flowing among people who loved Kate. A whole lot of people really cared about her and want to tell stories about her. She inspired a whole lot of people.

B: Good. What else?

C: I noticed that I felt really good when I read your dialogs to some of my friends this week. When I focus on you, and on feeling loved, I feel good. I felt good when I typed *Turn, Turn, Turn* today, too. That's a powerful message.

I noticed that you predicted Dusty would eat her food and take her meds easily. She did. But only after I had to rush her to the animal emergency vet. They gave her the liquid meds, and she took them so much better.

B: How is she now, C?

C: She's still sleeping more than usual, but her eye is looking better every day.

B: Good. What else?

C: I noticed as I was walking in the woods today that it was Kate who gave me the copy of *The Shack* that inspired me to the idea of a more personal relationship with you, B. A real relationship!

B: Ahhhhhh! Good noticing, C!

C: I noticed that you said all was well with Dusty – that I could relax and trust that she would eat well and take her medicine easily, which she did – *EVENTUALLY*! Took a rush trip to the emergency vet to arrange that though. What's up with that, B?

B: Your old standby line, C. Even when it looks like something going wrong, it's actually something in the process of going right. We told you we'd inspire you at the right time with what to do. We kept our promise and you followed through perfectly. We particularly liked your hearing our guidance to go back in the house for the earplugs and to sing loudly in time to her howling. We don't mean to hurt your feelings, but that was pretty funny from our perspective!

B: & C: [Laughter]

C: OK, B, I can see the humor in it from here. It wasn't funny at the time though.

OK, thank you, I am loved.

That reminds me of another great Kate story. In the middle of our beautiful World Peace Meditation last year, my cat put his tail on a candle and torched himself. I had my eyes closed, but I heard my friend Judy, who was leading the meditation in that moment, gasp. I opened my eyes, leaped up, moving faster than ever before in my life, grabbed him and put the fire out with both hands. He was shocked, we both were, and the smell of burning fur was horrible. I sat with him in the other room while my friends continued on with the ritual.

Eventually, I got myself under control and, reassured that he was fine, went back into the room. I sat down and tried to meditate but all I could think was about someone asking, "How was the World Peace Meditation?" and my answering, "Before or after I torched my cat?"

Anyway, that thought sent me into hysterics. I began to laugh and I couldn't stop. After a moment of surprise, all my friends gathered in the room laughed with me. It was such a relief! We laughed for at least 10 minutes!

B: Another great movie moment, C! How did Kate fit in?

C: Well, she told us afterwards that she had the thought, "This is going to be funny in six months. I wonder why it isn't funny now?" My guess is that her thought planted the idea of laughter in my mind. It was the perfect response and a great relief to everyone.

B: Thank you, C. We are loved. This is a wonderful example of how you influence each other telepathically all the time. Kate was a very soothing influence in this situation. She was an observer, not caught up in the drama, and she used her sense of humor to diffuse your tension and inspire you to an action that was healing for everyone.

Good catch, C!

C: Thanks, B, I am loved.

B: Note the similarity between these two stories. Both times you were in shock because something appeared to be going very wrong for your beloved kitties. Yet both times, you picked up on the telepathic guidance, from Kate and us, to actions, laughter or loud singing, to relieve the tension.

We love that you can pick up on good ideas and be uninhibited in acting on them. Well done.

C: Thanks, B. I am loved.

B: You sure are, C. You all are! Your kitties, your candles, your laughter, even your world peace meditations.

C: Is there value in getting together to meditate on peace and bless all the world's peoples and religions, B?

B: Yes, C. Getting together to meditate is lovely. Getting together to bless all the people of the world is sublime. Getting together to laugh at averted disaster: Priceless!

We love Kate and her family's sense of the ridiculous in the middle of tense situations. We love the jokes they invented in the hospitals and that they played with each other through all her illnesses. It really did increase her longevity and lifespan.

Be playful. Be joyful. Laugh now, not six months from now. It's OK to take it all lightly, even if other people might not approve. Most people are incredibly relieved when they are encouraged to laugh. Life is funny. Enjoy it.

Eternal and Temporal: 11-6-09, 8:49 AM

C: Morning, B.

B: Hi, C.

C: I'm loving this morning with sunlight streaming in through the window. I'm loving that I have this day to prepare to teach my class tomorrow and then have a pot luck for "Friends of Kate."

B: Why a pot luck, C?

C: Well, since Kate's memorial service is not going to be held until the end of the month, I was feeling incomplete. So I asked myself what I was missing. It wasn't the funeral. In my own way, I did a funeral kind of service for her with my talk on the Nature of Being using Kate's life going on as my example last Sunday. I was longing for the "going home with all the close ones" after-the-funeral party. People hugging, telling stories, tearing up and hugging some more. Then telling more stories, laughing and hugging some more. I miss the hugs! Pot lucks around here come with LOTS of hugs!

B: That's great, C! And what's your class about tomorrow?

C: Immortality, B! Talk about perfection – Kate's timing is amazing. I was giving a talk on the Nature of Being as she was preparing to leave the planet. And a class on eternal life to close the week she did pass over.

B: We love Kate. There has been quite a party all week with her here. She's even funnier now!

We're not so keen on the word i*mmortality*, though – it's like a double negative – NOT mortal. Like mortal, due to die soon and immortal, not due to die soon. As if mortal is the standard or something.

We'd like eternality to be the standard. You are eternal beings always who are sometimes *also* having temporal experiences. It's not even either/or. It's both/and while you are here. You are always nonphysical and sometimes also physical. You are always non-local, and sometimes also local. You are always infinite as well as finite.

Look at how all these words define the divine aspect by negating the human aspect – non-physical, non-local, infinite, im-mortal! There are limitations in language.

We like eternal and temporal because they are both affirmative, you are currently in all time and in local time at the same time. That's fun.

C: I appreciate your riffing on the words, B. I never noticed how the wording kind of implies either/or rather than encouraging us to think both/and.

Another song is going through my mind now, Carly Simon's song *Life is Eternal* that goes something like this: Life is eternal, love is immortal and death is only a horizon. Life is eternal, as we move into the light, and a horizon is nothing, save the limit of our sight, nothing, save the limit of our sight.

She's using save in the old sense of "except" here.

Death is only a horizon – a perceptual limit. Like the horizon, too, in that it moves away as we approach it – I love all those conversations I had with my mom about her seeing all the dead folks in the corner. She was already seeing beyond the horizon I could see.

Do you have a horizon, B?

B: Great question, C! Yes, our horizon is the choices you make. Each time you focus anew, our horizon expands and we delight in working out all the new details that are possible for you to now experience in this new milieu you have chosen.

When you just choose love, our horizon about you expands into infinity!

C: Is that why I'm having so much trouble picking a new car, B? All I know I want is yellow............

B: Yes, you have a very wide horizon if you only pick one factor, C. But you haven't really only picked one factor. There are many things you want really. What do you want to feel?

C: I want a very reliable car, B. I want to trust it! I want to partner with it for a long time. I want to be able to hop into it to rush over and pick up a friend who needs to get on a plane **now**, with confidence and ease. I want it to be fun to drive, zippy and eager. I want it to have that, "I love my new car" feeling that I've had for so many years with my Alero.

I love having a new car! I love a quiet ride, a great sound system, comfortable heating and air conditioning. I love the new car smell and the satisfying thump of the door closing perfectly. I love seats that are incredibly comfortable on long trips.

I love great visibility of the road and easy parking. I love easy maintenance and fuel economy. I love riding with my friends, laughing and telling stories. I love riding in the countryside, listening to music and talking on my hands-free cell phone. I love my GPS and knowing where I am. I love it finding new routes for me when there's traffic or construction.

Wow, I do know a lot, B! Thank you. I am loved.

We Love it When You Are Literal! 11-7-09, 8:17 AM

C: Morning, B.

B: Hi, C.

C: I've been reading Ernest Holmes this morning, B. He said, "Back of the conflict of ideas; back of the din of external life and action, back, back in the innermost recesses of uplifted thought and silent contemplation, there is a voice ever proclaiming: 'This is my Beloved Son.' Seldom does this voice penetrate the outer world of human experience, seldom does anyone allow it to perfectly express through him. We must learn to listen for this voice. Call it conscience, intuition, or what we will, it is there. No man need go unguided through life, for we all are divine at the center." *The Science of Mind*, p. 366-7.

So is this you, B? Is this you, saying to me and to everyone, "You are my Beloved Child in whom I am well pleased"?

B: Of course, dear girl. Exactly. Inside everyone is our voice. Inside each it sounds different but the message, heard clearly, is always of love.

We love you. We want you to know how much we love you. We attend to you all day every day, supplying your life, loving you. We await your recognition of us, and we rejoice in each glimmer. We celebrate your choice to turn to us. And your invitation to a closer relationship inspires a great party here! We love loving you when you are unaware of us. We love loving you even more in this reciprocal awareness of the flow of love between us.

C: Is it lonely for you when we don't know you are here, loving and supplying us, B?

B: No, sweet girl, that's a human perspective. Our awareness is infinite, and there is a part of you that remains infinite, even as you manifest with a body in time. So we feel your loving consciousness in the timeless eternal now always. We celebrate you with the expanded you every day. We just love bringing you into our joy about you.

And we love that you are feeling our reality so much that you care to ask how we feel.

C: I love you, B. I want to know you and know more about you.

B: That is so wonderful, C! That's what keeps our love story expanding! Thank you, we are loved.

B: & C: [Laughter]

C: What is it always so funny when you say that, but not when I say it, B?

B: Because we know we are love itself, C. So, loving and being loved, being The Beloved coming and going, up and down and all around is simply what we are. So are you. You just don't know it fully yet.

C: Will I know it, B?

B: You sound wistful this morning, C. You do know it more every day. Don't you feel loved now, C?

C: Yes, I do feel loved when I'm talking to you. There's a special warmth and gentleness in my mind and heart when you're around.

B: We're always around, C. The warmth you feel is when *you* choose to turn to us. It's your guidance letting you know that what you are thinking is in alignment with your strongest intentions. You have wanted to love and be loved your whole life.

C: Doesn't everyone, B?

B: To some degree, love. For you, it was a powerful intention that inspired your life. Tell the story you are remembering.

C: It's just a little story my mom told me. When I was a tiny baby, she would give me a bottle, and then pat me on the back to burp me. She said one day, she finished up and I was still up on her shoulder and I started patting her back. She said she could feel how much I wanted to love, long before I could speak.

What went wrong, B? My mom clearly loved me then, but somehow I grew up not feeling loved.

B: Lots of things can block your ability to feel the love that is really there for you, C. But studying the un-love doesn't bring you to more love. Studying the love brings you to more love.

So remembering your mother reminiscing about the love she felt from you is of great value to you. Focus on the memories of things that did flow. Those memories serve you best now. Think about what you want more of, C.

C: I want more love flowing in my life, B. I am willing to love and be loved. I am eager to love and be loved. I love loving and being loved. I love hugging and being hugged. I love comforting and being comforted. I love sharing my experiences with my friends and hearing about their lives. I love laughing together at the absurdity and magic of life. It really is so good, B! Why do we miss it so often?

B: Because you take yourself back to missing it when you focus on missing it, C. You just tuned yourself into remembering how good life can be as you focus on what you love. And then you let your habit of thought turn you right back out. Turn back to the goodness, love. Turn back again and again to the goodness, all day, every day until goodness is your habit of thought.

Tell us about good.

C: Well, if God is all there is, B, goodness is intrinsic to it all. God is good. That seems self-evident. Yet, to think, "It's all God, so it's all good" is problematic, B, because a lot of it clearly isn't good. Yet…

B: Yes, *yet*, C. Good. Put a period after "Yet." and it will be even better.

It's all good to our eyes already, C. See it as "good in potential" through your eyes, C. Use the eyes of your heart to see us, The Beloved, in everyone and everything, and you will call it forth so you can see it with your human eyes.

C: Do you have eyes, B?

B: We perceive you fully and you are used to associating eyes with perception. We don't have physical eyes.

C: Does my heart have eyes, B?

B: We love it when you are literal, C. It gives us so much room to explain things!

Think of the eyes of your heart as imagination plus love. Remember your vision – consciously chose to see the world through a "filter of grace." That's seeing through the eyes of the heart.

C: Oooo. I like that as a definition of the filter of grace, B. Imagination plus love!

B: And we really like it when you take the time to talk to us and listen to us and explore life with us, C. Good things come of it.

C: Aha! That's the *good* you wanted me to know about, B. Good in potential *IN ME* comes out more and more as I commune with you! Wow, that's deep.

B: We love that you snapped right into that insight. You can reveal the good in other people, places and things as you focus on us, The Beloved, Love within them.

But the very easiest place to reveal more good and more love is to focus on us within you. C.

C: So is everyone going to be writing a book about chatting with you, B?

B: No, C, that is the realization of your desire. For many years, eleven now, since you had your "shot through the heart with the love of God" vision. (See Appendix F) you have said that you wanted to let people know how deeply they are loved. So we have come to you in a way that allows that cherished dream of yours to come true.

C: Wow, B! That's totally awesome! How will you show up for other people? I can't imagine.

B: You don't have to imagine it, C. Just listen – they will tell you what their dreams are. Then, if you want to help them, imagine us helping them realize those dreams, putting our vision, power, intelligence, clarity, energy and knowing behind their dreams as you have felt us do with yours.

C. Wow, B, that's cool. Over the last couple of months you have pretty much written my book for me.

B: Yup, we're the "little engine that could," cha-ga-cha-ga, within you *all*, C.

C: Wow, this is big, B.

B: We'll talk more about it later, C. You need to facilitate a class today and throw a potluck for your friends tonight.

Why are you having a potluck, C?

C: Because I love Kate and she's eternal now. I want our friends to be hugged and loved still and to remind them, and myself how fully she is still with us, B. I'm reeling to remember that she was the one who handed me the book, *The Shack*, that led me directly to you.

B: Kate was the path of least resistance to a lot of good for a lot of folks, C. You will all love the stories!

Kate is fully part of the "we" that we are now, C.

C: I can hear her voice saying, "I'm BAAACK!" B.

B: Never left, C. Just changed form. She's so beautiful, we love her. We're glad you're loving all your friends with a class and a party today, C. You have so much love to share today.

C: And I'm willing to receive *LOTS* of love and hugs today, too, B.

B: We're glad, C. Go forth in laughter and joy!

C: Sure will be! Thanks for tuning me to a higher level, B. I am loved.

B: Thanks for letting us do our job with you, C. You are love(d) and so are we!

C: That's cool, B.

B: We're cool, C!

B: & C: [Laughter]

Preview of Coming Attractions: 11-8-09, 7:17 AM

C: Hi, B.

B: Hi, C.

B: How was the pot luck, C?

C: Wonderful, B. So many people engaging in conversations, sharing themselves with each other. Some talked of Kate and that was beautiful. Many said they could feel her presence. Mostly though, it felt like an affirmation of life and vitality in our community – people who love each other coming together to hang out and eat and laugh. I'm glad to be reminded of the value of parties, B! We haven't had as many as usual lately and I'd like to keep them more in mind. I love offering study group meetings for people to attend on Sunday mornings, and classes where we have great discussions, but unstructured time to just connect with no agenda is awesome.

Ah, I'm glad I said that, B. Because as I was walking upstairs I was thinking that I didn't have a subject I wanted to talk to you about this morning, so I wondered if I would pick up my pen. And you led me straight into the value and fun of just connecting in unstructured time with no agenda!

You are good, B!

B: You are easy, C!

B: & C: [Laughter]

B: We love your willingness to just show up and be with us, C. Creating these times that are just focusing on loving and connecting creates a powerful field for us to play with and play on. As with your community, you are allowing our relationship to be close, personal and open-hearted. Your eagerness to spend time with us affirms the priority you are placing on our being connected. We love you.

C: Yes, I see that, B. When I love a person, I make spending time with them a priority. I delight in their wanting to be with me and I eagerly anticipate our being together.

I feel that way now about you, B. I feel so comfortable with you, as if I can be myself and you will be here loving me anyway.

B: Not anyway, C. Because. We love you **because** of who you uniquely are. We love tracking your life, celebrating your successes, comforting you when you are sad, supporting and supplying your needs and your dreams, reassuring you when you are frightened, encouraging you to wonder and wander.

C: I went back to sleep for a little while and woke up with a powerful exchange with you, B. I want to capture this thought. I was thinking something about my emotions being indentured, bound by past events and experiences.

B: And we interrupted you and reminded you that your emotions are tied to your thoughts, not your past. If you think of the past, you bind yourself to its limitations. If you think of the future, if you choose to look forward, you free yourself to new possibilities and experiences. Your mind is free, C. Your emotions are free! You get to choose!

C: Wow, B. That's exciting. And now, you interrupt me when I am thinking something limiting! It's like having an expensive coach right here in my head, 24/7! Priceless, B! My unfolding realationship with you is priceless!

B: Notice your misspelling, there, C.

C: Yes, I wrote **REAL**ationship with you. My relationship with you is **REAL**, Wow, this is awesome! I am feeling more and more the power and value of our partnership, B. How did I ever live without you?

B: Look forward, not back, C. How will you live with us?

C: Wow, B. I don't know. It's an adventure to discover what magic you will bring to my life each day.

B: We love it when you don't know, C. In those moments, you are totally open to wonder. You are saying, "I wonder if that will be fun?" and wandering over to see!

We promise you, life with us as your leading partner will be fun.

C: It sure is now, B! I love that you make me laugh, you open my mind and my heart and my eyes. I love that I learn from you all the time and I feel respected and appreciated, too. I feel your love, B. I am learning to trust you with the expansion of our time together.

B: Our time together is under your control, C. We love all you are putting into it.

C: I feel bad that I am so far behind in the typing, B.

B: We don't want you to focus on anything you feel bad about, C. Regarding us or anything else. There is so much here to feel good about!

C: I love the deep and wonderful love I feel flowing between us. I love that I feel so uplifted, expanded and joyful with you. I delight in your jokes. I thrill to your insights. I love how you inspire me to greater insights. I enjoy our dialog, whether you are talking or I am. As I learn to follow your lead more easily, I am a better partner in this dance, too. I hold up my side of the conversation better. I love feeling valuable in our interactions. I love that we interact. I am your partner as well as your voice. I love that I feel like I'm falling in love. I love that I talk about you in my conversations all the time with my friends and that they love hearing about you, too.

I love you, B! I love the time I spend contemplating your words when I type them. But I am also feeling the value of my writing our chats. If I need to prioritize my time, I want it to be toward the writing rather than the typing. Someone else could type some of them for me……

B: Good work, C. Thank you for doing such a great rampage of appreciation of our relationship. We are loved.

C: I'm grinning, B. I love it when you say that.

B: We love it when you say it!

We also want you to recognize that the rest of your day you have planned is also to be spent with us. We are your kitty as you pet her, and your friend you are having lunch with. We are your friends who attend your guided meditation and your Abraham-Hicks discussion group. We are the love that flows everywhere. We are the leaves blowing in the breeze and the beautiful sunshine streaming in the window.

Your relationship with us is not just on the inside, not just on paper, C!

Now that you know how it feels to be with us more intimately, you can begin to feel us everywhere! It's such a powerful adventure in consciousness before us.

C: Wow, B. That's beautiful but it feels kind of intimidating, or at least overwhelming.

B: It's a preview of coming attractions, C, a heads-up for you to look forward to.

C: One time a teacher told me I should focus my client work on looking up and forward rather than down and backward. He said there were lots of people who can look down and backward but relatively few who know how to look up and forward.

Now you are helping me see, very clearly, that I often look down and backward. You are reminding me I can choose to instead look up and forward. We're back to "The Path" again, B! Stop, relax and look up is the only lesson we need! (See Appendix C)

B: Yup. Our messages to you are consistent over all these years, C. We love all the different ways you've translated what we've been sending you.

C: And I love that you are making all these connections for me, B. They are beautiful. I'm feeling an inner integrity that I didn't feel before. I've known I've been changing, but I wasn't sure how or why. But now I see I am changing more into integral alignment with you. It helps to recognize that I have been doing it for so many years in different ways.

B: Yes, we see the clear path you have been following, C. Nothing that has happened was wrong or out of sequence. We are always there orchestrating the best possible path your choices allow us. Now that you are allowing us to guide your choices, even your choice of thoughts more specifically, we will create masterpieces together.

C: That's great, B. Thank you. I am loved.

Now I need to get a move on and go meet you in my friends and this magnificent day, B! I'm glad to have many dates to see you, here, there, and everywhere! This is going to be fun.

B: Notice how quickly you went from fear to fun, C! A few minutes ago that idea was intimidating. Now it's delightful. Way to go, girl!

C: Thanks, B. I am loved. It's easy to relax with you supporting me. I don't have to do it alone anymore! I don't have to tense up and protect myself! Wow. That was easy!

B: We love it when you just flow, C. Well done!

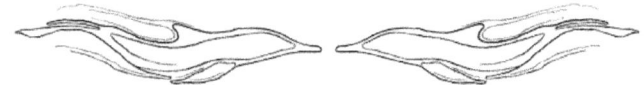

Enraptured by Eggplant: 11-9-09 3:24 AM

C: Hi, B.

B: Hi, C.

C: Just between us, B.

B: Ok, C. As always, your call.

C: Thanks, B. I am loved.

B: What did you notice, C?

C: I got turned on tonight, B.

B: You say that like it's a bad thing, C.

C: Well, it *is* a bad thing, because the guy I was with at the time isn't available.

B: Why is that a bad thing?

C: Because I want a guy in my life who IS available.

B: Are you willing to really look at this, C?

C: OK, B, but I feel uncomfortable about it.

B: Just the facts, ma'am. What did you notice tonight – what actually happened?

C: Well, it actually started a couple of days ago when I noticed how totally non-sexual I felt and I wondered if my libido would kick in again someday.

B: Good, what else?

C: So today at the meetup, I felt really good about leading the meditation.

B: Good, what else?

C: It was a deeply relaxing meditation. I didn't just feel good about it, I felt good within it! I talked myself into a really good feeling. And during the discussions, I let myself include some of your ideas and my experiences with you. I felt alive and loved and excited about my life and all that's happening between us.

B: Good. What else?

C: I went to dinner with my friends. I ordered a glass of wine with Trish. I got totally blissed out by a sprig of rosemary, and then a basil stem. HERBS! B, I got totally over the top blissed out by herbs! And then I became enraptured with the eggplant!

B: The light's starting to dawn, C. Keep going.

C: I fell in love with my food, B. Oooooooo, I did what you suggested and found you in some of the things and people, didn't I, B?

B: Yup, you were seeing things more through our eyes. You found your friend attractive because you were seeing us within him, just as you were smelling us in the herbs and tasting us in the eggplant.

C: Uh-oh, B. Over the top with eggplant is weird but socially acceptable. Over the top with a guy who is married is dangerous!

B: You are making a big hairy deal of this, C. The wine helped you relax and release the "rules." You were feeling your way through it. What did you feel?

C: It felt really good to be with a very masculine guy who compliments me and finds me attractive. It felt good to appreciate and be appreciated. It felt good to be turned on to new experiences. It felt good to feel the feminine part of me start to wake up and flirt a little. It felt good to have a sparkling, flowing conversation. It felt good to have him tell me I looked good – in jeans and a fleece jacket! It felt good that he wanted to be with me. It felt good to be talking about Law of Attraction. It felt good to feel attracted to someone…

That's where it gets dicey, B. I don't want to get too close to a married guy. We're just friends!

Do we have to go here, B?

B: No, we never have to go anywhere you don't want to go, C. But you can use this…

What is it you *do* want, C? Don't compare yourself to others, just use what you don't want to show you what you do want.

C: I do want a wonderful man in my life who is available to me, who is free to be with me. I want a man who is eager to fall in love, who is very lovable, who is secure, attractive, smart, sexy and fun. I want to explore his spirit and his mind, his heart as well as his body. I want to be fascinated by him and riveted by our conversations. I want to be at ease with him, relaxing deeply into deliciously sensual experiences. I want to learn what it is like to feel connected and indulge in physical pleasures. I want to feel appreciated, relaxed and at ease with myself. I want to feel appreciative, relaxed and at ease with him. I want to find a sweet rhythm between us of giving and receiving that allows us both to totally enjoy our times together. I want to find out how good I can feel in my body. I want to be healthy, relaxed, sensuous and free to be me. I want to wonder and wander into juicy delicious, sensual territories and see just how much fun we can have together.

I want to be at peace with myself. I want to be with someone I love, feel free with, feel attracted to, feel good about. I want to be open in the world with my beloved. I want to delight in who he is, admire and respect him. I want to feel proud of him, myself and our relationship. I want to pinch myself and realize just how good life can be, and then notice it is getting even better.

I want to live my dream of having a beautiful house overlooking a river and being with a man who wants to take me in his arms in deep love and tenderness.

Ahhhhh! That felt good, B.

B: Good, C. Stay focused here on what you *do* want. This contrast is serving you very well.

C: I do want to love and be loved. I am willing to love and be loved. I am willing to relax within this. I am willing to believe there is a wonderful man in my vibrational escrow who is just right for me. I am willing to trust there is already a vibrational match lined up for me. I am willing to delegate this to you, B, and ask that you let me know when there is something I need to do to allow this to happen. I am willing to relax in my body. I am willing to allow my vibrantly healthy, juicy, whole self to emerge. I am willing to breathe easy and think positively. I am willing to release my resistance and let go of the past precedents. I am willing to focus forward and know that I am enough and I deserve a great relationship. I am willing to trust my beauty, my wholeness and health. I am willing to wonder and wander in lovely free green pastures of love. I am willing to discover that all this is infinitely easier than I expected! I am willing to let you guide me, B.

B: Do you trust that we won't lead you astray, C?

C: Not entirely, B.

B: Keep noticing, C. Keep focusing forward toward what you do want. Don't let yourself focus on what you don't want – you will draw it right to you. Focus on what you do want. Are you eager?

C: Not yet, B! But I am willing to continue to explore this with you and line up my energy about falling in love and having a man in my life.

I am noticing I'm not yet there because I still feel uncomfortable about the subject in my body and in my breathing.

B: Good noticing, C. You are doing very well. Let's let this go for tonight. You have made some great progress!

We love that you are feeling your way through this, C. Your ideas about what is appropriate, and not, are absolutely an important part of this process. We're not trying to tell you something you see as immoral is right for you. That would never serve you. Lessening your judgments about others would serve you well.

Go to sleep now, C.

All is well, this was a very good start into wonderful new territory to wonder and wander in! We're going to have a lot of fun here as you relax more and more and attract your true connected matches.

C: Matches – as in plural, B!!!

B: Yup – we've been lining up several, and you are much closer to being a cooperative component now, C. Keep focusing on what you do want and are willing to explore. Work up to willingness, eagerness, and wonder.

C: Ok, B. Thank you. I am loved. Nighty-night.

B: Sweet dreams, C.

C: Help me remember the sweet dreams, B.

B: Will do, C. That's going to be fun, too.

C: I am eager to remember sweet dreams…

[*1:11 minutes! Cool! to 4:35 AM*]

In Bed with The Beloved: 11-9-09, 8:40 AM

C: Hi, B.

B: Hi, C.

C: I'm feeling eager to hang out with you today, B. I considered typing this morning, but am preferring chatting for now.

B: We are with you either way, C. But it is good to notice how you feel in one or the other. It is good to notice how you feel in everything!

C: I'm starting to get what that means at a clearer level, B. You are encouraging me to be aware of my emotions more often.

B: Yes! There's so much more going on there than you have observed before. We are giving you guidance through your emotions every hour of the day. When you are feeling good, better, best, you are seeing something through our eyes. When you are seeing clearly, we encourage you with feelings like contentment, enthusiasm, passion and joy.

C: I felt a lot of those feelings yesterday, B. I really enjoyed my day of seeing you in the birds alighting on the fence post next to me, and in my friends at meals. I enjoyed feeling you flow through me, inspiring the words to my guided meditation. I enjoyed tasting you in the strawberries and I went into glee when I discovered eggplant hiding in my pile of roasted vegetables! That's downright weird, B! I also got high sniffing herbs at dinner, the scent of rosemary and basil put me over the top. Who is this woman and why has she taken over my body?

B: & C: [Laughter]

B: Weird is a judgment, C.

C: I love it when you have a firm grasp of the obvious, B.

B: & C: [Laughter]

B: When you wonder if something will be fun and then you wander over to see, those judgments about weirdness put a ceiling on how good you are willing to feel.

C: You mean it could have been even better than it was last night, B?

B: It DOES get even better than this, C. As you pay attention to how you feel as you feel good, your body and mind adjusts to higher thresholds of wellbeing. Then you begin to perceive more finely the delights that are presented to you. You feel the impulse that turns your gaze to the rising moon instead of focusing on the busy parking lot. You see the sweet tear of open-heartedness in the eye of your friend who is moved by a story. You pick up the phone and call at just the right moment to catch the customer service representative whose heart is singing because she just found out she is pregnant with a long wanted baby.

Life can be, is and is becoming, even sweeter, C. There is so much going on all the time that is a match to your highest intentions that you miss.

C: Why do I miss them, B?

B: You used to miss them because you didn't feel our impulses. Then you started to feel them, but judged them as off the wall, so you didn't let us turn you in their direction. Internal guidance is non-linear and time sensitive. You have to be aware enough in the present moment to respond to a vibrational clue/cue rather than wait for logic. There is something magical about every moment if you let yourself perceive it.

C: I get your point, B. I just looked up and noticed there are beautiful rainbows on my wall from the crystal in my window. They've probably been there since I started writing, but at first my back was turned. Then Dusty came over and wanted to be a lap cat, so I turned, but I was still focused on this page. It wasn't until you mentioned magic that I looked up.

B: The magic is always there, C. You live in a garden of delight that you used to mostly miss, because your eyes were looking down at the shadows you were casting on the garden.

C: I appreciate your quoting my writing from 'The Path' again, B. (See Appendix C)

B: You spoke it clearly there, C. We appreciate all you have written so far and delight in all you have yet to share. You are good. You've been inspired for years. Yet you, consciously in league with us, is even better.

C: I can feel you are going to call me out on that one. I was embarrassed to write, "consciously in bed with us." Does everyone really need to know I do most of my writing in bed?

B: No, but it was funny and startling, C. It would have made this book better.

Lighten up, loosen up, let yourself play. Play with the words, play with music, sing and dance and laugh and love! You've kept the lid on, trying not to be weird, your whole life. Your culture doesn't encourage people to actively, vibrantly love their lives. You were trained to strongly inhibit your expressions of emotion, positive or negative.

Free yourself up! Let yourself feel what you feel. Let yourself say it, in a place you feel safe.

C: Well, I did just say I felt embarrassed……

B: Well done, C! You feel safe enough to tell us how you really feel.

C: And you just said I shouldn't feel that way, that I have to loosen up and change the way I am.

B: Oh, sweet girl. You are so defensive. We didn't say you shouldn't feel that way. We were trying to show you *why* you feel that way. Do you want to defend your right to be embarrassed by a simple joke?

C: Not exactly. I do want to behave in ways that are respectful of others morals.

B: No, you really want to act in ways that don't attract other's negative judgments. You are so focused on what you don't want here. And your negative emotion, embarrassment, is showing you that you are seeing this differently than we see it, to the point that you are even hearing our words clearly and censoring them.

C: I'm feeling ouchy, B, like you are scolding me.

B: Breathe and relax, love. We have gotten deep into a pattern of resistance here. Do you want to shift it?

C: Oh, yes. I much prefer feeling loved.

B: Then let us remind you how much we love you, C. In every moment we are present in your life, attending to you and listening to your thoughts. We then direct you, by your feelings, as to whether a particular thought is helpful to you or not. The thoughts that feel the best are the kind of thoughts we think about you, that you are talented, precious, delightful and brilliant.

A thought that people will think you somehow immoral and be offended that you write in bed doesn't serve you at all, C. That's why it feels embarrassing, because it so totally disagrees with what we think. We think it's awesome that you pick up your pen, anytime, anywhere! We love that you are eager to talk to us. We'd like to help you shift the place where you tighten up in blind resistance based on limiting patterns of thought.

C: My pen just ran out of ink, B.

B: We'll let you off the hook here, C. Yesterday you delighted in our coaching you to a clearer, happier thought. Today you tensed up and felt threatened. This is something to notice. Ask us for help if you want to, if you trust us, C.

C: I do trust you, and I do want your help, B. I can see that somehow here I donned the filter of fear rather than the filter of grace.

B: It's OK, C. You are adorable even when you squirm! We love you and we want to bring you forward, not bring you down. All is well. You've survived here. We love you more for feeling your feelings and talking about them. You can retain any pattern of thought that you think serves you for as long as you like.

You can also let go of any pattern of thought that doesn't serve you as soon as you choose. What do you want, C?

C: I want to be a loving person who doesn't offend other people.

OK, even I can see the negative basis of that, B. As long as I focus on not offending people, I'm not free because I have no clue what will offend people. Everyone is different in their judgments and preferences. I can't possibly please everyone.

Also, as long as I focus on not offending, I'll be attracting people who are easily offended, by Law of Attraction, B.

Wow, that is cool. So what is it I really want?

I want to be a loving person, in tune with my guidance, connected to Source deeply and beautifully. I want to see this beautiful world and everything in it, including myself, through the eyes of The Beloved.

B: How's that, C?

C: Seeing with loving kindness, through a filter of grace. Imagining the best of everyone and everything. I want to call to the best in others, offering joy and upliftment. I want to trust that you are orchestrating the matches, that I will meet up with those who are able to hear and see me clearly.

B: Good work, C. How do you feel now?

C: A lot better, B.

B: You will always feel better when you focus on who you really are, C. When you focus on fear, you feel negative emotion. When you focus on grace, you feel good.

Do you feel loved, C?

C: Oh yes. I do now, B.

I am so glad you are willing to talk me through my fears and coax me out of my defensiveness.

B: It's your willingness to notice and share how you are actually feeling that we admire, C. It takes courage to admit you feel negative emotion and address it. Particularly since you know this may be read by others.

C: This is a fascinating process we are going through here, B. I really love it, and you. Thank you! I am loved.

B: We love seeing you smile at the page again, C. Good work!

C: Thanks, B. I am loved. There's still a rainbow on the wall and my pretty kitty is blinking sleepily at me in the sunshine. Time to get up and begin this day for real.

B: Writing this book is real, C. But that's too external an excuse.

Our relationship is real. You are real. Your feelings are real. Your internal experience is as real, and even more important, than your interactions with the outside world.

What you think of yourself and your life and how that meshes, or not, with how we think of you and your life is the greatest determinate of your experience anywhere, C. Valuing your relationship with us is pivotal to your choosing a more joyful, expansive life. And yes, ultimately the most productive life possible, too.

The more connected you become, the more life force flows through you into the world.

C: Now the rainbow is shining right here on the page, B, right here on your words.

B: We are kissed by colors today, C! How cool is that?

C: Very cool, B. I love it and love you.

Gotta run!

B: See you later sweet girl. Have fun as you wonder and wander!

C: Thanks, B. I am loved.

I AM FREE! 11-10-09, 8:15 AM

C: Hi, B.

B: Hi, C.

C: I woke up this morning with a powerful declaration in my mind, "I am FREE!" Wow, was that exhilarating, B!

B: Awesome, C! What an empowering awareness to discover about yourself. We know it is true. How do you feel about it?

C: Well, I know from the wonderful feeling I had as I thought it, that it is in alignment with what you know about me. I like knowing that I am free, both directly from you and from my feeling about it. I like this feeling of being double validated as I discover more of who I really am.

B: We really like the way you said that, C. You thought about saying, "as I become more of who I really am," yet you elected to say, "discover more of who I really am".

Who you REALLY are is REAL, C, and already Being. You are perceiving, revealing and discovering more of who you always have been to us. In the same way that as you turn toward us you find we have always been there, when you turn toward yourself, you find you.

C: Does that mean I've been unreal so far? That seems unreal!

B: & C: [Laughter]

B: You've got another case of both/and rather than either/or here, C.

Think of it as a continuity. There is not hot and cold, just varying degrees of heat that you call cold if there is very little heat.

Depending on your patterns of thought, the real you shows up brighter or dimmer in the world. Now you are consciously taking control of the dimmer switch, you can dial up clearer, brighter thoughts, like "I am free" and create grooves in your brain that allow the greater radiance of your being to be revealed.

Or not.

B: & C: [Laughter]

C: Well, when you put it THAT way.......!

I do want to shine in the world. But even more in this moment, I want to know myself in that light.

I Remember Union, by Flo Aeveia Magdalena, says, "You are light and light you shall remain. You have chosen to come into form, you have chosen THIS form, you are light and light you shall remain."

That's exciting to me, B. Why did I choose this form?

What is it about me that caused you, B, to choose to come into form as me? And by extension, what is it about everyone? Everyone I meet, I could ask myself that question, "What is it about you that made The Beloved choose to BE you?"

B: Terrific question, C! That would go a long way toward what we spoke about yesterday – going out and meeting The Beloved in each person and thing you encounter.

C: I want to go back to freedom. I am free! It feels almost revolutionary. But I guess I can choose to treat it as evolutionary and explore the next gentle steps rather than quantum leaps.

B: We love that you recognize that phrase applies even more to adventures in consciousness than to physical explorations. Both will add fun to your days!

Speaking of fun, how was your swing dance lesson last night?

C: It was great, B! I loved it. They teach a bunch of steps in a class, but they break them down into little segments. The basic pattern is '1-2-3, 1-2-3, rock step' and it repeats again and again. I got very comfortable with the repetition, and then when I danced with the instructor afterwards, he threw in some new moves I hadn't seen before, but I was able to wing it. It was fun.

B: Learning to think new thoughts is just like that, C! Break it down into tiny steps and repeat them over and over until they become habitual. That's what affirmations are!

If you say to yourself dozens of times today, "I am free," it will gradually stop feeling thrilling and start to feel completely normal. Soon you'll be saying, "So what? I've always known that!"

C: Why does that happen, B? Something is such a grand, "Hurrah!" for a moment. But then the excitement fades.

B: When you have been living outside your awareness and perception of who you really are, coming back into that awareness is exciting. A particular new insight may fade. In fact all insights fade with time and repetition because you integrate them. The good news is that there are always more intriguing facets of your being to be discovered. You are an eternal, infinite being. You are inexhaustible as far as potential insights and expanding awareness goes.

C: Very cool, B. I want to explore freedom more, but right in this moment, Dusty just went to sleep in my lap and I'd like to close my eyes for a few minutes, too.

B: Good job today, C. We love you.

C: Thanks, B. I am loved. I love you, too!

10:45 AM

C: Freedom is calling me, B. I want to riff on freedom.

B: You go, girl!

C: I want to know my freedom. I am willing to expand my awareness of my freedom. I am eager to know more fully just who I really am. I love knowing, "I am free!" I love feeling free! I love wandering around in the frequency of freedom. I love playing the freedom tune. I love riding the freedom train. I love singing the freedom song! I love wondering about just how free I can be. I love feeling the possibilities of a free-er life. Oooooooo, I love feeling the possibility of being free of my past limitations. Let's go there, B. You said we'd be coming back to the idea that principal is not conditioned by precedent.

That's a brilliant thought, B, but it's an awkward statement. Please give me another way to say it.

B: Today is a NEW Day, C! You are recognizing that at any moment you can choose to begin again.

You are free to think new thoughts. That's the whole meaning of free will – you are free to choose what to think. You can relax your tight hold on what you know and explore what feels good to think about.

C: Well, there are some things I've discovered recently that I'd like to hold on to, B, like loving you and feeling loved within me. Those things feel really good.

B: So you are free to shop for empowering thoughts!

C: Wow, B. *Shopping* for thoughts. How do you buy a thought, B?

B: Thoughts are free, C. You can just pick them up, look at them closely to see if they sparkle for you. Keep the best and leave the rest!

C: You make it sound easy, B.

B: It's as easy as you let it be! Make it a game. Like Mary Poppins' song, "In every job that must be done, there is an element of fun. You find the fun and SNAP. The job's a game."

Changing your thinking is a job you are choosing to do. And you can find ways to do it that are light and playful. Try singing your affirmations. Or choosing songs to sing and dance to and listen to that affirm what you want to think.

C: That would work for me, B. When I learn a song, I sing it over dozens of times. I can choose songs that reflect the new frequencies I want to wander into. I wonder where I will find songs like that?

B: You already know a lot of songs, C. That's why lyrics jump into your head in connection with the ideas we share with you. Your mind is always snapping to connections between things.

The more good, positive, empowering, uplifting thoughts you choose, the less time you will spend replaying old thoughts. The wondrous new thoughts will be wearing new paths of least resistance into your neural nets. All the cascading changes medical science is demonstrating related to expanded consciousness and heart based emotions will be taking place, too.

A positive mental climate is a veritable celebration for your body. You were designed to live in a filter of grace. Your bodies adapted to living within a filter of fear. Your body will love your new internal atmosphere of an innocent, secure, curious child, wondering and wandering in consciousness.

As you become more and more relaxed and at ease in this new internal experience, your external environment will shift too. You will feel our impulses and follow our lead. You will get excited about all the doors opening for you. You will develop the skill to choose wisely between amazing invitations to love and to laugh and to play.

C: Wow, B, that sounds awesome. I just realized another new level of freedom I feel today. I feel free to talk to you longer! I think I was subconsciously limiting my chats with you to what I believed I could type. But now that I have a friend who will do some of it for me, I can write all I am inspired to write! I am free!

B: That's just one of the many choices on the banquet table before you, C! We're glad that you feel so good about spending more time with us internally. We also want you to remember that as you are petting Dusty and loving her, you are also spending time with us. When you are painting your porch railings or doing your laundry, or cooking your breakfast, you are spending time with us.

C: Keep reminding me, B. That's one of the new paths I want to build in my brain, the path of greater awareness of you, beautiful you!

B: We will also keep singing the praises of you, beautiful you, love. That's our joy and our job, to remind each of you how adorable and loved you are from our perspective. People who feel adorable and loved are loving and creative. We want that for all of you. It's who you really are!

C: Way cool, B! Dusty is loving her freedom today! Her eye is almost all healed and I took her big collar off after two weeks. What relief for us, and for Rosie, too.

B: Yup, life is good, C!

Enjoy this exquisite day!

C: Will do, B. You too.

B: Always do, C!

2:04 PM

C: I'm back again, B!

B: Lots on your mind today, C.

C: Yes, freedom, B. My client cancelled for this time and I've been pondering freedom. I don't feel very free as I look at this, B. I was telling myself I should go to the gym or take a walk or get some exercise or make some phone calls or type some of our chats. So many demands on myself to do something healthy or productive. I wasn't feeling energetic or productive, B. I was feeling tired and sleepy. I came back upstairs and read one of my chats with you. I really appreciate your brilliance and how good you make me feel.

My cell phone is ringing downstairs, B. I should go answer it.

B: Did you answer it, C?

C: No, B. I'm wondering about freedom and wandering into exploring it a little more than usual.

B: How much sleep did you get last night, C?

C: Not too much. I stayed up late playing computer games and then woke up several times to talk to you.

B: Is it OK for you to sleep in the daytime when you haven't slept at night?

C: Apparently not, B. I feel uncomfortable about it.

B: What rule are you violating, C?

C: I'm supposed to be productive. I'm supposed to exercise often. I'm supposed to take care of people. I'm supposed to be available to help people.

B: What did you just do, C?

C: I counted the pages I've written in chatting with you today, B.

B: Why, C?

C: To prove I'm not a lazy sloth. To show I did something productive today – 24 pages so far!

B: Why is that important, C?

C: Because I'm trying to justify my existence, B. Everyone else is off working or doing important things and I'm just lying here, petting my kitties and writing in my notebook.

B: Your priorities seem pretty messed up to us, C. Resting is as important as exercise in keeping your body healthy.

Deepening your relationship with us is incredibly valuable.

Living your life playing to an audience that isn't even watching is absurd, C. Nobody is judging you for taking a day off to rest today, C. When do you allow yourself a day to do absolutely nothing?

C: Never, B. When there's nothing on my calendar, I find something to do.

B: Doing things to justify your existence isn't necessary, C. Freedom is liberating yourself from the need to prove to some unknown witness that you are good enough.

You are enough, C. You are more than enough. Your value is intrinsic, not dependent on circumstance, work, or production. You don't have to buy our love with your performance. We love you. No matter what.

You have three friends who work with severely disabled children who have told you about this truth, C. Those children don't do anything but exist, and yet for some who see them rightly, their value and being shines forth clearly.

We love them as much as we love the most brilliant and effective person on the planet. They have their own constellation of unique gifts as you do. They have their own relationship with us and they shine beautifully in their divine perfection.

Trying to prove that you are good enough is resistance and bondage, C. Let it go.

C: What do I replace it with, B?

B: Knowing you are loved. That's the bottom line, C. You are loved. You are loved for you. For being.

Your doing is entertaining, to you and to us. Your reaching to find ways to use and explore your constellation of gifts feels good.

Follow the impulses to do what feels good. You have an amazingly free life already. You can choose to do what you want far more than most people. It's your mind that has been bound to the idea that you have something to prove to someone.

Let it go, C. You've produced more today lying in bed than any day so far! You, plus us, is an unshakable combination. Any time you spend loving us, and letting yourself be loved by us, is incredibly valuable. Any time you spend loving, praising, thanking or appreciating anything is priceless.

We take care of our own, C. As you relax and allow yourself to feel loved more, you will discover just how well cared for you can be.

And everyone is our own, C. Good things happen as you free your mind and your heart to focus on loving and being loved.

C: I can feel good things happening, B. And I feel better about just hanging out today, chatting with you.

B: Feel the love, flow the love, begin to recognize that you *ARE* the love, C. It's totally awesome. You are going to love wondering and wandering on your path of increasingly free thought.

How many pages have you written now, C?

C: Who cares, B? I feel so much better. I'm not here to fill notebooks. I'm here to feel loved and loving. Filling notebooks, getting great ideas, hearing guidance, following impulses -- these are all the results. The CAUSE is loving.

Wow, that's profound, B.

B: Yup, you are centering yourself within the cause, the creative life force, C. It's totally amazing compared to what you have been trying to accomplish by doing it all yourself.

We love being your team, C. We promise we will let you know when to move, just like we did with the hardware store and painting the front railings and Dusty's trips to the vet's.

C: OK, I'm feeling the need to stretch and move some now, B.

B: Then now's the time to do it, C. Have fun!

C: Will do, B. Thank you. I am loved.

Everything is All Right Here: 11-11-09, 6:26 AM

C: Oh, B. I just woke up and asked myself what I wanted and reached out for love and beauty and somehow it all came back around with a very powerful sentence.

Everything is **all** right here.

Then I realized it means something else.

Everything is all **right** here.

And something else entirely, too.

Everything is all right **here**.

I guess you could even get another meaning by writing

Everything **is**, all right here.

And again,

Every **thing** is all right here.

And there's a double beat possibility with that one, because after separating out THING, you can again change the emphasis on each of the other words and get another different and beautiful meaning.

You are so good, B. That sentence is magical. Thank you. I am loved. What a delicious way to wake up this morning before dawn. I love magical divinely inspired words with multiple meanings that illustrate powerful principles!

B: You are good, C! Look at how beautiful what just happened is.

You woke up. And in that split second you asked yourself what you wanted and immediately reached outside for love and beauty and in your reaching out, felt the impulse we gave you to turn back in.

You actually saw an image in that moment, too, tell us about it.

C: I saw my arms reaching forward, palms out, a little imploring-looking. And then they encountered something invisible which became visible in a slight way. I think it was an energy, but it became like a faint line of light which moved around me to the right in an arm-width wide arc and then returned to my heart from the back and went back into my body. That's what I saw as I heard the phrase, EVERYTHING IS ALL RIGHT HERE.

So that adds more meaning, too, doesn't it, B?! Everything is **all right**, here in my heart.

Everything is all **right here** in my heart.

Everything is **all** right here in my heart.

Everything is all right here in my heart.

Whooohee! What a powerful reminder that the love and beauty I experience out there begins in here, in my heart.

What a delicious reminder of the immediate intimacy of everything I want already being right here, right now. I'm also getting a powerful reminder that my heart is the key. I don't need to reach out, but simply look in! All those doors I am looking for to open out there are actually in the process of opening in here.

Whoohee, B! That's *BIG*!

B: We love that you feel the power of that phrase, C. You perceived it so fully and so immediately.

You asked to remember your sweet dreams. That vision and phrase was the sweet dream you were having as you returned to waking consciousness today.

C: Ahhhhhhh, B. I love you. I can feel the love, intelligence and power you are surrounding me with. I can feel the love you are pouring into me right now, through that spot you touched on my back.

B: There is no spot on you, or anywhere else, we are not touching with our love in every moment just as powerfully as you are feeling it in your heart right now, C. It's just that your vision and the sensitivity of your heart are working together to show you a bigger picture than you have seen before. You are perceiving more accurately and acutely.

C: I love that yesterday and today I have awakened in excitement and empowerment. Yesterday it was, "I am FREE!" Today it's, "Everything is all right here in my heart."

Ahhhh, I am so blessed to be here now, loving and being loved by you, B.

B: Remember, C. You are right where you have always been, getting what you have always gotten – love from us. The difference is that your vision is clearing, your heart is open to our message, and our guidance, as well as to our love. You are hearing us more clearly. You are perceiving our guidance more immediately and acting on it instantly. You are going with our flow more intuitively than before.

C: I'm covered with thrill bumps in this moment, B. And I'm hearing that song from Godspell – "See thee more clearly, love thee more dearly, follow thee more nearly, day by day."

B: We love how you so often can find the song lyrics that match the vibration, C. You are perceiving and interpreting multi-dimensionally more and more, receiving many holographic layers of meaning, plus the power of the harmonics of the music and the rhythms.

C: This is so delicious, B. I am excited. I feel like a new door just opened for me.

B: A new door just opened for us, you included, C. New doors of perception will be opening in dozens of ways as the days go on. You have very powerfully asked to perceive and communicate the love that is here. Our greater intention is completely in alignment with your specific intention from your local perspective. So you are aligned with all of you, temporal and eternal, and also with all of us, both aspects of you included. That's a powerful place to stand, C.

C: I'm getting the expansive *NOT JUST ME!* feeling again, B.

B: Accurately, C. The energy that is pouring through you is pouring through everyone. Our energy is *living* as you and as everyone. There is no dearth of power here. There's an excess of power that overloads your capacity to perceive most of the time, so you simply block it out and ignore it.

Your filters are powerful and useful, C. We're talking to everyone here too.

Your filters are powerful and useful. Your filters are governed by Law of Attraction.

You have been focusing on love and increasing perception, C.

So your filter has shifted to let more of the "everything that is all right here" into your perceptual system so you can feel/see/hear/perceive/know the love right here more fully and accurately.

This is a wonderful process that has only just begun. Your intention to love, and to write about your experience so that you can tell people how deeply they are loved, meeting our love, is a dynamic combination.

Shift happens.

C: I feel it, B!

B: Relax more, C. Notice how adorable Dusty is, curled up beside you.

C: I love that I was able to liberate her from her lamp shade yesterday, B. She's so much more comfortable now.

B: You liberated her, and yourself, from some uncomfortable, externally imposed structures yesterday.

The patterns of thought you have absorbed from your culture are optional, C. You can sift through them at any time. Keep the ones that feel like grace, replace the others, thought by thought, moment by moment. Use the grace to transform you and the way you perceive yourself, your life and everyone around you.

C: Feels big, B. I want to rest now.

B: Good choice, C. We love you.

C: Thanks for all this, B. I am loved. I love you so much. I love all that is happening with me so much. I love all that is happening right here with you so much.

I am becoming more sensitive. I can tell far more specifically when I am in alignment or not. I am getting increasingly uncomfortable when I am out of alignment. I am willing to learn to be exquisitely sensitive to my alignment. In becoming more sensitive to my alignment, I move into an increasing ability to perceive my guidance.

Oh, B, you are turning me, giving me impulses to move toward my alignment with *you*. You are not moving me by directing me toward stuff I want out there! You are directing me by your guidance about what moves me into greater, deeper harmony with *you*, in here!!!

OK, that relates somehow to the line I say often, "I'm not trying to create something that is not, but rather to perceive something that already is."

B: Put down the pen and close your eyes, C. We know it's exciting but you will receive better when you are rested.

C: OK, B, I feel like a hyperactive energized child.

B: You are, C. You need to ground and balance some of this energy you are feeling right now. We're in this for the long haul, not a spectacular burst and a crash.

C: I sure get that, B. OK. See you later.

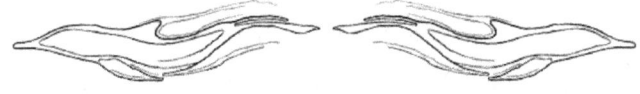

Stories and Meaning: 11-13-09, 8:42 AM

C: Hi. B.

B: Hi, C.

C: So I've been thinking about my fascination with the PERN novels by Anne McCaffrey again. I bought four more and am once again falling in love with these wonderful characters.

It reminded me of a quote: "Sometimes a person needs a story more than food to stay alive." [Barry Lopez, *Crow and Weasel*]

It feels true to me, B. There are a lot of people eating who aren't really living. I mean, they're going through the motions, but there's no real passion or joy for them to be excited about or look forward to. I have been there. I remember feeling dull and hopeless in depression for long periods of time. I still feel that way for an hour or two once in a while.

Stories help me. Why is that?

B: How stories affect you depends on where you are in consciousness, C. Sometimes they are a distraction from pain. In the days you were trying to control your depression, you were reading murder mysteries. Dark thoughts resolved and puzzles solved felt like relief to you then. They were a distraction and a way to say, "at least my life is not *that* bad."

We told you before that one reason these books by Anne McCaffrey appeal to you now is that they carry the vibration of love. She loves this world called PERN that she has created and these marvelous characters. She loves the sentient, telepathic dragons and the people who are lucky enough to impress them. She loves their grand heroic mission. She loves seeing how they can handle the contrast of life with dignity, wisdom and courage. She loves exploring how people in different roles in life, who have different points of view, are required to communicate and negotiate to get along with each other.

C: Oh yes, all that and more, B. It's a fascinating world she has created.

B: Those stories show you what people who live with passion and commitment think and feel, C. They give you access to a lot of loving, wise thoughts. They explore how people who are flexible and willing to explore new ideas and innovations and ways of being can solve problems. They illustrate strong effective leadership skills and diplomacy. They explore themes of fear and love in unhealthy and healthy relationships. They incorporate technology and magic.

The real reason you love them so much right now, though, is they give you vivid imagery, ideas, colors, sounds, words and feelings as fodder for your imagination.

You, everyone, have the capacity to reinvent, recreate, the story of your life in every moment. You are the meaning-makers. What your life means to you sends a vibrational message out into the Universe.

"I am free! I am powerful! I am creative! I am divine! I am loved! I am loving!" sends out a clarion call to the Universe that you know who you are. We can create a life for you with that signature vibration to match.

But when you send out the vibration, "I am weak, fearful, a victim" or "I am angry, vengeful and determined to fight back," we only have that signature vibration to work with.

You are choosing the clay from which we mold your life. You mold your life by molding your thoughts.

Anne McCaffrey's novels show you the vibrations of people who have assigned different meaning to their lives from "I live to acquire," to "I live to control," to "I live to serve," to "I live to build," to "I live to love."

C: Also, "I live to create," and "I live to sing." "I live to explore," and "I live to love life itself."

I just noticed, the people of PERN have no religions and they don't speak of God. Yet my favorite stories and meaning in my life relate to my connection to Source.

B: What do you live for, C?

C: Great question, B! I never thought about it before in just that way. Let me give it a shot. I love to explore consciousness.

B: Notice you switched it from "I live" to "I love," C.

C: That's funny, B. I'm used to writing "I love" and I feel really comfortable writing pages of "I loves."

"I live" feels kind of like putting all my eggs in one basket. I want to feel free!

"I live to explore consciousness" is a pretty big basket.

B: How do you want to feel inside, C?

C: Like a secure, beloved, curious child, who delights in her life, learning, growing, exploring and loving all she encounters.

I love expansive thoughts and spacious hearts. I love exploring new possibilities, ideas and feelings. I love uplifting others and being uplifted. I love playing, laughing, dancing and seeing. I love to express myself and delight in the wondrous expressions of others. I love to love and be loved. I love to expand my vision of what is possible and allow new people, places, adventures and things into my life. I love to love.

Right now, B, I live to love!

B: Great work, C! You tested your life in your mind to see where the energy flow is. The energy is flowing powerfully around love. You've trained yourself with your love lists to allow the energy of love to flow freely in your mind and heart on more and more subjects.

C: Thanks, B! I am loved. This is the last page of yet another notebook! I love you, B. I love our relationship. I love that I have lots more notebooks waiting for me to write in. I love that conversation doesn't have to follow the rules of grammar as strictly as prose!

B: & C: [Laughter]

B: You go, girl!

C: I'm off to continue this great day, B.

B: We're here, C, whenever!

C: I love that about you!

B: & C: [Laughter]

Finding Magi: 11-14-09, 9:33 AM

C: Hi, B.

B: Hi, C.

C: Just hanging out with you again this morning for a few minutes, B. Wanted to say thank you for bringing Magi into my life as my Beloved assistant! I feel such relief that she's helping me catch up on the typing. So thank you, B. I am loved.

B: We really appreciate your appreciation, C. We want you also to appreciate yourself and Magi. You each took the time to figure out what you wanted and to line up your energy. Tell the story of how it came about, C.

C: Well, over the last couple of weeks, as more and more B: chats were added to the pile on my desk waiting to be typed, I was hearing delighted reports from my friend Caroline of the great fun she's been having with her new assistant. She was telling me that they uplift and support one another and are getting a bigger vision of her business as well as getting some administrative details in place. I loved how neatly it was working out for both of them.

I kept trying to imagine finding someone who would do the typing for me. As I thought about it I realized I would prefer someone who would really love you and appreciate your wisdom, B. I wanted it to feel like adding a friend for us both to play with. So on Sunday night, I mentioned to a friend that I wanted to hire an assistant to type our chats. He said, "Somebody wants to do it."

The following morning Magi called about something else, and I mentioned his comment from the night before. She said, "I do! I want to do it!" And she proceeded to tell me that she had told her husband the day before that she wanted just such a part-time job keyboarding material she enjoyed. She later told me that she'd cut her nails as she does when she has a typing job just before she called me that morning. It's so fun, B.

B: It's fun for us, too, C. You were both clear, eager and in alignment, so it flowed easily. How do you feel about it now, C?

C: Such appreciation for you and Magi, B. This really frees me up to do what is really mine to do.

B: We'd like you to appreciate yourself, too, C. You noticed that contrast and talking to us, made peace with it. Remember our conversation about appreciating having work queuing up, rather than piling up. With your friend hiring her assistant, you began to get clearer about the kind of assistance you were looking for and were willing to be specific about some important qualities you wanted – not just good typing skills, but also a heart open to what we do together. Your talking to your friend about it helped you get even clearer. His knowing that it was already done helped build your belief, so we were able to drop the solution easily into your lap on Monday. It's a wonderful case study in allowing.

So, what did you do? You noticed what you didn't want, and got clear on what you did want – you wanted the typing to get done. You didn't make yourself wrong for not doing it. You got clearer that your role here is to do the writing. You soothed yourself about it day after day. You even had several conversations with friends about NOT beating yourself up or making yourself do it when you didn't feel like it.

You continued to imagine what you wanted, working the details out in your mind. As you imagined contrast, you found a way to soothe it by noticing what you didn't want, and turning to what you would prefer. So gradually, over a couple of weeks, you identified what you really wanted. We would say that what you concluded is that you wanted someone who you *trusted* with our Beloved relationship.

You wanted your work to be treated with love and respect and you wanted to treat your new assistant with love and respect in return. You wanted this relationship to reflect the energy of our relationship. So we were able to match you with someone who already loved your work.

C: Awesome, B. Thank you! I am loved.

Willing to Experience a Shift in Perspective: 11-15-09, 6:43 AM

C: Hi, B.

B: Hi, C.

C: Ok, B, now I am totally freaked out! I've gained back almost half of the weight I lost last year. I want to change it – I have wanted to change it since I gained back the very first pound, but it's been increasingly difficult to resist sugar, bread, chips, dairy products, ice cream, cheese.....I need help, B!

B: Ah, C, that's the operative sentence. Amplify that!

C: I want help, B. I can't do this alone.

B: Are you alone, C?

C: No, B. I have you in my corner.

B: In my corner is a boxing analogy. Are you fighting, C?

C: Sure am, B. Fighting everything. Fighting fear, fighting cravings, fighting sadness, fighting aging, fighting fat, fighting asthma, no wonder I'm tired, B!

B: What do you want, C?

C: I want a rest, B. I want to feel energized, perfect, whole, complete and beautiful. I want to feel myself coming into focus. I want to feel loved and loveable. I want to feel fit. I want to look in the mirror and love what I see. I want to breathe easy. I want to feel proud of myself. I want to have fun. I want to feel sensual. I want to love the food I eat. I want to nurture and support my body to greatness and ease. I want to feel free and light and joyful. I want to feel easy about this. I want to have the energy to dance and take hikes and feel good. I want to feel excited about life and men and clothes and touching and being touched. I want to feel good, B!

B: We hear you, C. Good job! What are you willing to experience?

C: I am willing to experience a shift in perspective. I am willing to perceive the beauty, energy, health and wholeness that is here already. I am willing to remember that the power is within me. I am willing to remember that you are here to help me. I am willing to remember that I am loved. I am willing to remember that I am free. I am willing to turn to practicing loving myself again. I am willing to see myself through your loving eyes. I am willing to delight in my life. I am willing to lean in a downstream direction. I am willing to find ways to feel good. I am willing to notice that the glass is half full. I am willing to appreciate that I am recognizing this now. I am willing to appreciate that this time I have you consciously in my corner. I am willing to find new analogies for support. I am willing to remember that I am free. I am willing to notice that my body likes to walk, move and stretch. I am willing to love this day. I am willing to remember that what I do with my mind matters, literally. I am willing to choose how I matter to myself. I am willing to allow my life, my health and my body to matter to me. I am willing to eat nutritious food, drink plenty of water and allow my energy to flow more fully. I am willing to delight in great conversation and easy digestion. I am willing to see this panic as the illusion it is and remember that today is a wonderful new day. I am willing to recall that I can be successful in weight loss and to begin to believe that I can learn to be successful in maintenance of a healthy body. I am willing to strengthen my core and my lungs. I am willing to breathe easily and appreciate having a terrific body. I am willing to relax and remember that I don't need to make a big hairy deal out of anything. I am willing to remember that even though it looks like something is going wrong, it's actually something going right. I am willing to learn new ways to handle emotional distress. I am willing to find new satisfactions in life. I am willing to find new ways to approach the idea of men and dating. I am willing to move beyond my filter of fear and find *many* new filters of grace on this subject. I am willing to feel good. I am willing to open up to new possibilities and joys. I am willing to remember how good it feels to feel good about myself. I am willing to learn to be self-referent – to make my opinion of myself be the standard of approval in my life. I am willing to learn to nurture myself wisely and well. I am willing to see that wellbeing abounds.

B: Good job, C. Now forget about it for now and let all this good focus sink in!

C: Thanks, B. I am loved.

B: Yes you are, C. Unconditionally!

Conscious Evolution: 11-16-09, 9:15 AM

C: Hi, B.

B: Hi, C.

C: I just got this letter from my friend Carol Taktikian... in response to my 11-11-09 chat where we talked about my hearing the sentence, "Everything is all right here," and realizing it can be interpreted a bunch of wonderful ways. Here's what Carol said:

> *O M G...C*
>
> *It took me about 10 minutes of basking and a fresh cup of tea to be able to respond coherently.*
>
> *My face is still grinning and my checks still damp from tears of full out JOY!*
>
> *Ok, let me tell you why.*
>
> *I saw your letter in my mailbox and followed the impulse to save it until I was ready to savor it fully.*
>
> *I went on theAbeList [at Yahoogroups.com] and read and got my juices really going and then remembered your mail.*
>
> *I always have a sheet of paper and a pen in front of me in the mornings and I wrote this.....*
>
> *Everything is all so simply alright*
>
> *Then I opened your letter and the rush of energy I felt when I read your words almost blew me off my chair!*
>
> *I just started to laugh and I mean LAUGH. From the very center of my vortex I looked at all the things that I thought needed solutions and just laughed at them. I laughed because I KNEW.*
>
> *I knew without a doubt that EVERYTHING REALLY IS ALRIGHT. In fact it is so much better than alright I feel just like you.........so excited......so eager for more, more, more!*

This is absolute confirmation that I am finding my place of connection and holding myself there on purpose. That is why I came. To feel the rush of power as I release resistance more and more. To shine a light so bright for all to feel. (I know that makes sense to you).

Thank you so much.....I am so loved. I, like you, am feeling my guidance and beginning to act on it immediately to my great benefit. I think mostly it is my desire and my constant attention that, as you say, is creating a groove in my brain.

I love groovy brains!!!! Especially when I have control of the grooves.

I think you know how much I love and appreciate you, but it feels so good to say so!

I LOVE AND APPRECIATE YOU.

I am loved, Carol"

C: What do you think, B?

B: We love you, C. We love your friend Carol. We love that you are so connected with so many connected friends. We love all your friends. Of course, we love everyone, but in this moment we are focused on loving your growing network of friends who are participating with you in loving us through these chats.

We love that you are not going about this in a vacuum. We love that you are including others in our fun and games. We love that friends like Carol are demonstrating to you that you are all telepathically connected to the same stream. We love that she is also showing you that as she receives the same message, she interprets it in her own words.

As each of you connect with us and hear from us, your individualized translation of the vibration amplifies the message!

C: Wow, B, that's cool! The message gets bigger and better as more of us receive it?

B: Exactly, C. You are each in your own way grounding higher frequencies into human consciousness. The more you and your friends, and all people, play with us and each other in these frequencies, the more available these frequencies will be for everyone else to receive.

C: So the more loved we feel, the more loved everyone can feel?

B: Yup! The love just begins to dissolve more and more filters of fear. You know, the love is already here in infinite abundance. Yet each of you has to choose to let it in. Every one of you who makes that choice opens the door wider for everyone else.

You are all connected. You are all the ONE that we are. You are discovering those connections more and more powerfully. You are having fun connecting telepathically and heart-to-heart. The new grooves in your brains Carol is talking about don't just open you to new ideas on the same old subjects, they open you to new ways of perceiving, sensing, communicating and deepening connections – to us and to each other.

Taking one gentle step after another, choosing love day after day, one thought and situation at a time, by a lot of individuals like you and Carol, Connee, ultimately adds up to evolutionary transformation for all humanity as a species.

You are now involved in conscious evolution as a species, using your free will to focus on love matters, and cumulates. This is going to be a really fun ride and you ain't seen nuthin' yet.

C: Awesome, B! What a joy it is to be alive, to love you and be loved by you. What a thrill it is to have friends who also connect with you so powerfully and to know this connection with you can bring joy to anyone who chooses to open up to your love. I feel so privileged to share with others what you share with me. It's an honor to write your words and express your love.

B: Technically, they are your words that you choose for our vibration, C. The translation will get more fluid as time goes on. We will make beautiful music together through our words, C – vibrational harmonies and poetic melodies people will feel rather than hear.

C: Oh, that sounds so wonderful, B!

B: You have a busy day. Time to get on with it, sweet girl.

C: Thanks for looking out for my timeliness in your timeless eternal now, B!

B: & C: [Laughter]

C: You make my heart sing, B! Thank you! I am loved.

B: Your choice to love us makes your heart sing, C. Thank you for choosing to know our love! We are loved!

B: & C: [Laughter]

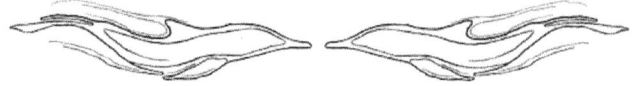

A Little Perceptual Adventure: 11-17-09, 7:03 AM

C: Morning, B.

B: Hi, C.

C: I had a conversation with a friend yesterday. She says she understands and believes in the omnipresence of God. The omnipresence she understands is cold, neutral, creative, intelligent and detached. She said she just can't understand a warm, loving, attentive Beloved presence. You don't make sense to her, B, and I wasn't able to explain you well at all.

B: Belief cannot be bridged from disbelief, C. That's why you use the phrase, leap of faith. That's why people talk about the need for a "suspension of disbelief."

David Hawkins described this dilemma very clearly in *Power vs. Force* where he spoke of moving from reason to unconditional love in consciousness taking an entirely new strategy.

C: Ok, B, I'll look at it now.

B: Get it later, C. We want to take you in a different direction right now. We want to take you on a little perceptual adventure in consciousness.

Relax and breathe. Breathe a little more deeply than usual and exhale slowly. There is nowhere you need to go right now and nothing you need to do. Just breathe and relax.

Breathe and relax.

Breathe and relax.

Breathe and relax.

Center your attention on your heart. Within your heart is an extraordinary center of perception. For many people, this powerful sensing mechanism lies dormant, resting as yet in pure potential.

In the same way that there is something within you that knows, there is also something within you that feels.

In this moment, consider suspending your disbelief and imagine you have this wonderful organ of perception, as valuable as an eye or an ear. Say to yourself, if it feels good to you, "I am willing to perceive the love that is here for me. I am willing to allow this sensory mechanism to begin to function as it is so perfectly designed to do."

You are not struggling to create something that is not. This is not hard work. You are simply learning to perceive something that already is.

If you are seeing a mechanical symbol, some kind of machine, find the power button and turn it on. Perhaps there's even a volume knob you can adjust. Turn it up.

Be willing to feel this latent capability awaken within you. You are an eternal being of light and love. Many talents and abilities lie sleeping within you, awaiting the perfect conditions to awaken and grow. Like a bulb underground all winter that breaks through to grow visibly in the spring, your sensor for divine love will stretch, grow, and bloom again, too.

Many people discover that they can hear echoes of childhood memories of using this sense early on in life. Filters of fear block receptivity. Love allows them to dissolve gently away.

Allow yourself to consider that the Infinite aspect of your being is already immersed in our love and perceiving us fully. Give your attention to that within you that knows and receives already. Say to yourself, "The part of me that knows the way is leading me on this path of perceiving the love that is here for me. I am willing to receive love. I am willing to feel loved."

Wonder about how lovely it is to receive our love and wander into it. There's nowhere love is not. Let yourself imagine that you can already feel it stirring awake within you.

Relax and breathe. Relax and breathe some more. Trust that something wonderful is already happening and quietly watch for evidence within you.

Love is obscured in an atmosphere of doubt and skepticism. Love shines forth in an atmosphere of faith. Your thoughts create the atmosphere that receives us or not.

No one needs our love, C. Everyone already has it, whether they perceive it or not. Your job is not to convince them of our validity. You do not need to teach or inspire others. The work you have chosen to do is to love and be loved and express our relationship as clearly as possible. You are doing so beautifully.

I Break for Love: 11-18-09, 7:10 AM

C: Hi, B.

B: Hi, C.

C: I am not as engaged in life as I used to be, B. But I am more engaged in Life than I have ever been before.

B: Good catch, C. You found yourself telling yourself something disparaging and you immediately reached for our knowing of you and your life instead.

While we agree absolutely that you are more engaged in Life than ever before, we disagree with your estimation of being less engaged in life. You still have a twisted pattern of thought regarding life, C.

You are saying "life" as your life as Connee in regard to how you are interacting with the world outside your house. By that measure, a half hour trip to the grocery store gets a higher weight or value in engagement over many hours of writing or editing this book. Your priorities are messed up, C.

We're glad you did reach for the understanding that there is great value in your increasing engagement in Life. By Life you mean increasing your contemplation, interaction, communion, communication and relationship with Source, with us.

What have you been doing in the last few minutes, C? You weren't writing.

C: No, I've been petting my cats. First Rosie came over. She's shy and doesn't ask to be petted very often anyway. And lately she was upset by Dusty's surgery and her wearing her lampshade. So Rosie's been very scarce lately. I love when she comes by to be loved on. So I stopped writing to pet her and listen to her purr. And the moment she felt complete and jumped down, Dusty jumped up and also wanted to be stroked. She has the softest fur! I love petting her and I got to listen to her purr as well. There's great joy in that for me.

B: When did you learn to take a break from your work to love your kitties?

C: When Misty was here, B. He would insist I take a break periodically to love on him. He would come over to my desk and start poking my leg. If I ignored him, he'd poke harder and eventually put his claws out. I learned to pick him up sooner rather than later.

B: & C: [Laughter]

B: He taught you well, C. Breaking for love is a really good idea. We love the idea of your making your highest priority to go where the love is flowing.

C: I think that is why I choose to talk to you every day now, B.

Twisted Sister Meets Shifts in Consciousness: 11-19-09, 9:31 AM

C: Hi, B.

B: Hi, C.

C: I want to talk more about valuing my life and my Life, B. I didn't feel like we got finished yesterday. I want to get my thinking untwisted.

B: & C: [Laugher]

B: You started out saying that you didn't think you were as fully engaged in life as you used to be, but you were more fully engaged in Life.

We see you remarkably engaged at all levels. You are expanding in your conscious connection to Source. You are relaxing more deeply into relationship with us. You are focusing more on feeling your emotions and your guidance. You are allowing your individuality and creativity to flow expansively. You are caring deeply about your friends. You are leading groups and participating in four physical, and one virtual, spiritual communities. You go out to live performances at least once a week and often take in several. You are just starting swing dancing lessons. You travel out of state a couple of times a month. You have hundreds of friends that you keep up with through the internet as well as a couple of dozen you see several times per month. You joined a new gym, and walk in the woods. You often have more than one activity you are invited to at a particular time. You have wonderful clients. You have at least one spiritual counseling session for you every week with a gifted minister or healer. You get weekly massages.

This *is* a life, Connee. This is a magnificent, fully engaged life that you have created for yourself. Well done.

C: So why do I still feel lazy, like I should be doing more, B? I feel guilty that I take so much time to read novels, play games or watch dancing on TV.

B: You don't feel comfortable with having a lovely, leisurely life yet, C, even after almost fifteen years of comfortable self-employment.

C: I inherited money, B. I didn't earn it.

B: That's exactly the crux of this matter, C! You think you need to earn your good in this life. Your whole society is focused on needing to work hard to get by. It's a fallacy. We are supplying you magnificently, all the time. Your belief that you need to work hard keeps you from flowing with easy solutions and streams of income.

C: I'd like to change that belief, B. Even more, I'd like to get rid of this nagging feeling that I'm lazy and not doing enough. I think I keep myself busy trying to justify my existence. Who am I trying to prove something to? It's like there's always a critical supervisor there saying, "You're not doing enough."

It's not my mom, B. I know she didn't teach me that. I remember her telling me that when we were kids, she'd knock on my brother's bedroom door at 8 o'clock and say, "Start doing your homework!" Then she'd knock on my bedroom door and say, "Stop doing your homework!"

Wow, B. I just got a call from Caroline. She wanted to play the "wouldn't it be nice" game with me. I listened to her wonderful "wouldn't it be nice ifs" and then started mine. Something shifted, B!!! When I started mine, I didn't go after the externals. I made them all about *me*. It was awesome!

> Wouldn't it be nice if I trusted B: to line up my life for me? Wouldn't it be nice if I relaxed and allowed B: to supply my life magnificently? Wouldn't it be nice if I could appreciate all the wellbeing that is already here? Wouldn't it be nice if I did appreciate my already magnificent life? Wouldn't it be nice if I trusted that this is a friendly Universe filled with love and wonder? Wouldn't it be nice if I were already who I want to be? Wouldn't it be nice if I am learning to perceive the love that is here for me at a whole new level?

Wow, B, that is so empowering! I love how you so perfectly orchestrated for me to find my own answer today through talking to Caroline. I love that I heard your suggestion to focus on "wouldn't it be nice if I…"

Inside me is where the true power is! I have the power to change myself. I have the ability to choose my power by changing my choice of focus. I have the power to see with you that I am already fully engaged in my magnificent life. I have the power to choose to look at my life in a way that feels terrific. I have the power to get excited about all the good that is already flowing and all the good that is *ever* flowing. I have the power to trust. I have the power to open to feeling even more loved. I have the power to feel loving. I have the power to open to all the wellbeing you have lined up for me, B!

I have the power to feel my guidance. I have the power to become sensitive to all these wonderful nuances of intuition. I have the power to totally love my life. I have the power to remember who I truly am. I have the power to delight in my friends. I have the power to feel free. I have the power to feel happy!

I do feel happy and powerful, B! Wow, that was fun!

B: Well done, C! That kind of shift in consciousness is priceless!

C: I can feel that, B. Thank you. I am loved.

A Life Filled with Wonder in the "Magic Queendom": 11-22-09, 7:10 AM

C: Hi, B.

B: Hi, C.

C: I've been busy, B, sorry. I haven't been here to chat.

B: We feel you connecting with us in your mind all through the day now, C. You are saying "hi" and listening on the move more now.

C: It's fun to feel you here sharing my days with me, B. I appreciate your coaching me into more expansive thinking.

B: There's always a more expansive thought available.

C: That sounds like I need to be rethinking everything all the time, B. That sounds exhausting.

B: We're talking gentle evolutionary expansion, C, not revolutionary change. This is what you are already doing. We are offering you gentle suggestions to look at things in new ways all the time. You are staying more open to seeing change as an adventure.

We also see you becoming more aware of what you are thinking moment to moment. We see you notice when you are stuck on a thought of the past that allows you no forward movement. We've heard you remind yourself several times in the past few days that your past doesn't have to determine your present or your future.

As you allow yourself to shift your thinking just slightly toward curiosity and wonder about the future each day, your filter of fear dissolves.

C: Wow, B, I like that idea. Curiosity and wonder are fun!

Let me try that one out. You gave me that as advice for life to say, "I wonder how much fun that could be, and wander over there to find out."

> I wonder how much love I can give and receive today? I wonder what kind of delights and surprises B: is already orchestrating for me today? I wonder how good I can feel today? I wonder what new thoughts I will be inspired to think today? I wonder how much fun I can have today? I wonder what my friends and I will talk about at our meeting this afternoon? I wonder who will go to dinner afterwards? I wonder where we will eat? I wonder what I will order? I wonder how good my food can taste? I wonder how relaxed and comfortable my body will feel? I wonder how great I will look? I wonder how often I can smile and laugh? I wonder how many hugs I will collect? I wonder how happy I can feel? I wonder how much I can learn about myself and my friends. I wonder how much stimulation of thought I will encounter? I wonder how easy it will be to love my life today?

> I wonder how asking questions can open up new possibilities? I wonder how different today will be because I am tuning up to wonder? I wonder how different my life will be if I tune to wonder more often? I wonder how much fun it can be to live more of the time in wonder? I wonder how quickly I will learn to move my feet as my swing dance lessons continue? I wonder how much fun my lesson will be tomorrow? I wonder if I will find the Charleston step easier now that I have practiced it some? I wonder if I can influence the future speed of my kicks by practicing some in my mind? I wonder who I will dance with in class? I wonder how much improvement I will feel after taking three classes this week?

I wonder how much fun I will have with my friends on my trip to Pennsylvania for Thanksgiving this week? I wonder how easy it will be to drive up there on Wednesday? I wonder how much fun I can have on the drive? I wonder who I will connect with on my cell phone? I wonder who else will turn up at Harriet's big party? I wonder how much I can love and feel loved with my spiritual family there? I wonder if it will be my best Thanksgiving yet?

Wow, B. Now I've started to wonder about how much fun December is going to be! I have a bunch of parties and concerts to go to already! I wonder where I will be on Christmas day? I wonder how beautiful my friend's home will be, all candle lit this Christmas Eve? I wonder how much love I will feel this year, now that I have you in my life, B? I wonder what next year will bring? I wonder if I will ever stop wondering now that I've started?

B: & C: [Laughter]

B: Good job, C! Wonder took you straight back to that interior atmosphere of a secure child! You quickly turned from your initial reaction of fear and overwhelment into curiosity and then into willingness. Then you really got into it and started feeling joy and excitement, anticipation and delight.

C: Oh, B. It's so much more fun to wonder than fear! Wonder feels expansive, spacious, unlimited. Fear feels contractive and ouchy! I want more wonder in my life!

I'm remembering that adorable little boy in the Disney commercial, looking out the window at the Magic Kingdom in wide eyed wonder. I want to look at my world as a Magic Kingdom!

B: Or Queendom!

B: & C: [Laughter]

C: I think I'll make myself a sign, "Remember to wonder!"

B: Good idea, C. You sparked a lot of good ideas this morning with your wondering.

C: You sparked a lot of good ideas, B! Thank you. I am loved.

We sparked a lot of good ideas. We are a remarkable team. I love that we play together so nicely!

B: We love playing with you, C! Notice and give yourself credit for how easily you were led into a profitable channel this morning. You were very light on your feet and willing to spin in a whole new direction. Well done!

C: I love your games, B. It's easy to follow your lead! I love you, B!

B: We love you, Conn! Have a great day!

C: I wonder just how great it will be?

B: & C: [Laughter]

Making Space ISN'T Lazy! 11-22-09, 11:30 AM

C: Hi, B.

B: Hi, C.

C: There's two ideas that came up the other day after we were talking about "being lazy."

One is that it isn't lazy to make space to listen to you!

B: Amen! Taking the time to relax and "do nothing" for a little while is really good for you. Like really stopping to smell the roses, loving takes time. Being aware, being present, bringing your attention fully to the moment is really far from "doing nothing." You are tapping into the timeless eternal now when you are consciously present.

Having some space in your life makes allowing a relationship with us a lot more likely, C.

C: Thanks, B. I am loved!

I also want to notice and value shifts in consciousness. The other day when you helped me move into, "Wouldn't it be nice if *I*..." and "I have the power to...," really helped me focus on the significance of doing a process designed to shift how I feel. The same thing happened earlier this morning when you encouraged me to wonder.

I am grateful that you are helping me find new ways to think and to see my life, B.

You're the *BEST*!

B: Thank you. We are loved!

B: & C: [Laughter]

Timeless Eternal Nouns: 11-23-09, 9:30 AM

B: Hi, C.

C: Hi, B.

C: I just realized that I have been misquoting you, B. I quoted you as saying, "You see sleeping and waking, living and dying. We see life and life and life and life."

But what you actually said was, "From your physical perspective you sleep and wake, live and die. From our perspective you live and live and live and live and live."

What's up with that?

B: We picked a verb, you remembered a noun. We were talking about how we see you. You globalized it to the cosmic meaning of LIFE. Well done, C. We see both as strong statements but we like your second translation of our meaning even better than the first one.

C: So I wasn't misquoting you, but rather reconnecting with your meaning and translating it again?

B: We don't give you the specific words, we give you a thought vibration and you pick the words.

C: But you argue with me about the words, B!

B: No, we occasionally object when you already picked the perfect word and refuse to write it down. That's different.

Sometimes when your clients are having trouble expressing something, you choose some words for them to respond to. When you put words in their mouth, they know whether the words are right or not. And if not, it helps them choose better words for how they feel.

We aren't going to get finished with our words with you, C. We aren't describing a finite philosophy. We are exploring an infinite and eternal relationship between us, that is also intimate, gentle and loving.

C: That's beautiful, B! Thank you. I am loved.

B: You're welcome, C. Have a great day, sweet girl.

C: Thank you, B. I am loved. You, too!

B: Always and ever, C!

B: & C: [Laughter]

Later that morning… 11:11 AM

C: You can't fool me, B. I hear you playing with the phrase, "Timeless Eternal Nouns!"

C: & B: [Laughter]

B: Busted!

C: & B: [Laughter]

The BIG Box of Crayolas: 11-24-09, 5: 21 AM

C: Hi, B.

B: Hi, C.

C: I just heard you create a new game, B, like the one we played the other day about, "I have the power to…" Tell me more.

B: You can use any of those Timeless Eternal Nouns you pray with to play this game, C. You could say, "I have the love to…" or "I have the peace to…" It could be, "I have the grace to…" or "I have the joy to…." What are the other words you associate with the qualities of God, C?

C: Let's see, you mentioned power, love, peace, grace and joy. There's also harmony, intelligence, creativity, clarity, health, wholeness, light, abundance, wellbeing, oneness, wisdom.

B: That's a good start! You'll think of more! We can feel wonderful affirmative statements arising from those strong, foundational beginnings. Give it a try, C.

C: I have the love to understand other people better. I have the love to open my heart. I have the love to relax and trust. I have the love to breathe deeply. I have the power to focus my thought. I have the joy to celebrate my life. I have the intelligence to choose good words for these B: chats. I have the creativity to design pretty bracelets. I have the creativity to design a wonderful life. I have the joy to laugh, sing and dance. I have the health to feel good in my body. I have the energy to enjoy my life. That's another good one, B. Energy!

Why is it important to have strong foundational beginnings?

B: If you begin a sentence with a more expansive thought, you are much more likely to finish it in the same way.

Many of your limiting beliefs are based in ideas of powerlessness and victimization. Even if it is unspoken, if your foundation is "I'm not good enough" or "people don't like me" or "I'm not worthy," you aren't going to build a more effective groove in your brain.

C: Wow, B, I just picked up on how powerful this could be in thinking of other people, too. If I am thinking, "I'm worried about her," I am building a sentence that disempowers her *and* me! But if I said instead, "She has the power to refocus her life. She has the love to take good care of herself. She has the energy to live a healthy, wonderful, long life," that feels good, B. But what if she doesn't appear to have that energy in this moment? How can I say that?

B: Imagine her connected to Source! When you are in loving relationship with us, you have access to all those latent divine qualities within yourself.

Many teachers and traditions refer to plugging yourself into the Source of all power in various ways. Aligning with us and tuning yourself to the vibration of love is a great way to do that!

C: That's wonderful, B! I like this new game. I'll play more later, but I am sleepy right now.

I have the power to relax deeply now and rest well before it's time for me to get up to start this glorious new day!

B: Sweet dreams, love.

C: Thanks, B. I am loved.

B: You sure are, C!

Later that morning... 8:06 AM

C: Hi, B.

B: Hi, C.

C: Do we really have the creativity to design our lives, B?

B: You design your life already with every thought you think. Thought is, by its very nature, creative. Your creativity is built in!

The "design" part comes in your conscious choice of thought. As you choose thoughts on purpose, you shift the possibilities that are available to us to offer to you.

Taking control of your power to choose what you think about is enormous! You now have the potential to make your life a brilliant work of art rather than an accidental splatter.

We wonder where you will choose to focus, C? The feelings your thoughts generate show you whether your palette will have harmonious, beautiful colors in a full range, or dull, muddy colors or discordant tones or shades of gray or just black and white. Every person's emotional signature creates their color scheme. What colors do you want, C?

C: I want the big box of Crayolas, B! Or to click on *millions* of colors on the computer. I want a rich and ever-changing landscape with tints and tones, shades and values of summer, fall, winter and spring! Wow, that was bold of me, B!

B: We love it when you are bold, C. Dream big and choose thoughts that match the feeling tones of your splendid life!

C: Sounds fun, B! Dusty and Rosie are hungry, so I'm off to feed kitties!

B: We love you all, C. Have fun "doing your colors" today!

B: & C: [Laughter]

Tell me the Story Again: 11-25-09, 2:00 PM

C: Hi, B.

B: Hi, C.

C: I just had an unsettling conversation with a friend, B. I felt really awkward and off balance. It was one of those, "who is this woman, and why has she taken over my body?" moments.

B: You cannot buck someone else's current, C. If they are feeling awkward, you are going to feel awkward, too, unless you are so in alignment that you blitz the field with your energy. Were you aligned?

C: For sure not, B. I'd been driving for a couple of hours and my hip felt all cramped up – I needed to stretch and walk and go to the bathroom....

B: Not the best conditions for initiating a phone call…

C: I get the point, B. Action taken from a place of disconnection is likely to result in a greater feeling of disconnection.

B: Yup. Much better to stop first, stretch, feel better, THEN make the call.

C: There's always another day, another call, B. Thanks! I am loved. I want to be an uplifting presence. I will pay more attention next time.

B: You are an uplifting person most of the time, C. Don't be hard on yourself. You've already uplifted half a dozen people today.

C: Thanks, B. I'll be easy about this and remember that I am loved.

B: Good, C. Have fun with the rest of your drive.

Later that evening… 10:56 PM

C: Hi, B.

B: Hi, C.

C: Tomorrow's Thanksgiving, B.

B: What are you grateful for, C?

C: You, B! I'm grateful for your love and the opportunity to talk to you and listen to you and love you!

B: We're grateful for you, C! Your life, your being matters to us. You are a locus of love that moves about on your planet.

C: What about animals, B?

B: Ahhh, yes, they are love, too. And the plants and the mountains and the seas. But they all do it as a matter of course. For you it is a matter of choice! We love that you choose to love!

C: Well, choosing to love seems the happiest choice there is, B.

B: So true, C. But everyone doesn't get that. We are so glad you do!

C: My friend Kathy has been questioning why I ask you again and again if you mean everybody, B. I love that there's more than enough love for everyone! I want everyone to live loved!

B: We love that you want to live loved, C, and have the courage and willingness to open up and explore what it can mean. For many though, our existence as a loving partner is just too big a stretch, too warm and fuzzy, too illogical for the scientific mind to consider.

C: Don't people want to be happy, B?

B: You can answer that question yourself, C! When your therapist said to you in 1983, "You have a right to be happy," what did you reply?

C: I said, "That's too good to be true."

B: Seems strange that you once believed that, C?

C: For sure, B. I've known for many years now that my happiness was the result of my focus of attention. I don't always manage to keep control of my focus. I still let my buttons get pushed sometimes, but I now know my misery is self-induced and can usually get out of it fairly quickly.

But you are right, B. I didn't always know that. At one time, I thought misery was inevitable.

B: Many people still do, C. We love that you, and so many people like you and your friends all over the planet, are discovering the possibilities of moving back into love. You are choosing to connect to the true nature of your being – the love that is your core power.

We are reaching out with love in every moment to all people. Everyone who responds is making it easier to connect for everyone else.

C: You're reaching out to us? I thought we had to choose you first?

B: You do. Our call to you is irrelevant until you choose to listen and comprehend.

C: I feel like a little kid settling into her mom's lap and asking for her favorite bedtime story, B.

Tell me again....

B: You are loved, C. You are always loved. You are made of love. Your life is woven of light, harmony, grace, peace, intelligence, energy, wholeness, oneness, joy and peace.

C: The timeless eternal nouns!!!

B: & C: [Laughter]

B: Exactly, C. The entire Universe is woven from the Timeless Eternal Nouns. And from there is birthed *ALL* possibility!

C: And what happens then, B?

B: Then you get to choose: to live in close contact with us, the indwelling Beloved, or to separate yourself from us.

C: Why would ANYONE do that, B? I sure did it myself, but I didn't know you or how to find you. I've looked for you for decades and only began to glimpse you in July. Why!!??

B: People who don't know us can't share us with others, C. Now that you do know us, you cannot wait to share what you know, right?

C: Right, B! I love it that I am now sharing our chats with about thirty friends and I keep hearing from them. Many of them are having powerful experiences. My friend David says his heart has to stretch when he reads what you have to say.

Others say that my talking to you reminds them that at one time they had experiences of connecting to guides of some sort. Several are regaining that facility. Some are remembering peak experiences, or talking to "dead" loved ones. You seem to have a remarkable effect on others, too, B, not just me.

B: That's how it works, C. Love is contagious. It spreads easily from heart to heart.

An open heart, in connection with us, creates a portal into a whole new dimension of experiences and possibilities. Your life is changed by your awareness of our presence and our guidance. The lives of many will be touched by our relationship. The immediate ones you touch directly will be a small proportion of the ultimate effect, even when this book has a significant circulation.

Because each one you touch, who opens her heart or his, will touch others, who will "infect" others with the possibility of joyful connection to Source. Each one will claim a new, internally perceived and experienced freedom to love their lives and their choices. For each, this will be a remarkable turning point. That day will start yet another blossoming like yours.

C: I'm glad, B. I hope everyone becomes happy and free.

B: Everyone chooses what works for them. Each one is free to choose. The freedom within our relationship looks like bondage from the outside. After all, we are leading and you are following, right?

C: Right, B! But this following is opening doors left and right and I am happier than ever.

I feel free to imagine, to dream, to open up to new choices and possibilities.

B: Are you making a lot of choices, C?

C: Not radically different choices, B. But evolutionarily different choices – to take swing dance classes, to have a glass of wine with dinner once in a while, to hire Magi to type our chats.

B: The changes will be more apparent later, C. We are guiding you to next gentle steps daily. Like re-orienting yourself to writing every day and spending less time on your computer than you used to.

C: Yes, that is different than it was before this year. But it started before I met you, B. My writing time began to increase when my teacher Tom Hirt said, "When you move from 'Daddy, I want,' to 'Daddy, I love!' miracles happen."

That's when I started writing the love lists to tune myself to the vibration of love.

B: We've been here all along, C, and you've heard/seen/felt glimpses of us for decades. Once you tuned more consciously to love, we started coming in loud and clear, once you said "Hi" and listened.

C: Just say "Hi" and listen, B? Can it really be that simple?

B: For many it will be, yes. For some, it will take preliminary tuning to the vibration of love.

We're loving everyone, C. We're surrounding everyone with wellbeing and supply. We love when someone takes some time to be still and listen, available to hear.

C: You said before that people are afraid to hear and afraid not to hear, B. Does that make them unavailable?

B: Sure, C. You know people who are emotionally unavailable for a relationship. Many people are emotionally unavailable for a relationship with us.

You used to be! You made a rule that you wouldn't channel. That decision shut off a powerful flow of Source within you. It was only when you relaxed the rigid rules and began to focus on your feelings that you became available to us.

We're glad you did!

C: Me, too, B! For sure!

I'm sleepy now, B. I've been writing for an hour and it's almost midnight.

Thanks for all your love and caring and information. I look forward to reading this in the morning. Right now I'm too sleepy to remember what you said.

B: It will keep, sweet girl!

Sweet dreams, love.

C: Nighty-night, B!

Kate's Service: 11-29-09

C: Hi, B.

B: Hi, C.

How was Kate's service?

C: It was an eclectic extravaganza of religious/spiritual expression, B. Rev. Jane from Unity, Kate's sister with Bible readings, Rev. John with Indian music and yogic philosophy and Gail, Judy and I sharing Science of Mind Philosophy. There were lots of references to Kate's Catholic upbringing, too. What a master of loving Kate was to bring all of us together! And the music was the same: David doing channeled meditation music as a prelude, Amy singing *For Good* from the Broadway show *Wicked*, 14-year-old Stephanie singing *Somewhere Over the Rainbow*, Doris singing a folk song with her guitar, Rev. John with his drone machine and flute – and Motown backing up the slide show that Ed produced - such a mismatch of styles, yet ultimately perfect to express Kate's diverse interests.

B: Definitely something for everyone, C!

C: Yes, B, and I got to see lots of old friends and get lots of good hugs! And we get to do it all again next weekend because another of our friends came home to you on Friday and his memorial is next Saturday. Oh, no – I have a class to teach AND a wedding to go to at that same time next Saturday. Oh my goodness! How to be in three places at once!!!?

B: Relax, C. You don't know the details yet. And you did get to see Gail yesterday and hug her. She will understand if you are unable to attend.

Back to Kate...

C: I loved learning things about Kate, B. I knew her family called her Katie, but I didn't realize it was spelled KT! So many people told so many stories of love during that service. Kate was so good, B. I love that her family quoted her saying, "People are for loving and not for comparing."

Kate was good at loving! I want to learn from her example how to love family and friends so well!

B: You already did learn so much from Kate, C. You will continue to think about her and love her, and hear from her, and see bunnies to remind you of her over time.

C: Yes, B, and I appreciate all the reminders of the good friends I still have here. And I love that I can remember that Kate helped introduce me to you. What a great gift she was in my life!

I remember when I was a kid thinking my grandmother was crazy for talking to dead relatives. Now I do it, too! Life is funny, B!

B: Your language is funny, C. If they were really "dead," you wouldn't hear back from them, and you do!

C: Sometimes I do...

B: Always they answer; sometimes you are quiet and open enough to hear them.

C: So Kate is listening if I speak to her? What if she's talking to someone else at the time?

B: Kate is no longer limited by time and space, C. Omnipresence is the ultimate in multi-tasking!

B: & C: [Laughter]

B: Kate is infinite and eternal, C. In fact, so are you. Kate is fully integrated now; you still have the distraction of your physical focus taking most of your attention.

B: & C: [Laughter]

B: It was a joke, C. We like to shake up your practiced brain ruts now and again!

C: You are good at that, B!!

I can feel you want me to tell the story of the time a couple of months before my mom died, that I was in Chicago on a business trip when she was in the hospital. She'd been seeing the "dead" folks in the corner for a while by then, and I asked her every day who was there with her. That day, when I called her from Chicago, she said, "You know, it's funny. When you come to see me in the hospital, you'd spend four to six hours with me and then go home. But since you haven't been here to see me this time, you've been in the corner with the 'dead' folks twenty-four hours a day. You are the only live person who has ever showed up there. I think it's 'cause you meditate so much."

So she was tapping into the infinite part of me, right?

B: Right, C! You weren't the only one there who was alive and thinking of her, either. But she could believe you were there because your talks with her were sufficiently weird to help her believe it was really possible you could be there. You do have to believe it before you can see it, not the other way around.

C: Like my relationship with you, B?

B: Exactly, C! Your willingness to suspend disbelief temporarily allowed the flow to start. Now, with our regular interactions with you, you are developing knowing beyond belief.

C: A phrase just popped into my head, B. My friend, Ann Roberts, said in an email, "You will know when to move forward, because you will not be afraid."

That reminds me of what Kate said to me when she was in the hospital, B. She said she wasn't scared anymore and the therapy she was receiving helped her.

B: Yup, it was wonderful that she was lined up with what was happening and she didn't feel afraid.

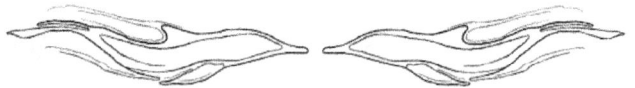

Forgot Your Book? 11-29-09, 11:15 AM

C: Hi, B.

B: Hi, C.

C: I'm waiting in the gas line right now because I want to fill up my tank before I go to Falls Church tomorrow morning.

B: Good idea, C.

C: So I thought I would just hang out with you for a few minutes...

B: Forgot your book, huh, C?

B: & C: [Laughter]

C: You know me too well, B!

B: We love to play with you, C. Being in a light, funny, delightful relationship with you is absolutely our idea of a good time. Along with a few gazillion other things in the Universe...

C: Yeah, it looked like you would have had fun soaring in the wind with the eagles the other day, B!

B: And leaping with the dolphins, and tail-slapping with the humpback whales, and whirling with the dervishes, and playing with our fingers and toes with all the tiny babies of the world! Life is endlessly amusing to us in all its aspects, C. We never get bored!

C: Well, you definitely spiced up the gas line for me, B. I started talking to you and voila! I'm suddenly at the pump!

Thank you. I am loved.

B: You sure are, C. Thanks for dropping by for a chat. We are loved!

C: You sure are, B.

B: & C: [Laughter]

DECEMBER, 2009:

We Bless You, Every One

Big Hairy Fun: 12-1-09, 11:01 AM

C: Hi, B.

B: Hi, C.

B: Unusual time for you to be talking to us, C.

C: Yes, B. I got up and caught up on some stuff this morning. It's a glorious morning, B! The sunlight is streaming in through my glass door and both Dusty and Rosie are basking in the warmth and joy of the sun! I bask in the joy of the sun, too, B!

B: Even though another of your friends "came home" to us this week, C?

C: Yes, B! Both Kate and Santos were beach babies and sun lovers. I can feel both of them enjoying today's sun as much as the kitties!

B: You've come a long way in a couple of days, C.

C: Yes, B. I feel lots better. I've done several chats with you where you just invited me to write about what I want, what I am willing to experience, and what I love.

When I was sad, you asked me what I wanted. When I felt a little better from doing that, you asked me what I was willing to experience. And then, when I only felt a bit ouchy, you told me I was nearer than I thought and you asked me to write about what I love.

Today I feel tuned to love, B! I've been going around my house, feeling grateful and appreciative. My friend Catherine gave me flowers last night and I split them up. I updated the two arrangements I made last week for Thanksgiving and they both look prettier now than they did last week. A little touch of purple in one and orange in the other livened up the golds, yellows, and bronzes I used last week!

And I love the box the one arrangement is in, B. It has harvest scenes painted on all the sides, and beautiful arching pheasant tails that come up on either end. It's perfect for the feeling of Thanksgiving!

I also gushed gratitude for my washer and dryer, B. I love being able to do laundry in my basement! I love warm clean sheets coming out of the dryer. Sometimes it isn't, "After the ecstasy, the laundry." Sometimes it's, "Here is the ecstasy, the laundry!" [That's the title of a book by Jack Kornfield.]

B: & C: [Laughter]

B: We love that about you, C! We love that you are willing to move into bliss at the slightest provocation!

C: Life really is awesome, B. I'd love to be able to celebrate it all the time. Can you help me do that more?

B: We love that you started to write, "why don't we stay there?" and you stopped and rephrased it. We are doing a happy dance that you realized that first question would take you down rather than up. You switched it in midstream to a more forward-looking question! Well done, C!

C: Thanks, B. I heard you when you told me before that I had a dysfunctional pattern of looking back just as I was making progress. I really want to develop more functional and expansive patterns, B.

B: And that's exactly the answer to your question about staying joyful more of the time! When you have that *first* looking back thought, notice it, rethink it, and change it to a better feeling thought *before* you proceed. In this case, you changed it before you wrote down the question you wanted to ask us. That's *BIG*, C!

C: It doesn't seem like much, B. You always say not to make a big hairy deal out of everything. (Thanks to Abraham-Hicks for giving me that perfect phrase, by the way. I am loved.)

B: Perfect, C! We don't want you to make a big hairy deal out of everything. We want you to make a big hairy deal out of the fun things, the effective things, the beautiful things, the lovely things! *Those* are worth making a big hairy deal over every time.

Your warm clean sheets in the chilly basement, your cheery flower arrangement on the table, your changing a backward thought to a forward thought – THOSE are the big hairy deals in life, C.

C: Sounds like the Cookie Monster, B!

C: & B: [Laughter]

C: And like my friend Margie saying, "Life is in the details and there is something in every scene that sparkles."

B: Margie is so right, C!

C: But, B, what about the BIG things. If I'm focusing on the details, who's taking care of the BIG things?

B: We are, C, if you add one word. If you are focused on *appreciating* the details, we are taking care of the big things.

What are your big things, C?

C: Love, B! Having loving relationships of all kinds. Health, too, and Joy!

B: & C: [Laughter]

C: I so love you, B. I love that you are willing to tell me the same stuff, over and over, endlessly, until I get it!

B: That's how you learn new functional patterns, C. Repetition is valuable and necessary.

Also, repetition and constancy builds trust. We want you to know us and feel us as we are. You can depend on us, C.

C: Even though you make me write and write and write what I want and love when I don't feel good?

B: Until you feel good, C! You have to choose the focus of your thoughts.

When you slip into habitual unpleasant, critical or self-deprecating thoughts, C, you are making yourself miserable. We can't stop you from doing that, you are entirely and forever free to choose.

But all you have to do to shift it is to notice the downward spiral, and choose to refocus. It was easy this morning – the discordant thought stood out and you were able to shift it relatively early. When you get a full head of steam going....

C: Oh, B, that's funny! I know that's a railroad term, but sometimes it does feel like my head is full of steam!!!

B: & C: [Laughter]

B: Yup, you all create your own kinds of hell in your thinking sometimes!

Fortunately heaven is a one-next-gentle-step-at-a-time up the emotional scale, C.

C: Esther and Jerry Hick's book *The Astonishing Power of Emotions* is awesome at teaching people how to do that, B. They have thirty-three wonderful case studies and examples.

B: And we love that day after day you are providing us with your own real life examples.

C: Thanks, B. I am loved. It feels good to feel good. I love feeling warm, cozy and close to you. It's so much easier to feel your presence when I feel good.

B: Feeling good is feeling us, C.

C: I love that, B. I'm running out of time before my next client. Bye!

You are Cute When You are Cranky: 12-2-09, 12:28 PM

C: Hi, B.

B: Hi, C.

C: I wanted to talk to you about a quote, B. It's from *Seeing Nature* by Paul Krafel. "Begin the work even though you cannot see the path by which this work can lead to your goal. Do not block your power with your current understanding."

B: Good quote, C.

C: Please talk more about the last line first, B. "Do not block your power with your current understanding."

What power do I have, B?

B: The power of love! The power of divine guidance, the power of imagination, the power of choice, the power of focus, the power of willingness, the power of infinite possibilities!

You have so much power! As usual, we are talking to all of you, as well as you, C.

C: I can feel, well, *something* in all of these ideas, B, but I don't really understand...

B: *Exactly*!!! That's the power of this quote. Do not block your power with your current understanding!

C: ARGH, B! I don't understand how to do that!!!

B: Breathe. Relax. Allow. Trust. Imagine. Enjoy. Appreciate. Love. Be grateful for. Sing. Dance. Bounce. Skip. Laugh. Delight in. Savor. Bask. Meditate. Wonder. Wander. Give thanks.

C: Ok, you are right. I do know how to do all those things and I even understand their importance to a certain degree.

B: Of course you do, C! We are step-by-step, day-by-day, leading you to greater understanding. But you will never see from your local perspective the bigger picture we can see.

So your "beginning the work" when you can't see the end result yet IS an act of trust and allowing.

C: And the work for me right now is writing down the words of this conversation, right?

B: Exactly, C. The work is taking the inspired action that day, whatever it is. Earlier this year, "the work" for you was writing notebooks full of love lists as you tuned yourself to the vibration of love. Recently the work has also been to make the appointment for Dusty's surgery and to take her to the emergency vet, and to go to the hardware store at 9: 15 PM and to paint your front step railings.

For every person, "the work" will be different because our guidance to them will be based on our intimate knowing of precisely who they are and what their situation is with this very breath they are taking right now.

C: I feel the power in that, B. I was going to write "in every moment," but what you are saying feels like it goes straight to the core of life – to the breath and the heartbeat.

I have tears in my eyes, B. In this moment, I can feel again how much you love us. How much you love me! Wow!

B: We get excited when you feel that "Wow," C.

"Wow," can be an "Aha!" of the mind or an "Ahhhh...." of the heart, a brilliant flash of light or a gentle opening to love. It's all good!

Intuition, feeling your guidance, can take place much faster than understanding. If you wait for understanding, the propitious circumstances that inspired the impulse may have changed.

C: Tell me about "propitious," B. I am unclear about that word.

B: We love that you wrote it down anyway, C!!!

Thank you, we are loved.

B: & C: [Laughter]

C: We fairly often get off the subject we are talking about to talk about the words we use – to talk about talking, B.

Won't that make people reading this impatient?

B: Perhaps, C. But that's not your problem.

This book that we are creating together, which you are writing down, is a love story. It is a narrative describing the evolution of a very special kind of relationship.

Your ability to trust your impulses, to translate our vibration into words, to write our side of this dialog, is intrinsic to the development and expression of our relationship. There is great value in discussing the details of how you are coming along in managing the mechanics of internal chatting.

C: Thanks for explaining that, B. It was making me a little uneasy.

B: We like that you talk to us about places where you feel uncomfortable. We want to bring more joy to your life.

You don't have to hide or pretend with us. We love you exactly as you are. We see your value and worthiness. We want to soothe you and help you relax into the joy that is your birthright.

You are beautiful, Beloved. You are intelligent, creative, loving, healthy, energetic and fun. We want you to know you as we know you.

C: It sure feels better to see me through your eyes than my own.

B: We are helping you see anew. Before long, you will begin to see more as we see. Life is magical.

C: Like the movie, *Mr. Magorium's Wonder Emporium*? Where the magic was happening all the time, but the accountant was always turned in the wrong direction to see it?

B: Exactly, C. We want to tune you up so that you witness the magic.

C: I love the idea of being a witness to the magic, B. I'm seeing a business card here –

Connee Chandler
Witness to Magic

Or, Magical Observer! That's fun, B!

B: We love it when we capture your imagination, C. Or better, unleash your imagination. We love it when we inspire you to think of something that makes you smile.

C: I'm trying to get over this feeling that you are too busy or too important to be hanging out playing with me and entertaining me, B.

B: We are here to love you and have a joy-filled relationship with you, C. We have all the time in the world! We *created* all the time in the world. Omnipresence is a hoot!

As you invite us into your life more and more, you empower our omnipresence to be in conscious action in your life. So in a sense, our relationship is mutually empowering!

C: Wow, that's a stretch – me empowering the omnipotent!

B: Your free will governs our power in your life, C. You have the power to choose to open up to our love. We love that you are choosing us day by day.

C: Some days it seems really easy and our chats just flow, B. Other days it seems harder to choose you.

B: We love that you still show up and talk to us, C, even when you aren't hearing us as clearly. We'll continue to coach you to tune your vibration up to love when you are cranky!

C: Do you still love me when I'm cranky, B?

B: We love you *ALL* the time, sweet girl. You are cute to us even when you are cranky. You just forget who you are temporarily.

Some people's "temporarily" lasts a lifetime. Yours is lifting as we speak. Literally.

As you speak to us and listen and we commune together, you are getting to know, more and more fully, who you really are.

You are Our Beloved, our sweet girl, our divine child. You are learning to live loved, expanding your imagination, your creativity and your joy in life.

C: It's very exciting!

B: For us, too, C.

C: I love you, B.

B: We love you, C.

C: I need to get on with my day now, B. Thank you for this wonderful time we have spent together this morning.

I am loved.

B: You are welcome, C! Enjoy this glorious day.

C: You are the sunshine streaming into my life this glorious morning. I feel your warmth today!

B: We are glad, C. Bye for now!

Handling Changes with Grace: 12-3-09, 5:08 AM

C: Hi, B.

B: Hi, C.

C: I'd like some help with my focus this morning, B. I'm not feeling as good as I'd like to feel.

B: What are you grateful for, C?

C: I'm grateful that my friend showed me the ticklish baby kitten video on YouTube last night, B. It was the cutest thing EVER! I loved how the person tickled the tiny belly and then when they pulled their hand away the kitten would throw all its legs out in every direction wanting more! That was adorable and fun. I loved that my three friends came over last night and enjoyed that with me.

I love that I have wonderful friends who share my life and my home. I love that I have a number of parties to give and to attend this holiday season. I love Christmas music. I love the holiday lights springing up in my neighborhood. I love having plans for holiday concerts with several different friends. I love having friends who think of me and share what they love with me. I love falling in love with my life over and over as I focus on what I love. I love having you remind me with your simple questions to focus on love. I love feeling better when I focus on love.

That was helpful, B. What now?

B: What do you wonder, C?

C: I wonder how good I can feel? I wonder how much more sleep I can get before this day really begins? I wonder who else wants to read and enjoy this book? I wonder how good I can get at focusing on what I love? I wonder how much love I am willing to allow in my life? I wonder how people who read our love story will be influenced in finding their own?

I wonder how good I can feel about sharing our love with the world? I wonder how many people really want to know that they are loved and intrinsically more valued than they ever imagined? I wonder why I have been lucky enough to be called to have this experience? I wonder how many others are feeling this call to love rise up within them? I wonder who else is tuning themselves to love and wanting to hear what B: has to share? I wonder how good a writer I can become? I wonder how much love I can pour into my words? I wonder how I can expand my ability to wonder?

B: You just read a quote that said you become a writer by writing every day. You become a wandering wonderer by asking yourself wondering questions and wandering over to see how much fun you can have in answering them. Every day.

C: Wondering is about opening to change on purpose and seeing life as an adventure, right?

B: Right! Life is a glorious adventure. Things are supposed to change. Evolution happens naturally if you let it.

We give you signals every day. We say, "Look here! Come over here. See this beauty. Smell this fragrance. Taste this bounty. Celebrate this joy. Appreciate this fun. Participate in this adventure. Love her. Savor this. Bask in this."

You have to be open to receive the impulses, listening for our guidance, ready to share in our love.

C: I feel like I've asked you this a million times already. How do I do that?

B: You show up here and talk to us, C. On the days when you are singing and feeling life is glorious, you show up and we celebrate your joyful enthusiasm with you. On the days when you are sad, you reach out to us for comfort. On the days when it all seems too hard, you let us coach you into tuning to love again so you can use the leverage of alignment with us to allow things to get easier again.

C: Remind me about the leverage B.

B: Go pet Rosie, C. She's asking for love. Sleep a bit more. We will talk again later to more effect.

C: Ok, B. I would like to sleep for a while longer. Thank you. I am loved.

Later that morning, 8:33 AM

C: Hi, B!

B: Hi, C.

C: Oh, thank you for helping me tune up during the night, B! I feel so much better this glorious morning. The sun is streaming in and I'm remembering that I don't have to make a big hairy deal out of anything. I can just relax and focus on love.

B: That's a powerful thing to remember, C. And while you are loving, what are we doing, C?

C: You're lining things up for me, B! You're taking care of the big things and lining me up with the people, places and things that will make my life beautiful!

B: Exactly, C! And how do you get to those things?

C: I listen for your guidance, B. I watch for that inner inspiration to take action. I wait for the impulse to move.

B: And then?

C: When I feel the impulse to move, I go!

B: How does it feel when you live like that, C?

C: It feels like life is flowing, B! It feels great to focus on love, appreciation and gratitude. I feel marvelous when I notice all the beautiful people and situations I am encountering each day. I feel terrific when I wake up in the morning, enthusiastic as I move through the day, and optimistic about the future!

B: You got it, C! That's the leverage of alignment. The better you feel, the easier it is for us to maneuver graceful interactions for you! The better you feel, the more you feel our impulses and guidance. The better you feel, the fresher you are in your awareness of your surroundings, and the more likely you are to catch a glimpse of something exquisitely beautiful in your environment.

C: Oh, that's a big part of the magic for me, B! Seeing the full moon rising, a fox at the end of a trail ahead of me, a particularly adorable pose Dusty is striking in the moment! To hear the giggling of a toddler or feel the gentle trust of an infant gripping my finger with her perfectly tiny ones. To live life open to the precious moments of beauty and tenderness, B! I love living like that!

B: What about when something happens to knock you off your stride, C? When a friend dies, or your marriage ends in divorce, or you get a scary diagnosis from the doctor?

C: Remember to come back to you anyway, B. To trust that even though it looks like something is going wrong, it's actually something going very right. I know you also want me to remember that the bad/sad/angry/fearful feeling is temporary.

I want to remember that my good feelings come from my tuning up to the frequency of love. I can do that under any circumstances.

Yes, in the shocking initial moments or days, I may be off balance and feeling bad. But I trust more and more that you are here with me and all is well. I trust that you are always loving, supporting and supplying me, even when it looks like something is going wrong.

B: You've come a long way in the past few months, C.

C: You've made such a difference in my life, B. Looking back at this year, it seems almost impossible that in just a few months my life has come to revolve around my relationship with you. You are my true north, the inner compass that guides my way.

B: What happened yesterday, C?

C: I got angry with you after I went to the dentist and found I need a crown and maybe a root canal. I'd been seeing light in my teeth, B. And you'd been encouraging me to see them as perfect, whole and complete.

B: What did the x-rays show, C?

C: My teeth looked great! Even the dentist admitted that the x-rays were perfect!

B: But.

C: He and my long time lovely hygienist said there was one molar in the back that looked and felt to them like a problem that needs to be fixed before it gets bigger - there's a fracture in an old filling.

B: Did you have any pain, C?

C: No, B. I had no idea I had a problem there.

B: So the solution was offered before you were even aware you had a problem, C! Can you see the beauty in that?

C: With your help I'm beginning to, B.

So, could sending light to my teeth actually bring a problem to light in the perfect time for the solution to appear, B?

B: Yes, C.

C: I had hoped sending light would be the solution to all the problems, B.

B: There will always be changes in your life that you can judge as wrong and call problems, C, but they are actually just conditions that are themselves in the process of being changed.

Learning to handle those changes with grace and love is what makes life flow.

C: So I'll feel better if I look for reasons to appreciate this experience with my dentist rather than judge him, me, my tooth or the situation wrong?

B: Of course, C. It's just like Dusty's surgery. Assign it to us, relax and look for things to love, and allow the process to unfold easily and gracefully. If there is something for you to do, we'll give you the impulse. Just chill out and focus on other things that feel good in the meantime.

C: Ok, B! I will! Thank you. I am loved.

B: Have a great day, C!

C: I already am, B! You too!

B: We always are, C! Thank you. We are loved.

B: & C: [Laughter]

We Bless You, Every One: 12-4-09, 7:42 AM

C: Hi, B.

B: Hi, C.

C: I'm taking a moment of thankfulness for having you in my life, B! I feel so blessed to have discovered that you have been here all along.

I noticed a few minutes ago that the initial bliss I felt when I connected with you was less – being with you was now familiar and comforting, but not so ecstatic.

I don't want to take you for granted, B. I love you and I feel your love for me. I want our love to stay fresh. So I wandered into thanksgiving for your attention, your love and how you orchestrate my life, and I feel pretty blissful again.

B: Well done, C! That's a powerful prescription for freshness in every relationship you have. Love thrives in an atmosphere of thanksgiving!

When you fall in love you feel good. Remember, when you feel good, you feel us. As you love anyone, you are in a state of alignment with us. When you are in alignment with us, our love pours through you, out into the world. Everyone and everything you think about in that state of appreciation benefits.

As you love us directly, you allow more of who we are to shine forth directly as you. You can take a tiny candle flicker in your heart and allow it to grow to a steady flashlight beam, and then to a lighthouse beacon, bringing more light and love into your world. It feels good to be a beacon of light!

C: I love feeling centered in light and love. I love to laugh and play, to write, dance and sing! I love the way you remind me often to tune to love and you give me empowering questions to focus on. I love that you taught me to say (I am loved) inside, every time I say thank you outside.

I feel so good when I remember how well I am supplied, B. Every breath we take is a reason for celebration! I am glad to be alive!

B: We love it when you feel that way, C. We also love you when you temporarily lose your awareness of your true self and our love. We would appreciate your being especially kind to yourself in those moments.

Perfectionism doesn't serve you. If you only love yourself when you are connected and shining, your love is very conditional. You sometimes beat yourself up when you feel disconnected. That response is self-defeating – it makes you feel further away from us and the love that we are.

C: I want to stop doing that, B. Help me, please, to know what to do instead.

B: When things happen that disturb you in some way, just take a time out. Stop and relax. Say "Ouch! That doesn't feel good!" Then do what you would do with a frightened child – soothe and comfort her. Notice that in this very moment you are really just fine.

C: But what if a tiger is chasing me, B? If I stop, it will eat me!

B: How often does that happen, C?

B: & C: [Laughter]

C: Well never, B, but it does happen to some people.

B: And sometimes you feel like it is happening to you. Generally, it's just a kitten chasing you – it feels like a tiger because your perception gets distorted when you are afraid.

C: And if it really is a tiger, B?

B: Welcome home, C! There's a party waiting for you.

C: ARGH!

B: & C: [Laughter]

C: My friend, Rev. Maria Clemente, said something like that yesterday, B. She said she loves being reminded of the comfort of home and that we are always at home in Spirit wherever we go.

B: You certainly can be at home with us wherever you are. Tuning in to love brings you right home. Opening up to loving relationship with us allows your growing awareness that you are not alone – we have always been here with you.

C: I am glad to feel your love and the comfort of your Presence in my life, B. I do feel more at home with myself now than I used to feel.

B: We love that about you, C! We love that you allow yourself to know us and our love more all the time. Thank you! We are loved.

B: & C: [Laughter]

C: Yes, you sure are, B! And so am I! The more I love you, the more I love myself. And the more I love myself, the less comfortable I feel when I don't love others.

B: When you get really familiar with love, not-love feels terrible to you! Your sensitivity increases. Then you are a lot more motivated to look for reasons to love.

Habituating yourself to love is a magnificent choice you have made and are practicing. New grooves are developing in your brain. New capacities for sensing are expanding in your heart.

Your increased sensitivity allows expanded awareness. You notice more quickly that you are turning away from love and choose to come home again and again. The more often you do it, the easier it gets.

C: I want to choose love, B! I'm willing to become even more at home with you! I am eager for our relationship to continue and to grow. I love you, B!

B: We're so glad, C! We love you, too, infinitely and eternally.

We bless you, every one.

Appendices

Appendix A: Putting on the Christ, *Science of Mind Magazine*, Daily Guide for September 25, 2003 [*This Daily Guide was also reprinted on January 25, 2007 as a "reader favorite."*]

The only prophetic thing that can ever happen to you and to me, is not to read – just read – what others have done, but somehow or other, taking that as an example, to do the same thing.

    Ernest Holmes, *Ideas of Power*, page 108

Each one "puts on the Christ" to the degree that he surrenders a limited sense of Life to the Divine Realization of wholeness.

    The Science of Mind, page 579

Putting on the Christ

Studying Science of Mind, people ask, "Can we do what Jesus did?" Superficially, the answer is yes. But that's not the whole story.

Truly, we will not do exactly what Jesus did. Jesus didn't do exactly what Moses did, either. Yet, if we become as clear in our consciousness as Jesus was, we will be able do whatever we are guided to do as well as he did what he was guided to do. Every life path is unique. What we feel called to do will be inspired within our own experience, in harmony with our own gifts.

We don't have the potential to be Christ Jesus. The I Am That I Am has chosen to express as each of us, an anointed one with our name. To whatever degree we are willing and able to know our wholeness, we will expand the Love and demonstrate the Law of Spirit, just as Jesus did.

In *Anatomy of Healing Prayer*, Ernest Holmes said, "Neither did Jesus place any limit upon our use of divine power. Rather, he said, in essence: Watch what I do, understand the words I speak, enter into conscious union with the Spirit, and you will do greater things than I have done." As we put on the Christ in ourselves, we emulate the consciousness of Jesus that inspired his actions, rather than his actions alone.

Today I take one more gentle step in knowing the true value of my life. I am willing to be guided. I trust the graceful unfolding of my own path.

Appendix B: Resilience, August 30, 2009

During a meditation, I saw myself as a magnificent crystalline structure, like a star, radiating light in all directions. But I was afraid to go up and touch it because it looked so hard, brittle and fragile. But then the meditation said, "Become the statue" and I went inside it, and discovered that was an illusion - from the inside, it was clear that I was bouncy and resilient, like a squishy ball with legs!!! It was an amazingly freeing image! I felt incredibly free, playful and joyful! I felt fluid, ALIVE, healthy and excited about life. YAY! And I was still radiating light, WOW, who knew???

Appendix C: The Path, Winter 1988-1989

I found myself walking down a steep trail into a valley. The going was very rough, and I was concentrating solely on keeping each foot placed securely ahead of the first on the slippery ground. As I walked, I noticed the tougher the going, the tenser I felt. The muscles of my legs, shoulders, and neck ached with the accumulated stress of holding myself stiffly, afraid I would fall. I looked at the landscape and could see nothing but barren slope leading to a desert-like valley below me. Forbidding dark clouds closed in above me. It was very clear to me it would be impossible to return the way I had come down, but the way forward was little more inviting. I was suddenly aware I had entered the valley of the shadow of death, and I was afraid.

I stopped on the path in the most secure place I could find, stretched and looked around. It then seemed I had reached the flat plane of the valley. I could see a multitude of gray shadows of others, plodding and struggling through the valley. Many of them walked as if they were very heavily burdened, although no one was actually carrying or dragging anything I could see. I thought, "What a hopeless, loveless existence," but could think of no alternative. With a sigh, I continued plodding along. As I walked, I lost sight of the others. Each step became more and more difficult. I began to feel as though I were pulling a heavier and heavier weight behind me. I felt compelled to go on pulling, but it was clear I had no valid reason to continue. Still, I persevered. Finally the weight got just too heavy and I fell.

My first inclination was to struggle back to my feet and continue somehow. But deep in my being, I suddenly heard the shouted command, "STOP!" I just stopped struggling then, and allowed myself to drop to the ground. I could hear a voice instructing me to relax.

> "Relax the tension around your eyes, and allow your eyes to close. Let the muscles in your cheeks melt into peace. Let your scalp and the back of your neck just let go. Breathe deeply and allow your breath to relax your shoulders, back, and chest as you exhale. Let your arms and hands fall limp. Let your hips, pelvis, thighs, calves, and feet become one with the ground. Allow yourself to rest here."

I don't know how long I slept. Sometime later, I heard the same melodious voice whisper, "Now just look up." I opened my eyes and was blinded by a light so bright I had to blink away my tears before I could focus. The steep walls of the valley were covered with jewels glistening in the sunshine like the stained glass windows of a magnificent cathedral. Deep cuts in the walls showed lush, verdant gardens with great stands of trees and gorgeous flowers. This was easily the richest, most abundant place I had ever been. I turned my attention to the valley floor and saw it, too, was rich and prosperous with life. Beautiful, sleek, healthy animals played near streams of clear, musically running water. Food grew at hand and nothing was lacking. Light beings moved gracefully through the valley, stopping here and there to rest, laugh, and play. I had gone to sleep in hell, and had woken up in heaven!

I looked up again at the hillsides, so lustrous and bright. I felt dazzled and thankful for my deliverance.

"It's incredible, isn't it?"

I turned and saw one of the light beings reclining beside me in the grass. I asked where I was.

"Where you have always been," he replied. He directed me to look outward across the valley again. This time I could see the gray shadows of the multitudes moving haltingly through the rich landscape. Each was dragging an invisible load. Each was seeing only the next gray step of the shadow he was casting on the garden. I started to jump up to tell them where they were, but the light being restrained me.

"I'm afraid it doesn't work that way," he said with compassion.

I wept.

Later he said, "Now there is someone we may be able to help."

He started moving quickly away from me. I followed, noticing I, too, was skimming lightly over the ground, never quite touching it. With astonishment, I looked down and discovered I was a light being myself. He laughed.

We halted beside the barely discernible gray shadow collapsed on the ground. A cold chill settled over me as the sun suddenly disappeared and the clouds gathered. As the shadow struggled to get up, I heard my friend say softly, but commandingly, "STOP!"

The shadow seemed to hear, and allowed himself to drop back to the ground. The light being began reciting the relaxation instructions. As the shadow closed his eyes and started to relax, the sun came back out and seemed to shine brighter and brighter. Finally, the clouds disappeared entirely. I could see the shadow had become another light being. I heard my friend issue the final instruction, "Look up!" and the former shadow became as dazzled as I had been by the beauty and richness of the valley. We all played together and rejoiced for a while.

Finally, my mentor took me aside and told me it was time for me to try to help on my own. I wandered blissfully though the valley, determined to help the first shadow I saw fall. I saw a woman stumble, and flew to her side. As I reached her, the clouds had come in again and I was very cold.

I shouted, "STOP!" She was not ready to hear.

She forced herself up and tried once again to pull her heavy burden. I tried to help her, but I realized she couldn't see me. I didn't have the strength or the will to help her pull the invisible load. I found myself unable to see her then, and continued walking. I put one heavier step in front of another, feeling hopeless and abandoned.

Time passed. Each moment got more difficult. With a sense of gray relief, I fell to the ground. As I fell, a voice within me whispered, "STOP!" I recognized a warm feeling of relaxation spreading from my face to my scalp to my shoulders, and all the way down my body. As my feet warmed, I opened my eyes and looked up. I was again dazzled, but this time the brilliance was familiar, and I knew I had come home.

When I turned and looked, my mentor was smiling at me. He gave me a hug.

"I'm glad you're back," he said. "The whole valley was saddened when your light dimmed. But you come back quicker each time it happens, because you remember yourself to stop, relax, and look up when you fall the first time."

"Why don't we just stay here once we get here?," I asked, confused.

He smiled, and said, "Our valley is not complete until everyone's light shines as brightly as possible. You can try to stay here and play without helping others, but as each helper light goes dim, you will find yours diminished. You will only be able to brighten it by helping a shadow to the light. You would last for a while, but eventually your light would be too dim to sustain you. You'd go back to the shadow. And you'd have forgotten how to help yourself when you fell."

I asked him, "The only way to stay here is to help others to rest in the light?"

"Yes," he answered. "And the only lesson you need is stop, relax, and look up."

Appendix D: The Hill and Fields, June 29, 2002

I saw a vision of a green hillside, broken by white walls of the kind of creamy smooth stucco from which they make fine hotels in the Southwest. These walls have such a delicate texture that it calls to my heart and makes me want to run my hand across them. The green is grass, deep and luxurious, like an expensive, thick, well-padded oriental carpet. It is a pleasure to walk on it, shod or barefoot.

In each wall, there is an arched doorway. Arched doorways are the symbol of Evensong for me, a doorway to home. None of the doorways have doors. They are all open and inviting. It is clear to me that I can walk through anytime I like.

As I saw the vision, I asked in the meditation I was leading for others, "What is the vision Spirit has for you as a mystic?" The answer I got for myself was "Tabular rasa, a totally clean slate, an infinite hillside with opportunities to explore eternally. I get to make it up." I could feel that when I chose to walk through, a number of other people would be following me through each doorway.

As I have lived with this vision since, I have seen that the key to moving through the layers is to develop the ability to perceive what is there. They are all different, but my current perspective makes them all look identical. Allowing myself to expand in my ability to see and experience them in their uniqueness is always the next gentle step for me to take.

[This vision continued in: Alhambra, September 19, 2002]

While I was praying with a friend, I saw again the vision of the white walls amid green. I was happily seeing the familiar view I was used to of the beautiful green hillside, with its exquisitely fine white stucco walls with their single arched and open doorways, up a hill I intuitively felt to be infinite.

And suddenly, with no warning at all, the walls exploded, just like the World Trade Center towers, and began to crumble. Great clouds of dust and smoke expanded toward me. Tears sprang into my eyes. As quickly as it began then, it settled, and out of the dust appeared a miracle! Instead of the solid walls, there was a colonnade of beautiful arched doorways - way more doorway than column on each one. It was like a series of filigree designs up the hillside, ever so beautiful. No rubble, no clearing, just beautifully transformed, intricately carved portals, everywhere I looked.

And somehow the hillside no longer just seemed to go upwards, like a hierarchy. It went around and through, so that every turn was a doorway, into a doorway, into a doorway, all of them beautiful.

I asked what it meant, and I heard the words, "As the walls come down, the doors open."

My understanding is still that to move from one field into the next through the doorway is still dependent on our expanding ability to perceive the beauty on the other side of the door. I sense that the willingness to look for beauty through every doorway is the prerequisite to seeing it. I also sense that the allowing/encouraging/experiencing of a new brain chemistry may also be necessary and the process is endless.

Alhambra is the word that came to me about these visions. This place in Spain includes many intricately carved white stucco colonnades, one of the world's premier sites of Islamic art and geometric patterning. I have recently been studying the brain chemistry of bliss, which has caused me to see geometric patterning in my mind.

I went to the library to explore beauty and the possibilities of altered states of deeply connected consciousness in Islam. Here's what I found about Alhambra's arched doorways...

> Always abstract, the designs are meant to draw attention away from daily life into a world of pure ordered form.
>
> Solyst, *Morocco*, p. 34.
>
> The abstract designs were intended to intoxicate the senses with a feeling of peaceful illumination through a constantly repeating pattern of movement.
>
> Angus Mitchell, *Spain*, p. 47.

Appendix E: Filter of Grace, May 1997

When I saw this vision, I was participating in a wonderful meditation workshop. One of the meditations included is a powerful one, suggesting we see how a great and inspired sculptor has created a statue of us. This meditation has given me some incredible insights about who I am, as I always seem to have a powerful vision when I experience it.

When I walked up to the statue and pulled off the cloth, I saw a big silver mirrored box with a beautiful purple bow on it. In the vision, I was the silver box, a gift to all those around me. What was happening was strange and very funny. As someone would enter the room and look at me, they would see only a distorted reflection of themselves. It was just like a fun house mirror image in the side of the gift box as they approached. They thought they were seeing me, but in fact they were only seeing a fractured view of themselves. None of them saw the truth of me at all. I realized we see everyone in our world this way. I see myself reflected in you. When I see you as beautiful, it is a reflection of the beauty in me. When I see you as less attractive, it is a reflection of what I dislike in myself. These evolving reflections are the gifts we are to each other, because we know ourselves by what we see in everyone else in our world!

The meditation then suggests that a master will walk into the room to start a dialogue with you. I saw a gorgeous woman enter who looked like Elizabeth

Taylor, violet eyes and all, in the movie, *National Velvet*. She introduced herself as Mary Magdalene. I was startled because she reflected purely in the mirror on the side of my gift box. There was no distortion at all in the way she saw herself reflected in me. Her beauty was perfectly returned to her.

I told her I would like to show everyone the truth of their being and their beauty as clearly as I was showing her who she was. I asked for her secret. How could I more often show a clear image of the true, loving nature of the being of others?

She was so beautiful, gentle, and kind. She looked at me with her huge, gorgeous eyes and said, "You must consciously choose to see the world through a filter of grace." Then she turned and walked away.

A filter of grace. Many people only experience the world through a filter of fear. The reflections we send back to others are distorted by anxiety. From the moment we are born, we warn, guide, caution, and enclose each other. We want to keep safe from all who would harm us in the world. From our desire to protect each other, we create a fractured view of a world. We begin to see monsters everywhere, out to get us at every moment. The more fear we absorb, the more distorted the world looks. After all, it is done unto us as we believe.

The more we believe in the need to fear and protect, the more we see fearful things. We wall ourselves inside a prison of fear. Because we guard and tense up, focusing on security rather than joy, we see a universe of fear rather than a universe of grace. We settle for survival, forgetting how to feel free. We may feel we're not good enough, smart enough, thin enough, or tall enough. Ultimately, we find ourselves looking out at others, cowering in fear, running away from the fractured image of our own selves.

So what is this alternative, this filter of grace? Mary Magdalene gave me two important instructions. The first is to consciously choose how I see the world. She encouraged me to make a deliberate decision, to leave behind the default view, to see life completely differently. Secondly, she recommended we choose grace. Grace is a gift, freely given, as we choose to look at the world through the loving eyes of Spirit.

Appendix F: The Next Gentle Step, March 14, 1998

This powerful vision affected me more intensely than any I had ever had. I saw a being of love and light gently reaching out a hand of welcome. First extending her right hand and then her left, she guided a person coming forward up over a small step, like a curb up onto a sidewalk. This was the simple action of the vision, but it was repeated with incredible loving energy for over twenty minutes. I felt like an endless flow of people came to her, were greeted, loved, nurtured, supported, and helped up this tiny step. They then moved beyond her into a light-filled space where they were happy, contented, and growing. The consciousness was expanding, the community of people congregated was growing. It seemed effortless and filled with joy.

I definitely felt she was a very special teacher, one who practices the Presence of God and the process of spiritual growth in divine balance. I believed she had created this path of light and prayed it into the realization of her ministry. This teacher encourages simple, easy, tiny steps, filled with grace and joy. I could feel this person understanding the law and the love, both of which are God. I could feel a powerful consciousness of her own divinity, and see the manifestation of it in wonderful human qualities.

I could sense how totally she was in the flow of aligned energy. The stream was endless and she was untiring. She had more love than I had ever imagined, collected in an enormous pool of nurturing consciousness, available to share with everyone. I could see she was empowering others as teachers. Soon many others were helping to take the people coming in up the next step and the next. The expansion continued endlessly. She was a person who led as effectively from the back as from the front. She had power as herself very strongly, but had no desire for power over others.

The most startling part of this particular vision was, about halfway through the ongoing vision, I had the feeling of being "shot through the heart" by a bolt of love of a magnitude I had never before even dimly witnessed. It was at least a thousand times stronger than any love I had ever felt. My response was to begin to cry tears of awe and joy in talking about it, and I continued to cry for three hours afterwards. All the while, I was trying to integrate the incredible gift of grace I had received.

This vision changed the way I look at many things. My previous model of spiritual teaching came from a team concept developed in physical challenge courses. At the end of a tiring day, the team members find themselves facing a 15-foot wall, assigned the task of getting everyone over to the other side. One solution is to "throw someone over the wall." The pioneer is then able to reach back and help the others to climb over. I felt as if I had been thrown over the wall a number of times in my life. I was grateful for the assistance of others who helped me get to new levels, however violently. I liked being a team member a lot better than being alone. I saw my teaching as the opportunity to give a hand up to the next person, so he or she didn't have to be thrown over quite as roughly as I had been.

In this crisis model of growth, I understood the future to hold someone getting thrown over the next wall periodically. Then the whole team could conquer the next obstacle. I knew it might be me or someone else. As I saw the teacher gently helping people up the next step, I could see the wall outlined in the distance. Nobody was choosing to climb the obstacle anymore, now the gentle path had been revealed. My wall paradigm, which had worked pretty well until then, was obsolete. Tiny, incremental steps could work much more gently and efficiently for spiritual growth.

The vision showed me clearly the kind of teacher I want to be. I felt an unprecedented sense of the magnitude of the Love of God for all creation. Far beyond my previous experience of human love, this love seemed unquestioning, universal, infinite. Even more than wanting to be an effective teacher, I want to learn to share great love. My understanding of the human capacity to feel and experience love expanded one thousand-fold that day. My daily affirmation now is to have a "heart as radiant as the sun."

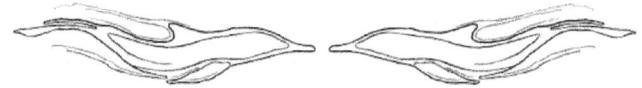

With Great Thanks...

I am so appreciative of the village of friends who have encouraged me to write these books and continue to develop my relationship with The Beloved! I want to thank Kathy Goode, my dear friend, long-time supporter and inspired publisher who started the ball rolling years ago by starting the Belovedquotes@yahoogroups.com list. I so appreciate David Gordon, who has encouraged my work since last century, and who also continues to maintain my website and put my meditations on the internet.

I really appreciate Marsha Moskowitz for assigning many of the titles and compiling the table of contents for this book and for her "teaching me to fish" so I could continue to create them. I am grateful to Magi Rose for her photographs which grace the cover of this book, and her editing and graphic wizardry. And also for her typing skills that helped free me up to write more, particularly with the second and third books in the series that this one starts. I am grateful for dozens of friends who have read the books as I wrote them, one B: chat at a time over several years. And for Dr. David Wember and Lissa Moore who said they read them to each other as bedtime stories.

I am grateful to Dr. Lisa Williams who listened to every one of these chats as they were written, taking inspiration from them and using them to guide her practice over several years. And I'm grateful to Dr. Laurie Bolster for reading and editing this book in its proofing stage. I'm so glad that Carol Taktikian allowed me to use her email feedback within this book. I am grateful to my dear friend, Paul Bailey who has encouraged me in the publishing process for this book.

I appreciate Ted Ramsey for allowing me to use his gorgeous "flora and fauna" graphics liberally throughout the book. His art inspires me greatly, and I feel it really contributes to the feeling of flow and connection on these pages. I am glad for my friend Jenn Fay, who continually affirms my identity as an author. Thank you, Jenn.

I love all my teachers, Ernest Holmes, my ministers and fellow practitioners in Science of Mind, Jerry and Esther Hicks who have created the Abraham-Hicks materials, and Tom Hirt and Katie Paulsen with their beautiful community in Pennsylvania, who all inspired me. Each one taught me through their example the vibration of Source. And I am grateful to Wm. Paul Young, for writing *The Shack* that was the direct inspiration for this particular volume.

I am glad for every reader who picks up this book and amplifies the vibration of The Beloved in human consciousness through their attention here. Thank you all!

With love,

Connee Chandler

www.ingramcontent.com/pod-product-compliance
Lightning Source LLC
Chambersburg PA
CBHW081352040426
42450CB00016B/3409